Once in a Blue Moon

Life, Love and Manchester City

'This is the best book you will ever read. So much so that it is certain to have a profound effect on the intellectual world many years into the twenty-first century. It is a literary masterpiece of pure comedy genius that any self-respecting football supporter would queue up to purchase; plus an extra copy just in case.'

Author's mother

'It won't even make it onto Ebay.'

Author's sister

'I don't remember any of that.'

Author's best mate

'I don't remember anything.'

John Eaton

'Read it and weep.'
  Tommy Muir, Chairman MCFC Supporters Club (Cheadle Branch)

© RA 9300 9284 4GB
Worthy Independent Mega Productions (WIMP) in association with Leon Yelyab Productions.

With special thanks and appreciation to Mr John Maddock.

Once in a Blue Moon

Life, Love and Manchester City

STEVE WORTHINGTON

FOREWORD BY
PETER BARNES

My good friend Noel Bayley once told me that, 'Everyone has a book inside them.' This is mine.

For Jane, Katy, Molly, Sam and hopefully a new shed.

* Certain names have been changed in order to avoid potential embarrassment to all of us.

First published 2010

The History Press
The Mill, Brimscombe Port
Stroud, Gloucestershire, GL5 2QG
www.thehistorypress.co.uk

British Library Cataloguing in Publication Data.
A catalogue record for this book is available from the British
Library.

ISBN 978 0 7524 5621 8

Typesetting and origination by The History Press
Printed in Great Britain

Contents

Foreword

By Peter Barnes,
Manchester City and England

I've only met Steve a couple of times even though we both went to Chorlton High School in Manchester during the 1970s. His descriptive style of writing certainly evoked long-forgotten images of my schooldays although I don't particularly remember Chorlton High to be the austere and Draconian place he recalls. Plus I don't recall being picked on as an argumentative, lazy and scruffy 'little Herbert'. The teachers actually liked me! Perhaps this was because, unlike Steve, I kept myself to myself, was good at football and I did actually lift a finger during lessons (albeit just the one).

Steve and I both love Manchester City and England, and his terrace tales of club and country made me smile. The passion and fervour of the old England v. Scotland experiences at Wembley and Hampden is something that has been lost in the mists of time and can never be recreated. His first attendance at Wembley in 1979 for the 'Auld Enemy' clash witnessed my equalising goal just before half time; a devastating volley from the edge of the box, which whistled past George Wood's left ear, bouncing only three times on its way in!

Steve's stories of being a spectator at Maine Road portray a side to the beautiful game often lost on players who are busy wrapped up in the pressures of performing in front of large and expectant crowds. I have my own cherished memories as a star-struck youngster sharing a dressing room with great players such as Colin Bell, Mike Summerbee, Dennis Tueart and Rodney Marsh. It's a great shame that Steve wasn't at Wembley in 1976 to enjoy my goal in City's last trophy win when we beat Newcastle 2–1 in the League Cup final. I wouldn't have swapped places with him that day for all the world (I never did like Burnden Park).

In later years when my professional career was over, I turned down Steve's generous offer to play for his Sunday League team Lee Athletic when he collared me one boozy Friday night in the Orange Tree in Altrincham.

Having read the book, I thank God for my foresight.

Peter 'Barnesy' Barnes, 2010

Everything you are about to read is true, but then again, don't believe everything you read. . . .

1

Out of the Blocks

I was a child of the 1960s, a '60s child named Steven Worthington – once nicknamed 'Worm', and these days known as 'Worthy' to my mates, and other various creative expletives to my enemies. Having informally adopted 'Worthy' in the early '80s, I've always found it to be an appropriate nickname, being a clever derivative taken from my surname. Thankfully my mum and dad, Kathleen and Derek, didn't trouble me with a middle name. Their considered reasoning was that there were more than enough syllables within Steven Worthington to cope with without having to learn a few more unnecessary additions, particularly if I should turn out to be a bit thick.

I was born – much to my mother's discomfort, I should imagine – in the 'master bedroom' of a two-up two-down terraced 'cottage' on 2 May 1962, at 239 Wythenshawe Road, Northern Moor in South Manchester. Our modest dwelling was set into a Victorian terrace of six, which conspicuously nestled amid the contrived conformity of the surrounding red-bricked houses. These newer homes had sprung up on the adjacent green fields and served to accommodate the post-war population explosion in the 'Baby Boom' years when Britons had, 'never had it so good', according to the original 'Supermac': Prime Minister Harold MacMillan. This not so grandiose address was our 'Worthington Towers', our working-class palace, complete with an outside loo and a newspaper hanging on nail. It was a humble abode and bigger than it appeared from the outside. Contrary to local belief, you could have swung a cat in our front room, but in doing so, you would have smashed its head in.

When first built in the nineteenth century, our row of cottages was marooned within a flat, rural area, located several miles below the dark, yawning shadow of a thriving industrial city. They were rooted just a stone's throw (well a stone's throw from the Olympic World Record stone-throwing champion, and then some) from the vast, green 250-acre oasis of Wythenshawe Park, which had been generously donated to 'the people' by Lord Simon of Wythenshawe in the mid-1920s. By the early 1960s, most of the rural land had been devoured by the seemingly relentless modern housing development. The park now unwittingly dissected the huge and ever-expanding area of collective neighbourhoods which came under the vast new suburban umbrella of Wythenshawe.

In those days 'Wivvy' (as it was known locally) had grown to become 'the biggest Council Housing estate in Europe'. It was a reasonably safe, if unremarkable and stereotypical, pay on the never-never land in which to commence my journey through life's trials and tribulations. A land where love and hate were emotions experienced with equal and extreme passion. These were also four-letter words indelibly etched into the knuckles of many a confused adolescent male. They were local badges of honour constantly serving as a crude reminder of the alternative choices always available for adoption at key moments within their lives; choices which were not always taken with the greatest wisdom in mind (such as tattooing their own knuckles with the words 'love' and 'hate' for example).

As a baby, life was uncomplicated. In later years, my mum reckoned that I – unlike my two sisters – was an angry baby. Perhaps I had suffered a disturbing premonition of what was to follow? Once I was up and running, I shared the smaller bedroom with my sister Julie. She was my sole, elder sibling and was to prove to be my arch nemesis through my turbulent, but happy, childhood – even though it was often fraught with major injury and minor illness. Indeed my earliest memory is of the pain and discomfort of Scarlet Fever, a disease I'd contracted during the days leading up to my third birthday. Scarlet was hardly an appropriately coloured fever to suffer and was, perhaps, an early seed of my deeply rooted psychological aversion to all things red.

Dad worked at the Kellogg's Cornflakes factory at Trafford Park, distinguished by the huge illuminated red 'K' which could be easily seen from the M60 motorway. Today, the 'Big K' is unfortunately obscured by the artificial neo-classical splendour of the 'cathedral to consumerism' that is the Trafford Centre.

Despite an eight-year apprenticeship as a photogravure printer, dad couldn't afford a car in those fledgling family days. He brought home the bacon on his trusty little 10cc Raleigh moped. His headwear was the most ridiculous looking white peaked leather helmet. It had straps on the sides which looked like he had Deputy Dawg's (a well known cartoon character of the day) ears buckled around his chin to keep it placed safely on his head. His biking attire also included what looked like snorkelling goggles, wicketkeeper's gloves and galoshes. Once mounted, he portrayed that cool Steve McQueen look in *The Great Escape*.

Dad's efforts didn't literally bring home the bacon; we rarely saw bacon for breakfast. In fact, he brought home the Cornflakes, the Rice Krispies and whatever else he could buy cheaply from the staff shop and carry home on his 'Superbike' without toppling off. My dad's employment at Kellogg's meant that we always had an abundance of free gifts, such as *Magic Roundabout* figurines, which lay hidden within family-sized cereal packets. These trinkets made up most of the contents of my older sister's toy box. He would also bring home Kellogg's Variety Packs, which were soon banned by mum as they caused more in-fighting than they were worth. She wouldn't allow us to open a new Variety Pack before all the boxes in the old one had gone. If the one that was left was an old boring packet of Cornflakes, then World War III would erupt between me and my sister.

Dad would be busy working hard at the cereal plant, while mum stayed at home. Not only was she a double agent (for Grattan's and Freeman's catalogues) she also had her work cut out providing all the necessary comforts needed for developing her tender offspring.

The background music was mostly provided on the 'wireless' by the Beatles during their commercial period in the early to mid-1960s. 'A Hard Day's Night' now seems particularly appropriate for dad, who worked gruelling treble shifts to earn his weekly wage and regularly came home exhausted. But he still managed to muster the strength to give his two demanding kids the love and attention we needed.

Bath nights were limited to Sundays, when I would bathe Cleopatra-like in the deep, square, chipped enamel kitchen sink, having my grubby knees tenderly wiped clean by a caring mother and Camay soap. As I grew bigger and the sink grew smaller, I graduated to the tin bath and second-hand water clouded by my elder sister's weekly grime. This was where caring mother would not so tenderly scrub muddy knees with an old Brillo pad and carbolic soap. Tough times, tough knees. Sometimes bath nights included a haircut: an obligatory short back and sides with a wobbly fringe. Mum didn't go as far as cutting around a basin placed on top of my head as a template – as was the desperate plight of some children of the day – but she did have some vicious hair clippers that always jammed in mid-chop. Whether they reduced my hair length by cutting or by wrenching my dark brown locks unceremoniously from my scalp was of little interest to my mother.

Any football I played during these dim and distant days between the early and mid-1960s was limited to kickarounds at the nearby Sandilands School Nursery. My lack of footballing opportunities changed when the Worthington family moved around the corner to our new abode. Technically it was two corners and a quarter-of-a-mile car journey in my dad's Batmobile-like Goodwood Green Zephyr 6. He had acquired this gas-guzzling monster by swapping his moped, 13,654 Park Drive coupons, 274 books of Green Shield Stamps and £83 in cash. We arrived at 8 Greenham Road in 1968, the year that Manchester City were Champions of England with the last and probably ever fully English team to win the league. This was also the year my football career began in earnest.

♦   ♦   ♦

Our new home had one more bedroom and an indoor toilet compared to the old place. To my undiscerning eyes it was a luxurious mansion. The extra bedroom came in handy as Julie and I had been joined by our younger sister, Joanne. This meant that I was both outnumbered on the gender front and wasn't the youngest anymore and in less need of TLC from my mother. This was no great problem as by now I was more than ready to face the world. It was a world limited by the boundaries of Orton Road to the north, Wythenshawe Road to the east, Sealand Road to the west and Moor Road to the south. It was a patch of about 2 square miles in which to roam freely.

However, first I would need some pals. I went out to find them under instructions from my optimistic mother to, 'go and make friends and play' (as in, 'get out from under my feet'). There were a couple of potential friends living directly opposite our house. The first was Billy Roddy at number 9. He was a tall, thin boy who turned out to be a year older than me (and hopefully still is). His next-door neighbour, Terry Stanton at number 7, was my second candidate for impending 'buddyism'.

Being a child of the '60s in Manchester meant that football, (footy, togger, etc.) was the most important thing in life. I soon befriended Billy and Terry, the latter being something of a hero despite him being from the dark side (a Manchester United supporter). Terry had a large collection of impressive silver boxing cups which he regularly 'won' at his annual family holiday to Butlin's in Pwllheli (or 'Puff Elly' as we pronounced it). I later discovered that you got one of these trophies whether you won, lost or didn't even fight but could hold the heavy gloves up properly! The trophies were proudly displayed in a cabinet in his living room which was decorated in a common shade of grubby yellow. This wasn't from the paint, but from his mum and dad's chain-smoked nicotine.

Not only did Terry have apparently impressive pugilistic talents, he had no fear of the dreaded crane fly (or 'daddy long legs' as it was ominously known). These were in abundance and terrified me on summer nights as their legs made a sinister scraping noise as they tickled against the polystyrene tiles symmetrically adhered to my box-room ceiling. One hot summer's day, Terry caught one of these ugly monsters in his mother's washhouse and made me pluck off its legs and wings until it was just a tiny little stump. Now it didn't look so frightening. My fear of that particular little monster had been exorcised.

With Billy also in as the tallest and the cornerstone of our gang of three, we became a tight little unit. We played games of 'war', 'garden patrol', 'rallivo', 'kingy', 'hide 'n' seek' and 'split the kipper'. But generally, we were never without a cheap and lightweight Winfield wonder or a Frido fly-away plastic football. Our contests were played at no less than six main venues. Greenham Road itself was our initial pitch, the goals being the entrance to the council garages between number 5 (the Sweeneys) and number 7 (Terry's house). It was reasonably devoid of traffic and was safe enough. On-road footy would be played between two players, mainly 'kerb-y', 'three and you're in' or 'Wembley'.

The 'ginnel' between our house at number 8 and the Steele's, next door at number 10, provided two players with our second venue which was mostly used for 'one-a-kick'.

The nearby secluded crescent of concrete and wood garages was our third main arena. This was locally known as 'the Bangers' because the loose stones on the hard black surface would bang against the bottom of the wooden garage doors if cars entered too quickly. The entrance at the near end would be one goal, and jumpers hung on bushes at the far end (the 'Bush End') would be the other. At this end of the pitch, our play would invariably be disturbed by having to dance around a stolen car left next to the large, green, humming electricity generator. This was until the local policeman bothered to turn up to remove it. games in the Bangers were for two players, where the 'one-a-kick world championships' took place on a daily basis. Such contests would help build up my long-range shooting ability. They also benefited my climbing skills when shots invariably flew over the Bush End and into the old folk's bungalows where biddies waited eagerly to confiscate our ball. In such an event, I quickly learned that an overly polite request of, 'please may we have our ball back please?' usually paid dividends.

Our remaining three venues included Wythenshawe Park, Button Lane School and 'the fields'. The park had an extra joy to behold. It was where the great Manchester City team of the era regularly trained on the cinder running track. This was a real bonus because I could collect autographs in my hallowed scrapbook from the players before they departed in their E–Type Jags, Mini Coopers or whatever other flashy cars were available at the time. Not that their wages meant they could easily afford such opulent luxury; these cars were usually the result of sponsorship or promotion from a local car dealership. Money wasn't king of football in those days and the players weren't overpaid mercenaries. It was great fun perching on the 5ft-high rusty fence which surrounded the running track to watch Malcolm Allison and Dave Ewing putting the team through their paces. This training mostly consisted of a run in the woods and several sprints around the track in their initialled drill tops and grey baggy 'tracky bottoms'. It was noticeable that Colin Bell always led from the front in the long runs, but Francis Lee was always ahead in the short sprints.

Button Lane School backed onto our garden and we were forbidden to play there out of school hours. Despite the warnings, we would chance a game or two. Great courage was needed to play football while keeping a nervous lookout for the much-feared school caretaker, Mr Timmins, and his vicious Alsatian dog, 'Mauler', as we dubbed it. Alsatians have a reputation for being big and nasty but, in reality, Mr Timmins' dog was called Sally and she was as soft as putty. Sure, she would come bounding after us if we were trespassing in 'his' school. But like her owner, she was fat and ponderous and her bark was even feebler than her bite. Had a burglar ever broken into Mr Timmins' 'Jesus House' (as we called it because it was white and square with a flat roof), Sally would probably have licked the offending scallywag into submission.

The final venue, the fields, hosted a different game altogether. The tradition of the day in Northern Moor was for a Sunday afternoon footy match involving most of the lads on the estate and sometimes even the dads. These were held on a croft of unkempt fallow land which abutted a tiny local farm and separated Northern Moor from Sale Moor. It was a historic battleground for many a fabled territorial and vicious fight between gangs of Mods and Rockers from either area. Fabled because I never actually saw any fights, nor Mods or Rockers come to think of it. But mainly in my little world, the fields were home to referee-less games of 25-a-side where all the local street urchins would congregate in eager anticipation of joining in. These keenly contested indiscriminate matches were my first introduction to the world of tactics.

I quickly learnt that with no referees or linesmen there to spoil things, the best chance I had of scoring was to 'goal-hang'. This meant standing around as near to the goals as I could. I'd wait around for the ball to come near, then bang it in like an offside mini-version of Gerd Müller (the West German goal-machine who never seemed to score outside the six-yard box). Unfortunately, I was just one of a posse of young forwards awaiting the ball to come our way from one of the older outfield players. Scoring could often mean blocking a goal-bound shot from one of my own players, then scoring myself – much to the annoyance of my bigger team-mates who had done all the donkey work of ploughing through their nine-man midfield and getting a shot on target. Since when was football a team game? As I saw it, it was every boy for himself. Goal-hanging would also be a source of annoyance to the goalkeeper who would have to dive over little pests such as me.

It was hard to impress in these mixed age games. Small boys would invariably get under feet and often tackled their own players in a bid to get the ball. But the bigger lads were always tolerant and these games were played in a happy, friendly spirit. They finished when it got too dark, or when one team or the other managed to score 25, or when the large-chested pinny-warblers, who were our mothers, called us in for tea-time.

If the inclusion of adults in the Sunday game on the fields made things difficult for one so small, then playing at school was where I could shine away from the goal-line – and I often did. The morning playtime bell signalled a mass exodus from the main school building located next to pets' corner. The girls ventured out in an orderly fashion with skipping ropes at the ready, while the boys barged them out of the way as they charged past into the playground, with jumpers for goalposts and an orange plastic Wembley ball.

First, there was always the ritual to get through of picking the teams, which we tried to organise during lessons. But we always got 'copped' by the teacher for arguing too loudly about whether the line-ups would be fair or not. The privileged owner of the ball usually captained one side and would have first choice. This was usually a well-to-do boy called Mark 'Diddy' Davies, whose parents seemed to have just that bit more money to spend on sporting equipment. He was always the one with the highly coveted 'Wayfinder' shoes, complete with a compass in the heel and an animal pawprint etched on the sole. Enviable features which unfortunately didn't accompany my bog standard brogues from Woolworth's. I'm not suggesting that I was from a poor home and it wasn't that I couldn't have provided the ball, but I was wise enough not to put mine under the unnecessary threat of theft, loss or puncture by bringing it into school. Of course I could have temporarily repaired the 'pop' by moulding surrounding plastic over the hole with a red-hot knife which had been heated up on the stove. However, such measures rarely lasted, although they did at least provide some hope and an extra 30 minutes of footy if you were lucky.

In the early days of school, picking teams was a difficult exercise. But as we all got used to each other's ability, the pecking order was soon established. I was an early pick. I had a bit of skill, and a good trick or two, where I would feint to shoot, dummy the shot then stroll past my marker. They fell for it every time. I also had a bit of pace and a good hard shot thanks to hours of practicing at the Bangers. Being picked early was a good thing as it gave you kudos with your mates. You really didn't want to be stuck with one of those pimply, specky-four-eyed weaklings picked near the end. As it got nearer to last pick, boys would shrink into their hand-knitted Aran wool cable jumpers while dreading the shame of being chosen last. Playtime footy in the schoolyard was fast, furious and often unfair. The boy who owned the ball often held sway and I had more than one goal disallowed by 'Diddy' Davies because I hit it into the goal 'too hard'.

Games could also become a bit confused, especially when there was an adjacent match going on with another class. With no touchlines to worry about, the boundaries became crossed, with us on their pitch and them on ours. Not only that, you had to remember whether it was 'goalie in', 'goalie out' or 'goalie fly' – the latter meaning that anyone nearest the goal could save it with their hands. Then there were the goals themselves. 'Jumpers for goalposts' were one thing, but they led to many an argument as to whether the ball was in or not. I quickly found that the best bet was to hit my shots low, hard and as central as possible so there could be no doubt that it was in. That was the morning match. If the game had been a close score, such as 16–15, the teams would remain the same and the score would carry on in the afternoon. But if the score was lopsided, the ritual of picking new teams would prevail after lunch.

I loved my school dinners and couldn't understand why anyone would want to go home or brought a packed lunch into school. They didn't know what they were missing! In the 1960s and '70s, Manchester's Education Committee must have used a menu and recipes which covered all of its schools. Most of my friends from that era salivate when in conversation about some of the tried and trusted meals which were on offer, without a chip or a pizza in sight.

Once into the dining hall, the trick was to encourage fellow pupils at your table to be as quiet as possible with arms folded to enthusiastic attention. This false piece of good behaviour by the best actors in the school always worked as you immediately qualified for the teacher to pick out your table as a priority for the serving hatch. It just didn't pay to lark about because sometimes there was a choice and, as in football, you didn't want to end up with last pick.

My particular favourite was the meat pie which came in a long, rectangular aluminium tray, about 1½in deep. The oblong pie was cut into generous squares by the dinner lady and served on a white pot plate with a two sumptuous scoops of mashed potato, cabbage and lashings of delicious meaty gravy. If you were lucky, you'd get a corner piece of the pie and some melt-in-the-mouth crust, which was simply heaven! I always ate my greens, whether I liked them or not, and I would even plough through portions of disgusting mixed carrot and swede for good reason. A clean plate allowed me to go for seconds of pie, should leftovers remain at the end. Despite being a skinny kid at the time, I had (and retain) an enormous capacity for pie. It helped that the dinner lady was Terry Stanton's bespectacled mam – who only had a fag out of her mouth when she was working. She always saw me right with a wink and a corner crust piece, bless her.

After the main course – washed down with water poured from a metal jug into a thick glass tumbler which had 'Duralex France' etched into the bottom – it was time for pudding. School puddings were brilliant. Whether it was served with white or yellow custard, Manchester Tart, cornflake pie, treacle or lemon sponge or currant pie always hit the spot with great accuracy. We all used to leave the dinner hall absolutely stuffed. This certainly slowed down the afternoon football . . . well, for the first 10 minutes at least.

For some reason, games lessons were always in the afternoon. These official matches resembled the famous football match shown in the film *Kes*. Once all the arguments had been settled as to who was going to be Colin Bell, Mike Summerbee or Neil Young (there wasn't much call for

George Best's 'Stylo Matchmakers' in our class full of enthusiastic little Blues), the game would begin. I still retain the comical memory of the games teacher, Mr Preston, a man who uncannily resembled Francis Lee in looks and appearance (overweight, blonde and balding), trying in vain to referee and structure the game. He would attempt to make us undisciplined players adopt the usual tried and tested positions of the day, such as wing-half, half-back, inside-half, half-wing-half and inside-half-wit, which was usually me. Nobody took a blind bit of notice of the struggling portly official and chased the ball all over the field like a speeded-up posse of Keystone Kops in pursuit of a baddy in a striped suit and black mask carrying a bag of swag.

The attire for these games sessions was varied. The boots were moulded stud, as any screw-in boots on offer in those days were not the coolest. They usually looked like a pair of Doc Marten's with studs on and resembled 'Billy's Boots', a well known cartoon character in the comic *Tiger and Scorcher*, whose footwear lurched over his ankles. Even though Billy's Boots had magical powers, you'd rather play like a clown than have to look like one. Our sartorial splendour also consisted of football socks, which had white feet from the ankles down and were accompanied by an enormous pair of cotton knee-length navy shorts. These looked like those Stanley Matthews wore during his famous cup final when he repeatedly waltzed around the hapless Bolton defence. Finally, our kit of the day was finished with a school football shirt which looked like it had been made from old sackcloth during the Second World War. The shirt had a natty pattern of yellow and navy blue quarters, into which the portly Mr Preston could easily have fitted into while hugging a bear. I also recall wearing homemade shinpads which I put together with old newspaper and Sellotape, as shown on *Blue Peter* or *Magpie*. I don't remember excelling during these matches. They often contained kids from the other forms in our year and I didn't know their game as well as my regular mates from our form. Besides, the pitch seemed enormous to a seven-year-old professional goal-hanger such as I, and with shinpads made from broadsheets, I usually ran around the field with all the agility of a knight in clanking armour.

My preference was for the smaller game and with fewer boys. I would have more of the ball and wasn't discouraged by a know-all teacher to pass the thing as soon as I got hold of it. No, games lesson football was not my favourite and neither was Mr Preston.

2

Goin' to the Match

Unlike these days, wearing a replica kit in the 1960s wasn't the norm, although some of the luckier children did have a cotton City or United 'Umbroset' shirt to proudly display on their fields of battle. In my case it would be a City shirt purchased from Insport in Northenden. Being a Blue was traditional in my family, therefore it was my natural birthright to follow suit and suffer a life of misery and despair.

What little I did find out about my recent ancestors from my reluctant and tight-lipped father was that his dad was a Blue and that his granddad was also a Blue. My great granddad regularly attended matches at Hyde Road – City's old ground – which was burned down and subsequently superseded when Maine Road opened in 1923. My granddad was one of the 84,569 present for an FA Cup sixth-round tie against Stoke at Maine Road on 3 March 1934 which City won 1–0. At half time he managed to force his hand into a pocket to fish out a flat fag, but he was packed in so tightly that he didn't manage to get it out again until after the match! That attendance remains an English club record for any game other than a cup final.

I didn't want for much as a child, but maybe that's because there wasn't much about that you would want. A new Chopper bike with Sturmey Archer gears perhaps? But that was way out of my parents' price range and, therefore, out of my reach. What I did want, however, was to go to M14 every other week with my dad.

I was brought up on stories of legendary players of the past; how Georgie Best wasn't fit to lace Peter 'The Great' Doherty's boots; how one of Frank Swift's giant hands would swallow up a cross with ease; how Bert Trautmann became a legend when he broke his neck in the 1956 FA Cup final and played on, and how Roy Paul threatened the whole of the team prior to that cup final, that, 'if we lose this year, you'll have me to reckon with afterwards!' Maybe that's why Bert played on? Being a City fan, and when you consider that we haven't won a trophy since 28 February 1976, it is unfortunately necessary to take a retrospective glance over your shoulder to find some comfort of glory. Bazooka Joe bubble gum, Esso football coin collections and Granada TV comedy *The Dustbinmen*, together with memories of cold but fruitful Saturday afternoons spent cowering under a leaky Kippax roof, evoke joyous childhood memories within the vaults of my mind.

Saturday was always the day I looked forward to all week for a variety of reasons, including the fact that it was pocket money day. My dad brought home his pay packet on Thursdays, but never failed to make his kids wait until Saturday before the penurious dishing out of the lolly. I wasn't one for chocolate; sweet things were for the girls and I had more manly commodities of which to invest my weekly allowance. I'd find myself running to Sproson's the newsagents to purchase packets of football cards, a canny bag of Tudor crisps and *Shoot!* magazine. I would devour my crisps while religiously scouring through the pages in a desperate quest for pictures of City players to cut out and paste into my hallowed scrapbook.

Saturday mornings were spent at the ABC Minors, Northenden, long before the Jehovah's Witnesses moved into the building and turned it into a hall of their own. My sister Julie and I used to attend and merrily sing, 'We are the Minors of the ABC,' at the top of our voices. We were accompanied by a theatre full of children and a small chap playing the Wurlitzer organ, which magically emerged from beneath the stage. Before the programme commenced, Julie and I would pretend it was our birthday and nip up onto the stage and take advantage of the free gifts on offer. These were available to all ABC Minors who had enjoyed their birthdays that week. I must have had at least seven birthdays in one year before I was eventually rumbled and sternly ordered not to go up on stage again. My sister and I would then settle down to the latest gripping episode of *Flash Gordon* and his weekly tussle with the evil and dastardly Emperor Ming and his equally despicable army of slugmen. Then we would be gripped by Lassie's latest courageous rescue act of digging out some careless local who'd fallen down the same disused mine shaft for the fourth time in as many weeks. It was tame stuff, but sometimes my dad would accompany us to the Saturday morning matinee to see films that were a little scarier.

When Julie and I returned home from the Minors, it would be time to focus on the afternoon ahead. Dad had taken Julie to see City before my Maine Road debut, but it wasn't in her soul and her visits usually served as an exercise to clear the way for mum to enjoy a Saturday afternoon shopping expedition.

I could hardly contain my excitement in anticipation of seeing my Sky Blue idols. Going to the match with my dad – my hero – at the grand age of six in 1968, couldn't come quickly enough and I managed to pester him into leaving the house as early as possible. He would park the car seemingly miles from the ground. I'd proudly trot the route march trying in vain to keep up with my dad's giant strides. I was kitted out in plimsolls, grey knee socks, short pants, doubled-up pullovers, an anorak and a sky blue, white and maroon scarf and bobble hat. Over the years my trusty scarf would fade to grey; the grey of the skies hanging threateningly over the Moss Side skyline, the grey of the windswept rain-lashed pavements and cobbled back entries, the grey of the people trudging towards the ground like characters in a Lowry painting. It was only once inside the ground that the real colour truly blossomed.

Maine Road had its own unique aroma. It comprised of the combined smells of pipe tobacco, cigar smoke and the rancid stench of brine from hot dogs peddled outside the ground by grubby, bearded unlicensed chefs.

While queuing to get into the ground, I would enviously study collections of button badges of Alan Oakes, Mike Doyle, Harry Dowd and Neil Young, strategically pinned on home-knitted woolly scarves; all while 'THE END IS NIGH' man (an eccentric religious chap who warned all in his path about the treacherous sins of which I was yet to experience) would optimistically thrust leaflets into unreceptive hands.

Who were we playing this week? Was it Wolves with Peter Knowles, Derek Dougan and Mike Bailey? Or was it West Brom with John Osbourne, Jeff Astle and Dick Kryswicki? Thanks to my collection of football cards, I could recite at least eight players from each opposition side without even looking at the back of the programme for reference.

At the turnstile I would be lifted over the barrier (my dad would still be trying this money-saving ploy when I was 13). The 'Can I 'ave? Can I 'ave?' questions would continue until the programme was purchased: a flick-through, straight to the black and white pictures and the action shots of 'Dinger' Bell, 'Franny' Lee and 'Buzzer' Summerbee strutting their stuff in the previous match. It was then into the Kippax Street

Stand to be lifted onto the crash barrier perch. This is where I would sit patiently (!) listening to Petula Clark, The Seekers, Nancy Sinatra and other sounds of the day bellowing out of the rotting tannoy as it swayed in the breeze while the interminable 45-minute wait until kick-off elapsed.

Finally, at last, out would trot the opposition. Boo! They were quickly followed by the Boys in Blue led by the regular mascot Paul Todd, the luckiest boy that ever lived.

'Will we win dad? Will we win?' came the question for the umpteenth time. The answer was usually 'yes', more often than not just to shut me up. He was usually correct.

The half-time whistle would usually signify the end, rather than the beginning, of the flask of Oxo and the start of the eternal fidget until the kick-off for the second half. The interval was a chilly time for the 'diehards' congregated on the Scoreboard End terracing as it had no protective roof. The usual mixture of 0–1, 1–0 and 0–0s would be slotted into the correct places on the alphabetic scoreboard, allowing the crowd to studiously check the back of their programmes to see how the other teams were doing.

Those dark, winter afternoons meant an early ignition of the floodlighting, steadfastly bolted onto the Eiffel Tower-like pylons under which the cavalier Blues would proceed to play the opposition off the park. The dreaded command of, 'Let's go up the top,' would usually come 10 minutes before the end so that we could take pole position in the race home with all the other Zephyr 6s, Ford Anglias and Austin Wolseleys. Once at the top of the Kippax Stand, there was one last chance to catch a panoramic image of the match. Then we were off, exiting the ground down the huge mountainous steps back into the car park, criss-crossed with other smiling 'early birds' heading home. City fans used to whistle a lot more in those days.

During the long hike back to the car there was invariably a loud roar. A penalty? A goal? Who's scored? Despite his best endeavours, my dad would always get stuck in the traffic queue on Princess Road. As we didn't have a car radio, I usually found out the final result from my mum when we got home, where the match-day routine would continue. I'd wolf down my tea, watch the end of *Star Trek* or Jimmy Clitheroe, then change into my City strip with a homemade number '7' crudely stitched on the back.

Once into the garden, barely illuminated by the kitchen light, the match would begin all over again, accompanied with my own

authentic crowd noises and Gerald Sinstadt commentary: 'As Bell gives
it to Lee, Lee to Summerbee, a great cross, and from nowhere comes
Worthington, who rounds the lawnmower and blasts in his sixth of
the game. Surely this lad will play for England one day?'

This was City's halcyon era. The Blues won the FA Cup later that
season and I was over the road at Billy Roddy's house to see Neil
Young's winner. I had aspirations of going to Wembley at the grand
age of seven, but my dad never offered. He'd gone to both the Newcastle
defeat in 1955 and the Birmingham City victory the following year, so
clearly thought another trip was unnecessary.

Into the 1970s –
Early Glory, Early
Disappointment

The dawn of the new decade brought two further trophies, the first being the League Cup on 7 March 1970 when the Blues beat West Bromwich Albion 2–1 in extra time, having come back from an early deficit. Once more I was forced to watch this one on the telly the day after the match on Brian Moore's Sunday highlights programme, as it wasn't shown 'live' on the day.

City then won the European Cup Winners' Cup (ECWC) against the Polish side Gornik Zabrze on 29 April in Vienna. It was also the night that Chelsea and Leeds played the FA Cup final replay. This meant that the domestic game was live on the BBC and City's quest for European glory was largely forgotten. The Blues' 2–1 victory in the old Praterstadion (now Ernst Happel) in Vienna meant that City were the first Mancunian team to win a European trophy on foreign soil – a feat which went largely unnoticed by the general population. Once again, I had missed out on City's glory in both the ECWC and League Cup finals. I was now eight years old, but unfortunately my dad was no glory-hunter and neglected to transport me beyond the boundaries of the magical, mystical world of Mancunia.

These absences weren't my only disappointments that term. 1970 was also the year of the World Cup in Mexico, which England were looking to retain, not that I knew anything about that. I was only four when Bobby Moore lifted the Jules Rimet Trophy in 1966. But even in those fledgling days I had a keen sense of patriotism. 'Back Home' I supported Alf Ramsey's boys. I don't know why I was an instant England supporter? Perhaps it was because Sir Alf's squad now included so many of my City favourites.

The England games I clearly recall were against Brazil in the first-round group match and West Germany in the quarter-final. Both the live pictures and commentary were somewhat blurred, but they didn't stop the enjoyment of what was, from a football purist's point of view, probably *the* best World Cup ever staged.

In the group stage and despite my prayers, England lost 1–0 to Brazil. We would have got a draw but for Jeff Astle's pathetic effort late in the game where he should have blasted the ball through the net. Instead he screwed his feeble effort wide of Felix's post. He hadn't made any mistake against City in the League Cup final for West Brom's goal a few months earlier.

The West Germany game was even more of a disappointment. Once more, I had prayed long and hard for an England victory. But even before kick-off at the high altitude of Leon, and unbeknown to the nation, severe and irrevocable damage had been done. Gordon Banks, England's No.1 – and arguably the world's best goalie – was left out for having what the papers subtly described as 'a bad case of the trots'. It later came to light that German-favouring Mexican hotel chefs had 'nobbled' Banksy's fish fingers.

England lost 3–2 in extra-time after Peter Bonetti, Banks' replacement, had made a mistake to let the Germans back into the match. Franz Beckenbauer's effort could have been stopped by my grandmother while wearing a strait-jacket. Bearing in mind that she normally played her football out on the left-wing, Bonetti's error was poor to say the least.

It was a painful defeat, which made me question the almighty powers of the Lord. Despite my intense praying, God's lack of fastidiousness had rendered my requests for victory unfulfilled. As I saw it, He even took the mickey by giving England a two-goal lead only to flush it away with the dose of diarrhoea he'd allowed to develop in Gordon Banks' nether regions. Either I was out of God's loop or some contemporary German boy had prayed just that bit harder and with even greater sincerity than I had. Either way, both this match and Jeff Astle's temporary 'squintness' made me realise that God was not an England fan.

Alf's boys returned from Mexico '70 without the trophy which was won instead, and in style, by Pelé and Co. – or 'Peel' as an old bloke called him in the Beehive before a City home game some years later.

My lucky set of Texaco World Cup England busts hadn't been so lucky after all. Perhaps it was because I didn't have all the players and had at least three Brian Labones covering gaps in the absence of Terry Cooper, Geoff Hurst and Peter Bonetti. Not that I ever tried to acquire our second choice goalie's white plastic cast after his woeful display although, years later, Bonetti briefly became City's goalkeeping 'expert'.

There's Gonna be a Nasty Accident

In addition to the official Saturday morning pocket money, further 'unofficial' money was to be gained by going on regular errands for my dad to get his daily packets of 20 Park Drive untipped. He smoked these things everywhere he went – even in bed; in the morning sparking up a fag was the first thing he would do. Funnily enough, none of the rest of the family ever thought anything of it. Nowadays he'd at least be expected to yawn first. Dad's favourite snack in those days was a bread and dripping 'butty' on a door wedge slice with copious amounts of jelly and salt on top. Yep, my 'old fella' was indeed a health freak. But happy memories of jumping into bed on Sunday mornings still remain. My dad with his fags and my mum with her weird and wonderful Goblin Teasmade, which tripled up as a lamp and a clock at the side of the bed, with me squashed into the middle.

One such Sunday morning, on 25 April 1971, came personal disaster. It was a disaster which was to curtail my already dubious chances of playing for City forever. Billy Roddy had knocked on at about ten o'clock to see if I fancied a kickaround. We left our house for the short journey down to Wythenshawe Park, eventually stopping at the corner of Northolt Road and Wythenshawe Road. God's flock were in the adjacent St Aidan's Church worshipping their master, who for a split second must have looked the other way as I walked out from behind a parked van having been waved on by a lady in a car waiting at the junction. By all accounts – well Billy's at least – the speeding Triumph Spitfire hit me side on coming from the left.

Billy legged it back to our house as fast as he could and burst in through the open back door. He ran up the stairs charging into my mum and dad's bedroom, frantically screaming the news, 'Your Steve's been hit by a car; he's a right mess! You'd better come quick!' – presumably interrupting dad's third fag of the morning. Meanwhile, I was lying there, gurgling in a pool of my own blood, face-up the road. I was surrounded by a circle of onlookers before the ambulance men finally arrived. They then scraped me up with the big spatula they used in those days, slapped me onto a stretcher and loaded me into the back of the white wagon.

I was accompanied by my mum. As she comforted me on the short but frantic journey to Wythenshawe Hospital, my dad was left behind. He had to be restrained by the traffic cops as he went into a complete state of panic and shock. But at times like these a child needs his mother, especially when providing the answers to my constantly repeated question of, 'Am I gonna die mam? Am I gonna die?' To which she gently held my hand and replied, in the calm and reassuring manner I so desperately needed, 'Yes son, you are' (a strange sense of humour has my mother).

Once the ambulance had screamed into the Wythenshawe Hospital grounds a mile or so away, I was thrust straight into casualty. My solitary pair of underpants were cut off by a nurse with a huge pair of scissors that looked to me more like hedge-clippers. I was then rushed onto a trolley and into theatre for the emergency operations which would save my life. It's strange how the mind blocks out the memories of such devastating events that may occur, and I was only ever visited by one flashback of that fateful day. A few years later I was wheeled into surgery on a similar trolley for a routine operation to remove some grit which had embedded in my elbow while playing football in my Secondary School playground. As I lay prostrate on the trolley with a small stone particle stuck in my arm, the sight of the 'moving' lights on the ceiling of the corridor triggered a fretful reminder, so much so that I had to get up off the trolley in a state of panic. For some bizarre reason I walked the rest of the journey into theatre screaming, 'Please mend those underpants missus or me mam'll kill me!'

The injuries I sustained from the car accident were life-threatening; a ruptured spleen and my right femur was broken in three places. But luckily for me, the surgeon, Mr Davies – who had been rudely disturbed from a Sunday morning round of golf without protest – managed to slip his surgical tools into a small incision he had made into my belly and safely remove my ruptured spleen. You never forget the name of the person who saved your life.

It took the best part of three days before I became totally compos-mentis. When I did, I found myself 'conked out' in Ward 9. I rested there for the best part of two months recovering from the trauma of it all while trussed up in a Thomas Splint, which helped support and allow the repair of my shattered right leg. These were hard times for me, and in hard times I usually sought comfort by sucking my right thumb. But this was well out of reach as my arm was hooked up on a drip that was providing me with what I was reassuringly told was liquefied and clarified bangers and mash. By the time the drip was removed I had no interest in using my thumb as a dummy. Getting 'wellied' by a car was perhaps an overly extreme way of kicking that particular babyish habit.

My class at school were so concerned about my welfare they all wrote me an individual letter, which I retain to this day. One was so emotional – from a boy called David Delaney – it still brings a tear to my eye. It read, 'Dear Steven, get well soon, soon, soon, plop, sorry about the plop, I fell in a hole, from David Delaney.'

Unlike my example, there was no punctuation. After all he was only eight years old, but he sure got the sentiments right. If ever a letter expressed the concern and heartfelt sympathy of my fellow classmates, this was it.

A week to the day after my accident, Sunday 2 May 1971, was my birthday and I had just about made it to nine years on the planet. It was indeed something to celebrate.

To help with my recuperation, the police who attended the accident had connections at City and they had gone out of their way to contact the club. Club captain and former Footballer of the Year, Tony Book, and chief scout 'Uncle' Harry Godwin came to visit me. It was mesmerising to see Book, the man who had lifted all the recent silverware the club had won, and an older bloke in a flat cap and Gabardine coat.

The following day Mike Summerbee turned up on my behalf, but not only to visit me; he took the time to go around the rest of the ward and have a chat with the other patients. I was in total awe of 'Buzzer'. He was an England international and had a reputation at the time as being a trend-setting, fun-loving socialite. For him to take time out on his day off and see me still means a lot today. The attendances of the players at my bedside cemented my allegiance to Manchester City, if such an adhesive was ever needed.

The next day brought the third and final visit from the City all-stars. Frank Carrodus was a promising young fringe player and he arrived to say, 'Hello. How's your leg little fella?' Embarrassingly, I didn't know who he was! Unfortunately, I hadn't managed to get a hold of a football card with Frank's portrait on it and, as he was mainly a reserve player, I wasn't overly familiar with his face. This was much to all of our embarrassment. Not only did the charming and affable Frank give up his time to see me, he gave me a get well soon gift of Subbuteo for which I will also be eternally grateful.

A couple of days later, City played United at home, in the shadow of the new North Stand's skeleton, which was under construction. I got a brief glimpse of the ground as Sir Matt Busby was featured on *This is Your Life*, which I was watching at the time. To my horror, the next morning I saw that City had lost 4–3. But worse still, while I was in hospital a heavily depleted team lost the second leg of the European Cup Winners' Cup final at home to Chelsea. It meant that we were not going to retain the cup, nor win anything else that season. A dark time indeed.

5

Holidays in the Sun

In the initial months after the accident, my right leg was 2 inches shorter than my left, which gave me a pronounced limp. Consequently, I worried about going back to school, although I had made a brief appearance in class on crutches just to say hello (I was a bit shy in those days). The girls proved as sympathetic as you would imagine, but I did hear a couple of muted calls of 'peg-leg!' and 'arr, Jim lad!' from the boys behind my back.

Before I went back to school full-time, the rest of the summer afforded the opportunity for a family break. Our destination was a field with a pronounced slope in Auchenlarie, located on the picturesque West Coast of Scotland. Our family holidays were supposed to bring calmness and serenity. Instead they brought mayhem and chaos and total trauma to my parents, with three argumentative kids to cope with. On this excursion, however, we had a special guest: my friend Billy Roddy. His welcomed presence brought restraint to the constant feuds. Billy's surrogate appearance was to be of great use as, after all, I was supposed to be in convalescence. To level up the gender score 2–2 could surely only work in my favour?

We always seemed to arrive on the camp site at some ungodly hour during a howling gale. These were testing conditions, in which my dad was expected to expertly erect a frame tent single-handedly which could reasonably be expected to accommodate a lavish wedding reception complete with a 24-piece band and a mobile catering kitchen. But once the tent and the poles were forcedly exposed to the elements, he never really had a clue what to do from one year to the next. My mum's impatient but usually concise directions on how to put the 'bugger' up were always issued with regal indifference from the warmth of the car. This customary practice didn't usually brighten my dad's mood. Yet, against all the odds and after about three hours, the tent would be erected. This was usually achieved not solely with my dad's unlikely aptitude, but with the considerable and ultimately necessary assistance from an army of helpers. These usually consisted of all the other campers on the site, including the camp site owner and a local farmer equipped with his trusty tractor. There was also the local scout troop hiding in the nearby bushes awaiting such an opportunity in order to get their 'Putting up a Marquee in a Hurricane' badge.

Once the tent was finally stable in the gale, we could all clean the cowpats off our shoes, hop into our pyjamas and dive into our sleeping bags. But before the inharmonious chorus of snoring commenced, there was still time for my mum to remind us for the 175th time, 'don't touch the wet canvas or we'll get leaks.' It was a theory I never failed to investigate.

This was about the time I put on my evil head and whispered horror stories about 'the dreaded man-eating crickets' into the reluctantly receptive ear of my little sister, Joanne. Those little devils made a noise which was far greater than the sum of their collective size and as our Joanne had never seen one, it was game on. She recently reminded me that most nights I'd wait until the lights were out, and then I'd torment her ear about the cricket monsters that lurked in the fields nearby. They were green and purple, about 5ft tall, with big, yellow, pointy teeth. They also had eight legs and four bums, from which they could fart poisoned gas. You could always hear them clearly at night just outside the tent and the incessant noise they made was just the sound of one of them brewing up in readiness for a quadruple-killer ripsnorter. Our Jo was absolutely mortified. Even so, it wouldn't be too long before she'd join the rest of the family fast asleep. After all, the journey had probably taken about two days and 17 hours. This was due to a combination of the lack of motorways in those days and the overloaded car struggling to get up the numerous 1-in-8 hills, a puzzling method of warning to the severe gradient which the overburdened car would have to ascend like an injured mountaineer while bending to almost breaking point on its suspension. This was always the signal for my mum to shout frantically, 'Derek, put it in first! PUT IT IN FIRST!' as we started rolling backwards towards the bottom of the incline. It didn't help matters that my dad was a fair candidate for the dreaded title of 'World's Worst Driver'. It took him no less than seven attempts to pass his test and he only succeeded in that one because he had a 6ft 5in examiner with him. My dad knew he was finally onto a winner when the oversized adjudicator commented from the outset on what a great pleasure it was to finally take a test in a car that had some leg-room. That old Zephyr 6 sure played its part in that particular success. It was just as well that my dad finally passed, because he spent the best part of a year driving around without 'L' plates having given up the driving test as a bad job.

It wasn't just my dad's lack of confidence behind the wheel that *also* prolonged many a journey. The regular mechanical breakdowns and the eternal wait for the RAC man to turn up made the trip so protracted, we'd have been quicker hiking. The rescuing hero usually arrived in his Morris Minor, resplendent in his blue uniform with peaked cap. He'd fix the car and then salute before departing. Ten minutes later we'd call him back from another RAC box half-a-mile down the road with yet another fault to report, and he'd turn up with yet another stupid salute a few hours later. It was no wonder we were all absolutely knackered once we'd finally arrived at our destination.

By the time the morning arrived, 'Hurricane Angus' had inevitably subsided, revealing a fabulous clear blue sky to be enjoyed by all. The day's first argument started with the row about whose turn it was to go down the hill and fetch the pail of water from the standpipe usually located in the bottom field, miles from where our tent was pitched. As I was the boy of the tent, this excursion was down to me, gammy leg or not. It was okay when I was going down with the empty water vessel. The struggle uphill on the way back was like being forced to watch a Rod Stewart concert at gunpoint. It was no fun lugging a container that weighed a ton and contained enough water to fill a small paddling pool. By the time it was hauled back to the tent, most of the water had slopped all over both of my goose-bumped legs. I usually had to go back and fill it up again! This was no job for which to volunteer, as indeed no job is. To volunteer is contrary to one of my dad's four great pieces of paternal advice to which I have always adhered to: (i) never volunteer for anything (ii) owt for nowt, take two (iii) always say you don't know and, finally and most importantly, (iv) never suppress a fart.

On the way back up the hill again, I would stagger past campers of all shapes and sizes, their towels draped over their unwashed shoulders while cheerfully whistling their way to the shower block for the ceremonial three S's. The aroma of sizzling bacon and eggs wafting up my nostrils from the surrounding tents was my incentive not to 'dawdle'. Not that we had bacon and eggs; my dad worked for Kellogg's, remember? It was Cornflakes for all, with another 37 boxes packed into the ample roof rack just in case.

It wasn't long before Billy and I set off on an intrepid exploration of the camp site in search of the flattest bit of ground on which to get our first game of footy underway. I wasn't really in a position to give Billy a good game. Due to my injuries, I couldn't run or kick the ball very far, so we spent most of our time crab fishing in nearby rock pools. That was until, to my horror, I actually caught one and had to get Billy to untangle the creature that was much scarier looking than the most fearsome daddy long legs. However, this was by no means my most frightening experience on this particular holiday.

In their wisdom, mum and dad decided to take us pony-trekking. I found myself perched on top of a fearsome looking beast with a terrifying name to match: 'Flopsy'. I was less than happy to climb onto the back of this animal and the pony looked somewhat underwhelmed about the prospect of giving me a ride up the well-trodden, boulder-covered, dirt track. But I was assured and reassured as to its safety by both parents, both sisters and indeed the pony's trainer, a local bloke curiously named Ginger McCain.

No sooner had I been put in the saddle when the docile pony did a highly accurate impression of a bucking bronco during an epileptic fit and bolted off down the hill with me clinging on for dear life. I was quick to realise that an unscheduled dismount could have shattered my right leg and I might have ended up a permanent cripple; this was not in my overall future game plan. As my life flashed in front of my eyes, there was a heavy jolt as the rampant nag came to an abrupt halt of its own volition about 10 yards further down the trail. I flew though the air in an impromptu Superman impression as I headed inexorably towards a bramble bush. Luckily for me, Flopsy's unscheduled gallop left me a few inches short of the thorny landing pad and I only suffered a few minor cuts and bruises.

A few days later football was to provide further danger. Billy and I had found a flat area of land on which to have our kickabouts. But the land ended abruptly with a 30ft cliff-face drop onto an array of jagged rock pools twinkling innocently in the shimmering sunlight of those long, hot Scottish summer days. There would be no problem unless we inadvertently strayed towards the edge. But one evening a rocket-shot from Billy beat my despairing arm and, given my upright immobile position, it was hardly surprising. That was the start of the catastrophe.

A sharp gust of wind helped the ball roll towards the unfenced abyss. The ball dropped over and disappeared; it had got stuck on a ledge a couple of feet from the top. Billy volunteered to retrieve it so I took a firm grip of his ankles and inched him, face down, over the edge . . . but the ball was just out of reach. Billy bravely shouted to move him out a bit further and I unquestioningly obliged until he could just about touch it with his fingertips. It was then when tragedy struck. Because my right leg was still weak, I was unable to anchor it properly to the ground and Billy screamed as he suddenly realised the impending doom. The ball had popped on the jagged rock and we only had plastic cutlery back at the tent so couldn't mould over the hole! Wait, you didn't think I'd have allowed Billy plummet to a certain death did you? We still had a mountain of Cornflakes to consume before we went back to Manchester!

After yet another hairy moment which she heard about from terrified onlookers, my mum got the message that I needed to benefit from more serene pursuits. So our extended and mostly terrified family (for one reason or another) went to nearby Newton Stewart and its local cinema to see a film called *Ring Of Bright Water*. This was a cheery little tale about a lovable cute little otter that ultimately gets slaughtered. To take our minds off this devastating semi-aquatic tragedy, that night we attended the weekly camp site barn dance. I particularly enjoyed this traditional Scottish affair as I received an ink stamp on the back of my hand to show that I'd paid in. To a nine-year-old boy, it was like having my first tattoo. Not only that, but there were real live bats flying around both inside and out, and with Christopher Lee and Hammer House of Horror films being the order of the day, these visually challenged rodents on wings certainly added to the excitement of it all . . . and by now mum was frightened to death as well.

After two weeks of holiday bliss, we were back on the dauntingly long return trip home to the magical mystical land of Mancunia. The car was once again crammed to overload and we were packed in like sardines, without a trawler or a seagull in sight. Just to keep up our flagging spirits for yet another 27-hour, RAC-interrupted journey, we'd all cheerfully sing our family's favourite songs. Songs like 'Bingo the dog', 'A sailor went to sea' and 'If you hate Man United clap your hands.' Ah, such fun; the time soon passed.

Billy had provided great support and friendship to me on that holiday and it was a shame he wasn't at Button Lane when I eventually returned for the start of the 1971/72 playground football season. Both he and Terry Stanton went to St Aidan's, the local Catholic school. Without their spiritual support or indeed the physical support of my crutches, I wasn't too sure how I was going to fare.

It had been several months since I'd ventured into class and everyone seemed genuinely happy to see me and the mature question of, 'Hey Worm, what was it like to get splattered?' had to be answered. For a fleeting moment, I was the centre of attention, but reality soon struck home at first break when I was last pick in the playground. My pals had clearly noticed that the built-up shoe on my right leg was going to be a hindrance to my turning speed and to my game in general.

The shoes weren't such a problem, sartorially speaking. This was the age of platform shoes and I was the only kid in the school to be officially allowed to wear them . . . well, one at least. However, it clearly had a negative effect on my football ability as I now had all the balance of a drunk on stilts and I wasn't the same dazzling goalhanger I'd once had been. Any hope I had of getting into the third year school football team had trickled into the tarmac on Wythenshawe Road on that fateful Sunday morning. I didn't play football at any level for Button Lane again. It was sad really, because my dad told me that I was a promising footballer before the accident, and he knows a good player when he sees one.

Unfortunately, my initial rejection was a sign of things to come. Rather than enjoy games lessons, I now disliked them. I could and did carry on playing football even though I'd been warned against it by the doctor. But it was always at the back of my mind that a bad tackle could put me in serious trouble. However, I continued to watch Button Lane and their star player Gary Blissett. Even though a couple of years younger than us, Gary played for the third year school team. He went on to become a professional footballer and – despite being a Blue – he scored a brace for Brentford against City in a 3–1 Cup victory in 1989. Gary later signed for the 'Crazy Gang' at Wimbledon.

It was a real wrench to leave Button Lane, and it marked the end of my personal age of innocence. At the grand age of eleven in 1973, I wasn't ready for the shock of 'big school'. Breaking up for that final six-week holiday before going on to high school left a tear in my eye and a lump in my pocket, as I got to steal a kiss from class pin-up June Illsley.

6

Earwig 'O'

ost of the kids in our class were down to go to one of the two local comprehensive schools available by choice: either Yew Tree or Brookway. The latter had a better reputation for educational achievement, but neither was good enough for me, or at least according to my mum. A couple of years earlier, she had sent my elder sister, Julie, to Chorlton High School. This was on the reasonable premise that it had only recently ceased being a grammar school due to the new introduction of the comprehensive system. Theoretically, it would retain most of its grammar school standards for the foreseeable future. Perhaps this was true when our Julie was there, but by the time I reluctantly arrived, the place had changed for the worst. Sending me to Chorlton wasn't the best decision my mum could have made and even though it was one taken with all good intentions, it totally backfired. Once I'd found out that my close pals had gone to the other, more local schools, I literally dreaded having to go to Chorlton-cum-Hardy and what was to prove a forlorn attempt at gaining a worthwhile education.

Predictably, the six-week holiday flew by during that final Button Lane Primary School summer and I knew my stay of execution would soon expire when my mum took me to Rosenfield's for my school uniform. This was located near to Victoria station in today's Northern Quarter in 'Town', as we always called Manchester city centre. She was soon to accomplish her determined mission to get me kitted out with the Chorlton High School uniform, while spending as little money as possible. This outfit consisted of a nylon tie (woven in the tasteful school colours of navy, light blue and yellow) and a box jacket known to the kids as a 'Woolly Joe'. This was cheaper and inferior to the coveted and more upmarket barathea jacket, which was crafted out of better material with vents cut into the rear creating a flap at the back. Not only did this look stylish, but it also proved a useful aid in wafting farts in the direction of someone you didn't like.

I was soon to find out that the owner of the up-market barathea gained instant playground cred in school – not that I knew this when being measured up and not that I'd have got one had I protested against the impending purchase of the bog-standard, ventless equivalent, made from fluffy sheep-twine. The final piece in this not so natty jigsaw was a pair of 'kecks' – 'strides' or trousers if you prefer. A pair of 'six hole' Oxford Bags with side-pockets stitched in the knee region would have been the fashionable choice, but I had to settle for a pair of itchy, unlined 'parallels' which were totally unstylish and proved to be the wrong colour (brown). This was only revealed when we left the dark, satanic shop and opened the bags the night before I had to start school. Even in my uncoordinated mind, I couldn't envisage that brown kecks on a blue uniform would help my already faltering personal image. I'd astutely realised that first impressions with fellow pupils would be crucial, but in this odd outfit I looked like a total turkey. It was a sign of things to come.

There were only two other lads in my year who joined me at Chorlton from Button Lane: Nicholas Phythian and Neil Cudbertson, or 'Cubby' as he was known. It was a pre-requisite of being a boy that you had to have a nickname and my mum shrewdly advised me to drop the 'Worm' tag I'd invented once at Chorlton. But I still thought it highly amusing and didn't realise its negative inference to the rapidly and outwardly developing girls in our form. Consequently, I got little action on that front as I naïvely plundered through my teenage years with such a misleading nickname. The only knockers I saw during my adolescence were the ones hanging from pieces of string that you banged together in pursuit of a broken wrist. Worm was a nickname that wouldn't have helped my cause but, having said that, Nicholas Phythian was called 'Python' and they weren't exactly dragging the girls off him.

Nick, a conservative and intelligent lad, lived on our estate, but he wasn't into football. His big passion was plane-spotting and he naturally became an air traffic controller when he left school. It was a fine achievement for a lad from round our way. I was also interested in aircraft and spent many an afternoon at Ringway (now Manchester International Airport) with Billy and Terry, watching the BEA and BOAC planes arriving from all over the globe.

In contrast, Cubby did like football and was an excellent player for the school team. But, like Python, he was in the other form from mine at Button Lane and our paths had never really crossed. My fear of going to Chorlton alone was uppermost on my mind as my 'loving' sister Julie had spent most of that summer winding me up with stories of rituals carried out on hapless first years.

My first challenge of day one was to get up an hour earlier than I was previously used to at Button Lane. Getting into Chorlton on time presented a whole new series of problems. Understandably, my older sister didn't want to be saddled with taking me to school, it just wasn't the done thing to be seen with a first-year sibling. Not that she was bothered in that regard, but we just didn't get on and so, as far as we were both concerned, the less we saw of each other, the better.

Chorlton High School was just shy of 3 miles from where I lived. Had it been 3 miles I would have been entitled to a bus pass. Being less than 3 miles meant that I received bus fare from my mother every morning. This was excellent as I soon found this to be a daily way of making money. My inward journey necessitated a two-bus exchange. I had the choice of boarding the 108, the 109 or the 111 to Southern Cemetery which, as the tradition goes, usually arrived at the same time. Sometimes the first bus would stop and the next two would sail past in the mistaken presumption that the job was covered. But when the first bus became full before I'd managed to get on, I was left high and dry as all three disappeared up Moorcroft Road. After that, I'd have to wait once more until the next three arrived 30 minutes later. Although legitimate, it wasn't an excuse teachers would accept for my lack of punctuality on occasion. For my complex daily journey I also had the money to get on the 306 for the second leg, virtually opposite the Southern Cemetery Crematorium. However, I soon found that I could bank this extra 5p fare in my pocket if I got off at Merseybank Avenue instead and walked the half-mile up Darley Avenue and into school. Nor did it take me long to 'cotton on' to an even better way of saving the 5p: by riding on the open, rear platform of the 306 and jumping off before the conductor could bag my fare. My final method of fare-dodging was to sneak in through the separate exit doors located in the middle of the bright orange SELNEC buses. I got away with this ruse, as the driver was always preoccupied with the mêlée of pupils boarding like a herd of demented cattle charging into an undersized pen.

On my daunting first day at 'big school' I entered the school gates with great trepidation into what appeared to be a bewilderingly large campus.

I paid a visit there a few years ago and the place was small in reality. But then so was I in 1973. For my initial incarceration day, the first port of call was the assembly hall where I was shepherded in to join the rest of the bleating pupils. Names were read out to allocate our class letter. These made up the name 'MANIFOLD' – why this word was used was never clarified, particularly as it contained eight letters and there were only seven classes. To my amazement, I was put into 1M, the top class. I quickly deduced that this lofty inclusion could only have been on the back of my sister's achievements at the school, rather than any of my great scholarly feats during my time at Button Lane.

At this point we were also sectioned off into 'houses', of which there were four. These were named after four local important historical characters: Egerton, Moseley, Trafford and Barlow – the last of which I was assigned to. Knowing who these people were was the first initiative test set by the teachers. But I hadn't a clue whom Egerton, Moseley or Trafford might have been and as for Barlow, well I'd never even watched *Coronation Street* in those days, so how could I possibly comprehend who he was? I was only allocated a class and a house at this point; the allocation of my own personal school bully would come a bit later on.

With my mum's encouraging words of, 'Be confident and you'll do well. You're as good as everyone else. You can achieve anything you want to if you put your mind to it,' and my dad's poignant advice of, 'Never suppress a fart, son,' ringing in my ears, I was ready to embark on a glittering academic career that could lead to fame, fortune, and eternal happiness. But then again, it might not.

♦   ♦   ♦

Predictably, my first thoughts on the first morning were not of lessons and studying. My first thoughts were of football and scoring a goal. But, to my horror and disbelief, we were quickly informed that full-sized footballs were banned in the playground. Any football played would have to be with a tennis ball or 'tenniser'. In questioning the teacher if we'd subsequently have to play tennis with a football, I had my metaphorical card marked within the first few minutes of my secondary school education.

A lad called Billy Jones – resplendent in his fabulously stylish Mitre Munich trainers – sorted out the players for the first game at first break and away we went. But it was not Button Lane. For a start, the ball was somewhat smaller and there were no teams. It was every-man-for-himself (or 'Wembley' as it was known). Once you had scored you could drop out of the game and take a rest. If you didn't manage to score once it was whittled down to the last two players, then out you went. This was where my early years of acquiring Gerd Müller's goal-hanging skills would come into place. It was initially an effective tactic to goal-hang, but it didn't bring much credibility or popularity with the rest, and so it was a tactic that I was soon forced to abandon. The 'goal' on the first year playground pitch was large, from one end of the metalwork block to a large concrete pillar that supported the main school building. It was a more than adequate target with a small ball, so scoring did not prove too difficult.

It was during these games that a trio of cocky third year pupils – Nicky Reid, Michael Barnes and Kevin Glendon – used to step into our game uninvited. They'd easily nick the ball while the rest of us 20-odd tried in vain to take it back off them. Michael Barnes was the most skilful young footballer I have ever seen to this day. He went on to reach reserve team level at City but had some health problems and never made it to City's first team. Michael was reputed to have had as much if not more raw talent that his older brother, City and England international player Peter, and it was a great shame that he didn't also make it to the top. Kevin Glendon also made it as far as City reserves and Nicky Reid made it to the City first team, playing in the 1981 Centenary Cup final against Tottenham Hotspur.

The early playground games were chaos, but as I had played football with a tenniser at home many times, I found that I wasn't too bad. Meanwhile as play continued, in other parts of the playground, ominous shouts of, 'Fight, fight, fight,' were heard as numerous scraps broke out. The outcome of these bouts would determine the pecking order within the first year's 'hierarchy of hardness'. I wasn't exempt from some of these desperate scraps, but I had arms as thin as cricket wickets and I couldn't punch a hole through a wet paper bag. It wasn't that I lacked bottle. I was game enough, but what I did lack was fighting ability, as I often discovered to my cost. In fact the only fight I ever won at school was a ten-second light chicken-weight bout against Steve 'George' Graham and even then I broke a finger in my right hand with the 'winning' blow. It now gives me severe gyp with arthritis whenever I bend it, so perhaps I didn't really win after all.

7

Settling in Nicely?

By the time I'd started at Chorlton, my broken right femur had knitted back to full strength and my right leg had grown longer to compensate for the size difference. The imbalance was now down to an unnoticeable ½ inch (thankfully unnoticeable to all but me and only when stood upright). This meant I had no worries about playing at full speed in a proper game. The only problem was that any pace I might have had was taken away in the accident. I was at a disadvantage from the rest as nobody else 'legged' it like they were towing an invisible tyre. Having beaten a defender with all the speed of a dying bumble bee, he now had time to re-tie both his bootlaces and read all 723 chapters of *War and Peace* before getting back to retrieve the ball from my possession. But I had a plan to compensate for my lack of forward velocity and, when the notice advertising trials for the school football team was put on the board, I was ready to give it a go.

My plan was to go for the goalkeeping spot, despite a previously porous exhibition for the local Methodist Boys' Brigade team when I was ten (managing to let in 23). Unfortunately, there was a lad called Pete Weston who turned up and proved to be way better than me between the sticks.

For the trial of the century, we were split into two teams. From the corner of my eye (the left one as I recall) I could see the games teacher Mr Taylor nodding in appreciation as player after player impressed him. He wrote down their names on his list. I hadn't seen any pen movement following any fumbling saves, and so I soon decided to go outfield. There was no quill movement after a play in which I'd been involved and I started to become desperate. I tried up front, but with my first chance to shine I missed a sitter. I slipped into midfield. I was hoping to give an impressive demonstration of my Colin Bell-like skills. But I'd never played in centre-mid and after I'd shown even less movement than a busker's dog, the nod of approval remained conspicuous by its absence. I was now so desperate that I went into defence, right-back to be precise – but as the old joke goes, right back in the dressing might perhaps have been better? But a miracle! The winger took me on, got past me for pace, but a beautifully timed slide tackle took the ball cleanly off his toes. Moments later he got past me again, but once more I was able to make up ground with another exquisitely executed Tony Book-style challenge. Finally, Mr Taylor nodded in appreciation and wrote down my name. At the end of the session, he read out the names of the team to face Bolton Grammar the following Saturday. He called out, 'Right-back: Worthington.' As there didn't appear to be any other Worthingtons around that night, I knew I'd made it over the first hurdle.

♦　　♦　　♦

On the academic side of school there were more hurdles than the Grand National. Placing me in the top class, or 'the grammar stream' as it was known, would take serious study to maintain this lofty position. As the supposed élite – the school brain-boxes – we were inundated with homework and books, none of which I ever bothered to open. I couldn't understand the concept of homework – the idea of carrying out further work at home was daft and unnecessary.

Nevertheless, my mum said she was as, 'chuffed as mint balls', when she found out I'd been drafted into the 'top set'. Prior to my new found lofty first year status, any 'mother's pride' in our house usually referred to a loaf of bread rather than mummy's little boy. Ever so briefly I took centre stage in the Worthington household. In fact mum was so impressed that she went out and bought me an imitation leather briefcase as a reward.

To be fair, my new piece of plastic luggage came in handy. Its vast size could easily hide my unwanted but regular early morning 'pocket spanner' which became evident as I stood up to vacate the top deck of the bus. I wasn't alone in using an improvised protective sporran to hide my feelings. I sometimes noticed other lads of my age shuffling off the bus holding their parkas or sports bags lower than necessary, and whistling innocently.

Another job for my plastic briefcase was a little less conspicuous. I discovered that Southern Cemetery had a lot to offer a budding pupil. In the 1980s, Stephen Morrissey of Smiths fame revealed that he had spent many youthful hours wandering around South Manchester's biggest graveyard. He enhanced his education with classical prose and verse from highly esteemed poets such as Keats, Yeats and Cooper-Clarke. This was to be admired on the numerous, precariously tilted, moss-covered headstones that marked the final resting places of many an affluent Mancunian.

However, I had shallower, less cultural pursuits in mind. Instead I wandered around the graveyard collecting as many conkers as I could fit in my briefcase. During my numerous daydreams, I envisaged taking on all challengers in the Playground World Conker Championships. However, I quickly forgot about the conkers and where they had been stored. They went mouldy and contaminated the inside of my new briefcase leaving a disgusting musty smell and rendering my big black bag useless (which it was to me in the first place). I had only used it for a total of one schoolday, which made it a brief briefcase. My quest for conkers rather than my quest for knowledge was indeed an indicator of where my mental development was at that time.

♦   ♦   ♦

During my temporary residence within the hive of study that was class 1M, I made no real friends. Nick Pythian and Neil Cudbertson – the latter fresh from his appointment of first year football team captain – were also in the class and sat next to each other rather than next to me. I didn't know anyone else and set out on a popularity quest, taking on the mantle of class clown. I didn't take the schoolwork seriously and spent most of the time coming up with one-liners or Mike Yarwood (the day's famous comedic mimic) style impersonations that would make everyone laugh but the teachers. After a while, my antics even became tiresome for pupils who wanted to get on and learn while I just craved attention. Had I put my mind to it, I could probably have held my own with the intelligentsia. But as I soon discovered, one can only realise one's full potential if one can actually be bothered trying.

Class 1M being the top class meant it was full of swats, the future prefects of the school and as such I was like a fish out of water. When the first term's lessons began I did try for at least the first 20 minutes of each one, but I soon realised that maths would be a major problem. Sir Billy Casio hadn't yet invented the battery calculator and there was no help to be had from technology.

The way I saw it, I didn't like school and it didn't like me. I couldn't see the point of listening to most of the *things* the impatient teachers were endeavouring to load into my cranial hard drive, or 'learn me' (as I probably would have said in those days). *Things* such as logarithms, for example. I simply couldn't imagine how these were going to come in handy later on in life, particularly when I was trying to calculate my bill at the local Co-op. Besides, I'd have probably forgotten to take my log book with me. I also questioned why we bothered to learn French. Just how many times in my life was I actually going to visit France? I'd never even been to London so what was the chance of going over to France on a regular basis? History was a thing of the past and knowing the difference between stalagmites and stalactites was all very well, but not worth the effort in geology class. As for chemistry, well even that soon lost its allure once I'd mastered the art of stink bomb-production.

Even some of the 'sports' seemed pointless. I could only just manage to pick up a javelin without dropping it on my toe, let alone project it a worthwhile distance. As for high jumping, I leapt in the air, crashed into the hard metal crossbar (raised about 3ft up at best) then landed on hard sand as the heavy barrier smacked me on the head as it followed me down. What about swimming and the quest to get my coveted bronze medal? For this I had to turn up with my trunks worn underneath a pair of pyjamas, then dive in to retrieve a rubber brick which weighed a ton, lying as it did 6ft down on the bottom of the pool. That was going to come in handy in the future.

Despite the various disappointments, I still had high hopes for Biology. My ears pricked up when we addressed the subject of 'Reproduction' in which the female naughty bits were illustrated on the blackboard with a diagram that looked more like a cow's head than a uterus. We were promised a revealing film on the subject, but rather than the 'bluey' I was hoping for, we were instead shown a clip of what appeared to me to be a tadpole colliding with a jellyfish in a sea of Gloy glue. If this was sex then forget it; I was rather hoping for a much more educational practical lesson with one of the girls on the well-flattened grass behind the back of the bike sheds. Our Julie told me recently my reproductive theory of the day was that, 'something comes out of the man's willy that goes into a cup and the woman drinks it and gets pregnant.' I was so naïve that I thought a Girl Guide was a sex manual.

◆   ◆   ◆

The football wasn't going so well either. We didn't have any formal training sessions prior to our first match at Bolton Grammar and were predictably beaten 9–0. Our defence showed about as much resistance as a nymphomaniac in an orgy. Speaking of which, I had been made vice-captain which, alas, didn't mean I was captain of vice and it didn't mean I was the second best player on the team. What it did mean was that I had a great big mouth and was good at organising the back four. A bit of responsibility did me no harm. I was also made house captain for the same reason and led Barlow to victory in the inter-house five-a-side competition with a team that was far better than the sum of its parts. This was to be my only football glory as the school team lost every single game we played in the first year.

Our poor form could have been due to lack of fitness. Nobody liked games lessons and as our games teacher always wore a rugby shirt, I thought he didn't know or care a great deal about football. Rather than have us play the beautiful game, he used to send our class on long-distance cross-country runs. The route took us up Darley Avenue then out into the open country along the River Mersey, in a big loop and back. On one occasion, Steve Wadsworth, Steve Graham, Jock Mathieson and I decided to try and give it a miss. As we were running up Darley Avenue we started dropping back, and as the games teacher was way ahead at the front, we ducked into Jock's back garden for a cup of tea and a sly 'ciggy'. We then waited 50-odd minutes for the mugs to come staggering back looking like victims of a methane explosion at the local sewage farm. In order to appear authentic, we threw mud pies at each other and rolled around in Jock's mother's flower bed in a vain attempt to illustrate we'd been running along the river bank. At an opportune moment, we rejoined the back of the forlorn snake of knackered-looking kids gasping their way back to school. The four of us were rumbled straight away. None of us had a sweat-on or were completely out of breath. Besides, Mr Taylor had done a head count at the turn and clocked that there were four boys missing. Our punishment was as severe as usual; Mr Taylor inflicting 25 laps of the school perimeter upon us.

Punishment could have meant any number of things but it was often barbaric. Mr Clarke, the metalwork teacher, had a tool – a steel ruler – which he thought clever to call the 'Double Diamond', because it 'worked wonders' (according to the beer advert of the day). But he wasn't by any means on his own. During my time at Chorlton I was regularly strapped and caned even though I wasn't really a bad kid. As a schoolboy I was often described to my detriment by my teachers as an 'impertinent child' but nothing more serious. I stepped out of line every now and then, but never really enough to warrant some of the violence that was dished out by the teachers.

The Scottish maths teacher, Mr Patterson, a man who looked like a sinister version of Fyfe Robertson (a mild-mannered 1970s BBC news reporter), made me temporarily deaf in one ear. I was sitting at my desk during one of his highly interesting and enlightening lessons nervously tapping my pencil as I couldn't understand a word he was saying (because of his heavy Caledonian accent and my lack of gumption on all things calculable). But I soon took heed when he sternly warned me to stop. Within seconds I forgot and started tapping once more. As my unwanted drumming recommenced he literally screamed, 'STOP TAPPING, BOY!' as he clobbered me with a crack on the head that left me deaf and dizzy. I failed to take in the rest of his teachings that day because I couldn't hear a word he had to say!

In virtually every lesson, there was the potential for some form of violence. If you stepped out of line with games teacher Mr Taylor, he did one of two things. He would either bend you over and take a run-up before whacking you on the backside with a large-sized plimsoll or, worse still, he could bend you over and then get the other kids to line up and kick you up the posterior as hard as they could! However, the worst instance of teacher violence was illustrated by Mr Tomlinson, the music teacher. He was a strange individual whose weirdness in both looks and actions were legendary. He was about 6ft 8in tall and as thin as a rake. The pupils called him 'Lurch' and had a song about the ridiculous looking 'ankle-stranglers' and 'winkle-pickers' that he wore (trousers which were tight at the ankles and outsized shoes in which he could have comfortably won the men's downhill slalom at the Winter Olympics). Mr Tomlinson was probably only in his mid-twenties and, although he wasn't one for shouting, he could be vicious. On this particular day he'd had enough of the diminutive Jock Mathieson's raucous antics, which were disrupting the class. He literally picked up the young irritant by the hair and carried him out of the class. We all went very quiet, very quickly.

◆ ◆ ◆

Despite my dislike for academic lessons, I didn't embrace games lessons either. Some of these took place on the football field where Mr Taylor took pleasure in playing football with us in his rugby boots. These had elongated rugby studs screwed to the soles, and he took great delight in slide tackling us as hard as he could just for the fun of flattening a physically inferior boy. Monday's games lessons meant a special bus trip to our school's home pitches located on the vast open space of Nell Lane. The pitches were overlooked by a huge if dilapidated, green, wooden pavilion which served as dressing rooms and reeked of that unique concoction of liniment, sweat and hot Vimto.

Nell Lane was also the home pitch for our school football team. The school team kit was all sky blue shirts, black shorts and socks. We were the Uruguay of South Manchester. Although Chorlton was no longer a grammar school we still used to play grammar school opposition and pitted our skills against Bury, Bolton and Stockport, all of whom gave us more banjo-ings than a hillbillies' barn dance.

Although my first year team was poor, the third year side were the total opposite and punished their opposition on a weekly basis. With Nicky Reid, Kevin Glendon and Michael Barnes – all future professionals – in their line-up, Chorlton Thirds really used to turn on the style. Our first year matches were only 40 minutes each way and so, after our game had ended in predictable defeat, there was always the brief opportunity to watch the older Chorlton team in action.

◆   ◆   ◆

I also had a poor season with the books and so I was relegated from the top class and put into 2LD which, if you remember the word MANIFOLD, meant that I was put into the bottom class with the so-called dimwits. This demotion took some explaining to my mother, but the explanation for failure was from me and only me as I conveniently forgot to tell her the date of parents' evening, adding that end of term school reports were no longer done in our year. I was gutted about taking such a humiliating drop and Vincent Turner (the only other loafer in the top set) took the same fall. It was the obvious move and we immediately became friends in our new class. This was just as well really, because I still didn't really have any at school.

8

Boy of Paper

It was around this time that I managed to gain my first employment. The pocket money my dad begrudgingly prised out of his wallet on a weekly basis was nowhere near enough to maintain my various and sophisticated materialistic requirements. At the grand age of thirteen, I started working as a paperboy (or Regional Information Distribution Technician Person as they are no doubt called today). The job interview consisted of 'Can you walk and carry a bag at the same time?'

'Yes.'

'Okay, you've got the feckin' job.'

That was my first formal introduction to Tom McGarry, the shop manager. He was renowned for uttering all kinds of obscenities under his breath as he went about his business. The shop was simply called 'McGarry's'. It wasn't just a newsagents; it was a veritable treasure trove of devilish temptations that tantalised its customers. The high internal walls were lined from foot to ceiling with huge glass jars, locked tight with rounded metal, screw-on lids. These contained every imaginable type and colour of sugar-coated sweet and toffee. The little old ladies who served behind the glass counters climbed rickety wooden stepladders to haul down the hard-to-reach jars towering above them on the upper decks.

These chastened shop assistants spent interminable hours trying to please awkward children such as me. We were armed with only a pre-decimalised 'tanner' or a 'thrupenny bit' as they waited patiently for us to make our minds up. The choice of whether or not to have an ounce of bonbons or a quarter of lemon drops or pineapple cubes or strawberry creams or bull's eyes or lemon sherbets or mint imperials or humbugs, was totally perplexing to one so young. Meanwhile, the boss-man Tom McGarry scowled as his staff were over-occupied by small fry for small potatoes. To us kids, the eventual selection of confectionary was serious stuff indeed and as the list of sweeties available was almost endless, the choice was totally mind blowing.

But it wasn't just the young 'uns who couldn't make up their minds fast enough. McGarry's also had an impressive array of pipe tobacco and cigarettes. This also blew the minds of many an urchin on the estate and at some point we all had a sly puff on the Woodbines, Turf, du Maurier, Park Drive, Player's or Capstan Full-Strength, behind the back of the shops. In those days, you could tell whether or not a man was working, middle or upper class by the brand of cigarettes he smoked. My dad lived on Park Drive – one of the popular drags of the working classes.

I was never sure if Tom actually owned the shop or whether it was his battle-axe of a mother. She used to pop in from time to time and stir-up Tom's infamous hot temper. Whether Tom owned it or not, he was certainly a slave to that, 'feckin' old boot,' as he often called her to her face (she was too deaf to realise).

Tom was a character, a well-kempt, God-fearing man who always wore a shirt and tie underneath his print-stained tweed jacket and M&S cardigan which served to camouflage his pronounced, but well-earned, paunch. He had a thick mop of hair, which was parted down the side and had a shade of un-dyed blackness which totally belied his years. His thatch also carried the unmistakable whiff of Dr Page-Barker's Patented Scurf & Dandruff Lotion, which was also the preferred cranial skin-flake evasion balm that my dad employed. It was an odour that gave a proper clue as to the Gaelic tobacconist's real age. Tom would have been in his late forties/early fifties when I started working and this was OAP status to a boy of my age. As for his mother, who must have been into her eighties, well she had comfortably reached the status of 'ancient' in my mind. As far as I was concerned there were Egyptian mummies younger than her.

Tom hailed from Sligo in the Republic of Ireland. Being a staunch Catholic, once the papers were despatched, he dutifully worshipped at St Aidan's Church every Sunday morning in his other, unstained, Sunday Best tweed jacket. His devoted attendance at Sunday Mass was probably to atone for the constant stream of foul language he used during his regular 'dickie fits'. He had many of these when his foul temper had been stoked by us 'unreliable little feckers' earlier in the morning. It was comical that he used to shout total abuse at us until a lady customer came in the shop when he would instantly become all sweetness and light.

Given his Irish background, it was remarkable that Tom hated United. His main team was his home-town Sligo Rovers, but somewhere along the way in his unique passage to Button Lane, he adopted the Blues and fiercely defended them against any Reds.

Tom was always okay with me, despite my cheeky tongue and unreliability in turning up for the Sunday morning paper shift. If I didn't, he'd send a more punctual and reliable paperboy round to chuck stones at my window, in a vain attempt to wake me up and, 'get yer arse in gear,' as Tom would say. I used to hate those perishing Sunday morning rounds, the frozen washing hanging rigidly in a state of rigor mortis on the lines adjacent to the nearby flats where I delivered. The mortified clothing looked like I felt. Despite my propensity to oversleep when he needed me most, Tom did take an instant shine in my direction. I don't know whether or not this was because he knew that I was a big Blue. However, it might have been that he was in the St Aidan's congregation on the fateful morning of my road accident and caught a glimpse of me doing an impression of a starfish covered in tomato ketchup while sparked out on Wythenshawe Road.

The pay at McGarry's was minimal, particularly for the hard work the proper paperboys put in. Their evening rounds were made up of 80 to 110 copies of the heavy broadsheet, the *Manchester (United) Evening News* (known locally as the *MUEN*). They had to lug these weighty sacks around the Northern Moor estate at risk of being bitten or mauled by huge, hungry dogs or their owners.

It was my dad who spotted the advert in the shop window: 'Paperboys Wanted'. Despite Moorcroft Road newsagents being nearer, my dad always waited for his *Football Pink* at McGarry's, located just that bit further in the opposite direction on Button Lane. This was because he knew Tom would have been to the match, so they could trade moans about how poor the team had played, despite winning 4–0.

When I began my employment at McGarry's I was given a proper paper round, which I soon realised wasn't for me. Not only did the extreme weight of the canvas bag dig uncomfortably into my shoulder, but my hands got covered in black ink. I was never happy get my hands dirty. Tom noticed this, particularly as I threatened to quit after just two days due to a severe red mark I'd developed on my collarbone. So, when a coveted magazine round became available, Tom allowed me to jump the queue for the most sought-after job in the shop. This was much to the chagrin of the other boys, but 'feck 'em all' as Tom would say (and I did).

A mag round was cushy because it wasn't a paper round. It was for the delivery of publications such as *Motorcycle Monthly*, or weekly magazines such as *Woman's Realm* or *Woman's Weekly*. Mercifully, they were light in weight, less in volume and didn't bleed ink. More importantly, I also delivered comics such as *Tiger and Scorcher, The Dandy* and *The Beano*, which I could read at my leisure in the shop before casually embarking on my daily delivery. This should have taken about 40 minutes, but the round usually took me longer. This was a cunning ploy to ensure that I wasn't available to do an extra – and proper – paper round if one of the lads had failed to turn up due to a severe bout of influenza during the middle of summer, which mysteriously and regularly occurred. Not only was my round cleaner and lighter, but it took me up a better class of garden path. One subscriber actually took copies of *Country Life* and *Cheshire Life*. This was bizarre as our Wythenshawe council estate was nowhere near the country, or Cheshire for that matter. It wasn't the hub of the Northern England social circuit either.

Nevertheless, a better class of garden path also meant a better pedigree of guard dog and as such, my canine attack risks were still there to concern me. But my fear of dogs was not due to the damage their bloodthirsty gnashers could inflict upon me. It always happened on a Thursday when my magazine round took me over the Sale border to No. 24 Sandford Road for the delivery of the hallowed *Weekly News,* a paper that gave me great football transfer tips. A couple of doors down at No. 30 resided a sexually confused Labrador. Far worse than trying to bite me or even lick me to death, the randy canine would spot me halfway down the road and gleefully try and mount my right leg while I was still on my bike. These unwanted amorous attacks gave me great concern. I suppose one good kick in the chops would have given it the message but to hurt an animal was never in my psyche and I didn't really know how to deal with the situation. My dad's pearls of wisdom didn't cover, 'in the event of a dog trying to shag your leg, give it a swift kick in the goolies.' I had to rely on either (i) asking it nicely to 'stop it' which it never did, or (ii) dismounting my bike and placing it between me and the dog, as we ritually went round in circles in the middle of the road for 20 minutes before one of the neighbours eventually came out and made it go away. If there was no neighbour about, I'd sometimes make a break for it, deliver the mag, get back on and pedal like mad up the road with the horny mutt in gleeful pursuit.

Despite these tricky moments, my hardships certainly paid off and my new-found wealth dribbled slowly into my trusty piggy bank. This would be mercilessly demolished as soon as I had saved up enough cash to build my own customised tracker bike, of which I was in dire need. After months of toil at McGarry's I had the money and the method to build my own modest dream machine. In pursuit of my goal, I swapped most of my remaining City programme collection for a bike frame, which, with a bit of hard work and elbow grease (of which my dad kept a large tin in the wash-house) I could turn into something special. I spent hours acquiring the necessary parts and got down to work sanding down the frame, greasing the cogs and chain, polishing the new chrome wheels, bull horn handlebars and short-sized aluminium mudguards. I fixed them all to the frame which had been lovingly painted in my trademark colours of sky blue metallic Airfix paint for the frame, and white for the straightened-out front forks. Once it had dried, I was ready to go. I mounted my new bike with great pride and rode up and down the estate like a peacock displaying his bright new feathers for all to admire.

After a few weeks of cruising around with a proud grin on my face I made a catastrophic error. I had cycled up to Sale town centre and popped into a shop for tights for my mum, but had forgotten to lock up my bike. As I came out of the shop I saw my prized possession disappearing into the distance. I kicked off my 3-inch platform shoes and gave chase barefoot. I must have got a quarter of a mile before I gave up and I wandered back to the shops totally distraught. My beautiful bike had been nicked. It was built with my hard work and money, but that wasn't all – some cheeky little fecker had slyly taken the opportunity to rob my shoes in my absence and I had to walk 2½ miles home from Sale in my dirty socks. It was devastation and humiliation all in one sad afternoon. What had made matters worse was that I hadn't even fully paid for that bike parts I'd assembled, and it meant I'd have to walk my mag round for the foreseeable future. I'd subbed a few weeks' wages from Tom McGarry in order to pay for the last piece in the jigsaw: a rear flanged wheel that cost £12. As Tom was only paying £1.20 week, it would be literally months before I'd worked off the debt. But then came a stroke of luck.

I wasn't the only paperboy to owe Tom, as most of the lads were in the red. All debt was written into the big black 'subs book' which Tom never let out of his sight, until the following Sunday morning. During the wait for the papers to arrive, there would be invariable requests to Tom to, 'sub us a packet of Parma Violets', or, 'sub us a bag of Black Jacks'. He was only too happy to oblige as it meant that we would soon literally eat into our wages and Tom would effectively have to pay us less, while making money on the sale. On this particular morning, Tom was remonstrating with the late delivery man, calling him a 'feckin' Commy bastard'. Meanwhile, Danny Griffin had located the subs book and popped it in his paper bag. Word soon got back to the rest of the boys. Within minutes, we all joined Danny round the back of the shops for the ceremonial burning of all our collective debts. It was a great moment.

Tom never found out who'd nicked the book, but we all started from scratch again, with strangely little protest from the boss man. His heart was in the right place. Eventually, Tom's mother died and Tom retired from the newsagency not long after.

Years later, my dad saw Tom McGarry one Sunday afternoon enjoying a pint in the Northenden Social Club. A few hours later, Tom went home, had an afternoon snooze in his armchair and never woke up again. The late, great Irish comedian, Dave Allen, used to finish his show with the words, 'May your God go with you.' I sincerely hope Tom McGarry's God went with him.

9

Away at Last

In the early years of the 1970s, Manchester United fell on hard times. George Best went through his 'I can't be bothered with it all' phase and some of their older stars were coming to the end of their sell-by date. By the end of the 1973/74 campaign, the threat of relegation was ominous as they found themselves second bottom of the First Division. United's penultimate fixture and final home game of the season was dauntingly a local derby match against their far superior neighbours.

Defeat against City would see United relegated. Most of the 'hard' lads in our year were United fans (or 'Rags' as they are 'affectionately' known to City fans) and they were bragging the week before the match about how they were going to stay up and kick a City fan's head in if they got the chance. I remember our Red Geometrical Engineering Drawing (GED) teacher, Mr Lowe, banging on about how relegation would be avoided as City had nothing to play for. It was a strange theory, as relegating them meant there was, in fact, everything to play for. He showed the class his Scoreboard End ticket for the match, which made me envious, as I hadn't seen City play away.

There was a big build-up to the derby in the *MUEN* and on the Friday night programme *Kick Off* in which Gerald Sinstadt had also been pontificating about United's precarious plight. The following morning I was in bed quietly minding my own business, when there was a sharp knock at the door. It was Mr Johnson, our neighbour, who had a job as a cleaner at Granada TV Studios. He wondered if my dad and I fancied watching the big match in the viewing room as the 'live' feed came through to the studios. Obviously we both jumped at the chance.

The drama unfolded at the end of the game. Colin Bell took possession of the ball and strolled deep into United's half totally unchallenged. He slipped it to Francis Lee, who in his words, 'played a nothing sort of ball into the box.' Denis Law, a United legend, back-heeled it into the net to send his old club into oblivion. My dad and I were the only ones in the viewing room to leap up as Gerald Sinstadt exclaimed, 'Denis has done it!' It was a great moment and one that my dad savoured in the hospitality room after the match with a pint or three.

City had also made it to the League Cup final that year against Wolves, only to lose to a John Richards goal late in the second half. My travel-shy dad didn't take me to that one either, despite my desperate pleas.

But all was not lost. Having a bit more money in my pocket from my paper round meant that I could go to the odd away game, not that I needed the extra dosh for my debut. My first excursion out of Manchester was on the 112 bus to Old Trafford for a night match: a League Cup third-round tie on 9 October 1974 against United. We lost 1–0 and it was a major cup shock at the time, what with them being lower league opposition and all that. My dad had been reluctant to take me to a City game away from Maine Road, and so I had decided to take matters into my own hands. Terry Stanton's mum and dad were a bit more liberal, and Terry was allowed to go to the match with his older brother, Fred, but Terry often went off on his own. We hatched a cunning plan. Even though it was midweek, I managed to persuade my mum and dad to let me go to Sale Odeon with Terry. The bus went to Sale Odeon, except we didn't get off until Warwick Road, Stretford . . . with Old Trafford looming.

On the way, Terry versed me in the skills of bunking in the turnstile by pushing through against the back of a slim fan. As Terry wasn't of such petite physique, our first job would be to find someone who fitted the bill. Jibbing into a ground was against my better nature, but Terry assured me that the turnstile operators rarely chased such scoundrels (and there weren't luminescent stewards or burly doormen lurking around in those days to contend with). We made our way towards the United fans' favourite part of the stadium: the Stretford End.

Terry and I waited until about 30 minutes before kick-off when the queues were pushing and shoving towards the gate. I nestled in between Terry and a smallish bloke and waited for him to hand in his ticket. As he did, the turnstile promptly clicked and I imagined we were on the edge of a cliff as I shoved him as hard as I could in order to make room for my diminutive physique. Before anyone could say, 'come back 'ere yer little git,' I was into the ground and off like a shot around the back of the stand. To my amazement, when I dared to turn around, nobody was in pursuit. I met Terry inside the gents' toilets, as we had arranged, and went into the ground to watch the match from a safe vantage point, away from the throng of coin-throwing morons behind the goal. United might have knocked us out of the League Cup that night, but at least I didn't have to pay to watch them do it.

When I arrived home late, I made up a cover story to my mum about the bus not turning up and having to walk home via the chippy, which she just about accepted. Although I knew I shouldn't have, I told my dad the next day that I'd been to the match the night before; I was so excited about it, I just couldn't contain myself. He took it well and didn't shop me to my mum. Not only that, but he took the hint. A few months later, he and I went to what I consider to be my first away game proper.

This was a league match at Elland Road, Leeds, on 1 March 1975. Dad finally booked us on a coach run by the MCFC Travel Club and stewarded by City's most famous gravel-voiced grandmother, Helen Turner. She had a preposterous blonde beehive, a bell which she rang by order of the Kippax, and a ritual pre-match kiss and good luck sprig of heather for goalkeeper Joe Corrigan.

Once we had left Manchester on the M62, we noticed the Pennines ominously shrouded in mist and blanketed in snow. This prompted me to ask my dad every 5 minutes, 'Dad, do you think the fog will lift? Dad, do you think it will be postponed?' He eventually replied, 'How the heck should I know, I'm not the ref or the bloody weatherman. Now give over.' By the time we eventually chugged into the away fans' car park, the visibility was so bad that you couldn't see Elland Road, easily within viewing distance on a clearer afternoon.

We arrived early and dad – who hadn't been to an away game since the olden days of Bradford Park Avenue – decided that we'd go for a walk around the ground. Leeds were opening their new North Stand that day and this was the area in which all the City fans had been herded. Dad and I were oblivious to this as we walked into the first paying turnstile to which he took a fancy. As we entered the stand, I realised something was amiss. There wasn't a blue scarf in site. We had walked straight into the mouth of the lion: the Spion Kop . . . Leeds' end! I started to hide my scarf but dad said, 'don't be daft', as we waited for the teams to come out. He couldn't comprehend that there was actually an away section, where we should have entered. But he had to concede the point 25 minutes into the game when the fog lifted to reveal a rippling sea of City fans at the other end of the ground.

Leeds were in all white with their ostentatious numbered garter-tags holding up their socks while City were resplendent in their traditional and mighty fine red and black striped away strip. The home side took the lead. Alan Oakes equalised. Leeds took the lead again. Willie Donachie equalised. It was an exciting game for my away debut!

On the way home I stared contentedly at the desolate snow-covered moorland speeding past my gaze while the charabanc strained back over the Pennines as the driver crashed the gears, like the sound of a tramp clearing his throat. Away games were the best. They were the most exciting things in the world and I wanted to see many more as soon as possible.

10

Colourful Times

My first school year had been one of abject academic failure, but once the six-week holidays had arrived, I could forget all my educational exasperations. It was 1974 and all avid footy fans were in for a treat as it was World Cup year in West Germany. Unfortunately, England had failed to make it thanks to Sir Alf's inconsistent qualifying campaign within a group of just three teams including Wales and Poland. England had to beat the Poles in the final group match at Wembley to go through, but Norman Hunter and Peter Shilton didn't help matters when they combined to allow Polish striker Domarski to score the goal that would ultimately deny England a place in the finals. However, Scotland had somehow made it through and my dad and I were looking forward to having a good laugh at their expense. So much so that he took advantage of a World Cup offer at the local TV rental shop. My mum must have temporarily taken her eye off the metaphorical ball as dad secured us a new colour television, finally persuading her to relent and let us ascend into a more colourful existence. Previously, she hadn't wanted any further excuses for me to spend less time studying, or my dad to spend more time idly gawking his 'square eyes' at the telly.

I could hardly contain my excitement when four blokes in white coats struggled up our front path with a goggle-box that must have weighed at least a couple of tons. It would hardly fit through the front door! Anyone who is of an age to remember the arrival of their first colour telly will recall the unadulterated magic it first brought, once two different blokes in brown 'Arkwright' coats had finally tuned it in ready for action.

The new set arrived right on cue on the day of the opening ceremony of the World Cup. My dad and I were mesmerised by the kaleidoscope of effervescent shades etched onto the bulbous glass screen of our Ultra set. The wondrous window into West Germany was framed by a mysterious black band within which the smiling participants from all over the globe paraded past the cameras on the Munich running track, which sparkled in the incessant rain on the day (and for the majority of the tournament).

The first game was played at Frankfurt's Waldstadion. Once the formalities were out of the way, we sat back to marvel at our new luxury in anticipation of the match. Brazil – *the* most colourful team in the world and current but troubled World Champions – were up against the Yugoslavians. We sat back, relaxed and made contented grins at each other, as we raised our respective glasses of Alpine pineappleade and Davenport's 'beer at home' and waited for the action to begin.

Disaster struck. Just as the teams were about to kick-off, there was a sharp 'PLINK' sound and a puff of smoke lifted from the back of the set as the picture disappeared, never to be seen again. At least not until the following Monday when half-a-dozen repairmen finally came round to fit a new valve. My dad ended up renting that set for the next ten years and for the next two World Cups. He must have paid for it at least five times over by the time it was finally knackered and obsolete.

Despite Brazil's reputation, it was the Dutch who provided the real colour in the 1974 tournament. Their 'Total Football' was played in a luminescent orange strip by pin-up players with their pop star looks, including Krol, Cruyff and Neeskens. But it was the West Germans and my old mate Gerd Müller who lifted the trophy in Munich's Olympiastadion. This was the venue where I would witness one of England's greatest ever triumphs in years to come.

♦   ♦   ♦

Once I'd prised myself away from the telly, 1974 turned out to be quite a summer. Not only did I have the family camping holiday, but I also got to help pitch a tent with the Cubs at Mevagissey in Cornwall. I was in 1st Wythenshawe Scouts, which included several of the boys I'd been mates with at Button Lane.

We trundled down to Cornwall in a clapped-out minibus. This heap was followed by both a cloud of blue smoke and an equally decrepit van containing the tents and the necessary equipment needed for a two-week survival trip. It was a journey of epic proportions and we didn't arrive until the early hours.

We pitched our tents in a farmer's field in Port Mellon and soon endured a scary walk through a field of imposing cows which blocked the pathway into Port Mellon Bay. I found cows to be threatening. Not that they carried flick knives or baseball bats, but they did hang about in gangs and their sheer size was rather worrying. In fact their obvious threat became reality when one inadvertently knocked me over as I tentatively crept past the herd. It was a frightening experience and I was completely covered in cow dung, but otherwise unharmed (apart from my pride, following the incessant mickey-taking from the pack for the rest of the holiday). Subsequently, I was quick to notice that cows aren't very big on manners, not that I ever held a grudge. In fact I now quite admire the cumbersome beasts. Let's face it, a beef vindaloo just wouldn't be the same without one.

While covered in manure, I walked down to the bay, which was romantically lit in the shimmering sun, and admired the Venture Scouts busily fishing for our tea. This would consist of the unlikely combination of mackerel and baked beans. If this was the type of food we were going to eat then I was going to go home very slim, although not as it turned out.

There were six Cubs in each of the three tents, plus a further tent for the Troop Leaders and Venture Scouts. The fortnight's holiday was an ideal opportunity for innocent young Cubs to acquire new skills and gain new badges, with harmless pursuits such as sea-fishing or canoeing. The most popular pastime, however, proved to be shoplifting in Mevagissey. Most Cubs on the trip won their advanced badges at this. I also earned a further badge, acquired for receiving stolen goods and then eating them! I was soon wracked with guilt for being complicit in the great Cornish confectionery heist. This taught me a key lesson – although crime could pay at the outset, it wasn't worth it as my conscience couldn't take it the guilt.

Following our delinquent little spree, by the end of the week most of the shops in this quaint little fishing village had handwritten signs up on their front doors saying, 'No Cubs are allowed in this shop'. I'm not sure that this was what Baden-Powell had in mind when he invented the Scout Movement. Numerous complaints from the village shopkeepers had led to the Troop Leader carrying out searches for contraband, but he found nothing as most of the sweets had already been scoffed and the chocolate had melted in our stomachs.

I have many good childhood memories of Cubs and Scouts, particularly during the lucrative 'bob-a-job' week where I operated on a one-for-you, one-for-me basis. Besides corruption, we were taught a lot of new skills, including a makeshift and impromptu music lesson. The Easter Whit Sunday Parades provided an opportunity for the local organisations to march around the neighbourhood proudly displaying their banners. These announced the arrival of the 'Women's Knitting Society', and the 'Men's Cat-Chucking Team'. Occasionally our Scout troop was invited to the jamboree march held in town. The Scout hierarchy must have been scraping the barrel in order to make the Scout Band at the front of the parade look a lot larger than it actually was. As they were short of musicians, 1st Wythenshawe was given instruments, although none of us could knock out a tune if a new badge depended on it. We were ordered not to try to play the instruments, but to march proudly while going through the motions. After 10 minutes of miming the bugle and missing the drums, some of us decided to give it a go for real.

As the rest of the band played *Colonel Bogey* with great accomplishment, the inane grins of the admiring onlookers lining the pavement, soon turned to frowns as 1st Wythenshawe and its merry band of half-wits marched joyfully past with all the harmony of a group of castrated banshees.

♦   ♦   ♦

Later that summer Chorlton High School held its annual Summer Fête. My dad and younger sister Joanne attended, as did City's goalkeeper, the red-haired and scrawny Keith 'Kipper' MacRae. He had come along, presumably at the behest of former pupil Peter Barnes, for the penalty prize competition. Each would-be Franny Lee (aka Lee One Pen) had to pay a small fee to hit six penalties at 'Kipper'. The winner had a fantastic prize in store: an all-expenses-paid day out for two to the radioactive surroundings of the Windscale Nuclear Power Plant. Most of the third year team had taken part including the star trio and five out of six was the best score. Our Joanne had asked my dad if she could have a go and I said I'd follow, thinking she'd make a mess of it. My dad was not yet used to watching girls playing football, but he bent down and whispered some shrewd advice into our Joanne's ear, 'Take your time and hit them hard and low and in the corners.' Armed with this cunning plan, up she stepped.

The first couple of penalties she struck hard and low and in the corners. I don't think 'Kipper' tried to save them perhaps as hard as he might have. But he soon took her seriously as she slotted the third past him with unerring accuracy and power. The crowd, particularly the women, started cheering. Meanwhile, the lads from the football team – who had already taken their penalties – started to look a bit concerned. My ruthless sister planted the fourth firmly past MacRae's left hand and did the same with the fifth. Could she get six out of six and carry off the big prize? Our Joanne, my little sister, calmly stepped up and mercilessly drove an unstoppable penalty to MacRae's right as he dived to his left. Six out of six! I didn't bother to take my turn, realising that I couldn't improve upon perfection. But Joanne's highly impressive spot-kicking feats did give me a great idea.

11

From Top to Bottom

Those six weeks in between the school years shot by and I soon had to face a different type of music in secondary school. Despite being put in what was virtually a remedial class for my second year in Chorlton, on the football front things were looking up and I was made school captain. But could my leadership skills inspire us to our first victory?

The second year team was still made up of the same players as the previous year and my sister's penalty prowess had certainly given me food for thought. As I was school team captain I could make decisions and the first one I made came against St Bede's at Nell Lane in the opening match of the season. After half-an-hour's play we were awarded a penalty. If our Joanne could put them away with aplomb then so could I. I ran all the way from the back and into the opposition penalty box. It was the furthest forward I'd ever been in twenty-odd appearances for the school! Once I finally arrived I informed our forward line that, 'I'm taking it!' As I was the skipper they couldn't stop my power-crazed assertions. I got my breath back as I waited for our long-legged games teacher to pace what appeared to be the 15-yard mark for the spot by the time he'd finished. I placed the ball, took a fast-bowler's run-up and smacked it low and hard and into the bottom corner of the net for my first ever school goal. Not only had I scored, it meant that we were in front!

It was a lead we retained until the 88th minute when disaster struck. Our defence, competently marshalled by myself, pushed up to the halfway line. One of their strikers spotted his opportunity and ran through on his own. With a defender chasing and our goalie coming out from his line, the attacker took the ball well wide. I was legging it back in a direct line to our goal and as I entered our box their striker chipped the ball over our advancing 'keeper. The ball dipped at the last moment, hit the crossbar and bounced down smacking me straight in the face and into the net. It was 1–1 and I had scored them both!

Any joy I'd had in leading our side to its first undefeated game was tempered by my own personal anguish. Far worse was to follow. There was a tradition at Monday morning assembly whereby the captains of the school teams would read out a match report. By now, word had circulated about my exploits on Saturday. By the time I was up on stage I was shaking like a celebrity in the Betty Ford clinic. After the usual prayers and covert trumps, I walked up the steps onto the stage and reported, 'On Saturday, Chorlton second years entertained St Bede's at Nell Lane. We took the lead after 30 minutes of the first half when Worthington expertly despatched a low penalty following a deliberate handball. Unfortunately in the second half, however, Worthington put through his own net with only 2 minutes to go to deny Chorlton Seconds their first victory.' It was a passage which was greeted with sniggers and chuckles from many in the hall and signalled yet another mickey-taking fest at my expense.

The following week we managed another draw, this time at Newall Green High in Wythenshawe. At half time we were 4–0 up, but as usual there was another disaster in the second half. We were all sitting on the coach outside the school gates feeling totally dejected, with the third year team losing to a late winner. Everyone was impatiently waiting for 'sir' to get on the coach once he'd finished his protracted sycophantic pleasantries with their games teacher – despite the fact that he'd been unbelievably biased towards his team as home referee. Suddenly we all noticed a young lad cycling past our window on the pavement. He spotted that the coach contained the players who had blown a 4–0 lead and immediately pedalled back gesturing with a tormenting 'Harvey Smith' sign and the pincer-fingered sign that rhymes with 'banker'. As he was doing this, the large flare of his trouser leg caught in his bike chain which jammed, instantly throwing the boy completely over his handlebars. He landed on his back with the bike on top of him and, when he finally managed to get up, his right trouser leg had been ripped clean off. A few moments later, sir got on the coach having missed the fun. He found us doing dying fly impressions on the musty maroon tartan seats and shouted sternly, 'I don't know why you lot are so happy; the thirds got hammered and the seconds blew a four-goal lead!' Nobody cared and it remains *the* funniest real life piece of slapstick comedy I've ever witnessed.

My last anecdote of any note while playing for the school team came in a Manchester Cup game against Yew Tree High. Their star player was Paul Stewart; *the* Paul Stewart who went on to play for City and England as well as Tottenham, Liverpool and Sunderland. He also played for Stoke, Wolves and Burnley. I knew him personally as he used to play practice games with Steve Wadsworth at the Manchester University playing fields where the affable former City full-back Roy Little was in charge.

Anyway, before Paul Stewart would be signing autographs of his own in later years, he had to come up against me in my own backyard at Nell Lane. Because I had prior knowledge of his game, I had evaluated his strengths and weaknesses. I knew what to expect and how to deal with him. Consequently, I volunteered to man-mark him. It was a cunning plan, which was to pay-off big style. I would have heeded our manager's advice of, 'give him an early kick and let him know you're there,' but I never got close enough to swing a connecting leg.

There are not many that can say that they've marked an England international out of a key cup tie, and I'm not one of them! Having said that, he didn't get a kick of the ball; he actually got four kicks and they all went into our net. Yew Tree beat us 9–0, but it was a moral victory for us because they were tipped to score ten. After I'd finished with him, Paul Stewart knew he'd been in a game, if only because he had a bit of mud on his left knee and had to wipe it off back in the dressing room.

12

Kung Fu Fighting

A couple of draws was the closest I ever came to winning a game with the school team. I also had minimal achievements in lessons. Unlike 1M – where I was the only class clown – 2LD, in which I now resided, had more clowns than Gerry Cottle's Circus, which regularly played in Wythenshawe Park. Being stuck in the bottom class was a real eye-opener. For starters, the behaviour of some of the class pupils was quite appalling. I was particularly alarmed at one early incident when the maths teacher, Mrs Jones, clocked fellow class 'mate' Kevin Williamson around the back of the head for persistent bad behaviour. He got up from his desk and grabbed her by the throat, threatening to 'knock her out' if she ever did it again. I wondered to what depths my sharp fall from grace may have taken me. Admittedly I had messed about in the first year, but this was several leagues below any poor behaviour I might have displayed.

The teachers seemed content to contain 2LD, rather than go out of their way to teach us anything worthwhile. This was understandable as we had pupils in our class capable of doing anything but study. The other real demonstration of such extreme behaviour came from Pete Weston, who was the ringleader of a group of baddies including the lad who attacked Mrs Jones. Weston had a reputation for being one of the toughest lads in Chorlton. One day he clashed horns with the woodwork teacher (the effeminate, but still potentially nasty 'Smoothy Boothy') and promptly locked him in his own stockroom during one of his carpentry classes. Mr Booth made all the muffled threats under the sun that if someone didn't let him out he would do this, that and the other to all of us. But Weston equally threatened, 'If anyone lets him out, I'll kill yer!' I was far more afraid of Pete Weston than Mr Booth and so wisely did nothing. I doubt that they could have punished Weston with any of their various methods of physical torture. He was as hard as nails. This was proved when he was smashed in the face by a flying rounders bat (when we were on a geography field trip) at a velocity which would have taken most mortals' heads off.

In a class with the 'bad lads' I wouldn't count as friends, there were two notable exceptions – Vinny Turner and Steve 'Wadsy' Wadsworth. I vaguely knew Wadsy from his days playing football for Rackhouse Primary School against my Button Lane. Steve was a keen Blue but, unlike me, he really could pack a punch and often did when his back was against the wall or even well away from it. He had one of the best left-hooks I've seen and I saw it in action a few times. My problem was that previous poor fighting performances in the gladiatorial arena of the playground hadn't gone unnoticed. I was best suited to holding someone's coat, rather than taking it off and getting involved in the ensuing scrap. In addition, most of the so-called hard nuts in that class were United fans and as such didn't like me or my brass City identity bracelet which was never off my green wrist. I didn't help myself by always mouthing off about City and never backing down in the many ensuing arguments about football.

A few of the 'bad lads' tried to intimidate me, although not as badly as it could have been because I knew how to lighten things up. As there were softer targets to pick on, they often lost interest. Unfortunately, Williamson – Mrs Jones's tormentor – took matters further than the rest and always accepted an opportunity to have a go. Whenever I spotted him in the corridor my heart sank and I'd deliberately walk the other way. He would do horrible things like gob in my desk, use me as a punchbag or trip me up as I walked past. He also derided me with his rapier-like wit, calling me names like 'fat boy' or 'fatty'. I wouldn't have minded, but I wasn't that fat. Okay, so I had developed a bit of 'puppy fat', as the history teacher not so diplomatically called it in front of the whole class. I was unable to explain that the silhouette of a pot-belly and a double chin was a totally natural shape and was how male Worthingtons were meant to look.

On reflection, Williamson's bullying was usually in the presence of his mates. A bully needs an audience or backup if their prey develops enough courage to fight back, which I didn't at the time. But I did many moons later when I saw him on his own and decided it was time for revenge – but for now I was the victim.

After our relegation into the bowels of the bottom class, both Vinny Turner and I resolved to get our heads down that year to win our places back into the top set. Despite my initial good intentions and an end of term exam score of 86 per cent in French – the highest mark of anyone in the whole school year – promotion back to the top flight was denied as the rest of my other exam results had rhymed with 'kite'.

13

Bully for Me

B y the time I'd progressed to the third year, I'd given up on the school and its football team. My right knee gave me serious gyp, so much so that I had regular appointments at Wythenshawe Hospital with my consultant, Mr O.O. Cowpe. The knee was heavily scarred from the accident I'd had when I was eight, the diagnosis being that I might have 'a foreign body' floating around near the joint. This was something I should never have mentioned in class, as I soon became known as 'frog-leg' – the hilarious supposition being that I had a dead Frenchman trapped in my knee.

The injury meant that I lost my place in the school team and I didn't actually play for Chorlton again. It was a sad end to a not-so-glittering school career. Not that I was too bothered. I was struggling to walk let alone play football, and there were far better players making themselves available. In fact, the school team started winning when I departed! As far as the school's footballing reputation was concerned, my knackered knee was perhaps a blessing in disguise.

The upside of the injury meant that on my way back from hospital to school, I stumbled across City's training sessions which had moved from Wythenshawe Park to the private Christie playing fields off Barlow Moor Road. I poked my nose through the chain link fence in order to get a better look at Tommy Booth, who always had a go at me for not being in school. It was surreal to see Francis Lee training with City even though he'd been sold to Derby County.

By the time the 1975/76 season arrived, United had now rejoined the top flight and they had drawn City in the fourth round of the League Cup at Maine Road on 12 November 1975. My dad drove that night and we took United fanatic Terry Stanton to the game. My dad and I were behind the North Stand goal which was odd because we nearly always went in the Kippax. City really turned it on and a great virtuoso performance from Asa Hartford inspired City to a famous 4–0 win. Unfortunately, it proved to be a pyrrhic victory as Colin Bell suffered an ultimately career-ending injury which robbed City prematurely of our greatest player. None of us knew this at half time, and as I looked around the ground during the break, I spotted Terry Stanton who was sitting away from us with his head in his hands as City were 3–0 up. He didn't come back with us, choosing instead to go home by bus.

The following morning I made my way to school, ready to dish out the bragging, as was my right. I was warned at the school gates that Williamson and his Red mates were on the prowl for Blues and that I'd cop for it big style. I walked into the playground unperturbed, but was soon spotted by the pack. I ran into the school building as fast as I could. It was still early and the building was empty. I legged it down the corridor with an angry half-dozen Reds in hot pursuit. Running out of options – and out of breath – I shot up the stairs to the top floor where I was cornered in a classroom. I was thrown around the room and took a kicking that gave me a fat lip and a bloody nose.

Although there wasn't much I could have done in the circumstances, word soon got around the school about what had happened and the bigger City lads went looking for Williamson and his crew at the break. I had mixed feelings on the news that Williamson and his henchmen had copped for some retribution. The threat of an all-out riot between the Blues and the Reds was looming, but the teachers had got wind of the situation and were out in force to create a stand-off. I was relatively safe because the tougher Blues told me to see them if I was picked on again. The problem was that none of them were in my form class and I was left to fend for myself. While most of the Reds had let it drop, Williamson did not and continued his campaign against me.

It was more annoying than disturbing and I didn't live in constant fear. Besides, at upper school I was to witness fellow City fan Joe Lawson give Kevin Williamson a bloody good hiding, and I lost a lot of my fear of him after that. When I eventually left school I didn't give him a second thought, until one night . . .

I must have been about twenty when I was out on a Friday night with my mate Terry Hyland. We'd started supping in the Snooty Fox on Princess Road near Chorlton and had decided to go for a rare pint in the Oaks located near to the junction with Barlow Moor Road and Princess Road. As it was a Friday night – lads' night out in Manchester in those days – the pub was packed and as we walked in, who did I spot at the bar?

With the words of the old Spanish proverb ringing in my ears that, 'If you sit by the river long enough eventually the body of your enemy will come floating by,' there was my old nemesis himself: Kevin Williamson. I couldn't believe my eyes. Without any delay, I told Terry that there was a bloke at the bar I was going to, 'sort out'. Initially confident in my chosen course of action, Terry asked, 'Do you want me to hold your coat?' (we were very chivalrous chaps in those days). He said it as if I 'sorted people out' every day of the week. But then, upon quick reflection, he asked, 'Do you want any help?' I declined.

Since the days of Chorlton High, I'd long since built myself up and had learned how to throw a decent punch; regular lunchtime bag work at the YMCA had seen to that. Confident in my own ability to exact revenge and knock his miserable, smarmy Red block off, I pushed my way to the bar. My belligerent frame of mind was driven by the memories of numerous torments this medium built (but smaller than I remembered him to be) lad propping up the bar had inflicted upon me. This was the same lad who had continually subjected me to so much grief as a child. As I pushed closer he noticed me immediately and gave me a greeting that took me totally by surprise.

'Bloody hell,' he exclaimed, 'it's Steve Worthington. How are you doing, mate? It's really great to see you. Are you having a pint?' I was totally taken aback and the wind was completely knocked out of my sails. I lamely said, 'Go on then. I'll have a pint of bitter.' Terry kept a discreet distance while Mr Williamson and I had a cosy chat. He even offered me another pint which, of course, I accepted remembering my dad's advice that if there's 'owt for nowt, take two', As Terry followed me out of the pub, he commented, 'You really sorted him out, didn't you!' I suppose in a way, I had . . . in my own mind at least. This wasn't the lad that I'd feared at school; in fact, he was a bit of a daddy long legs-type character. He was something that I shouldn't have been afraid of in the first place. Besides, it was obvious to me that we'd finally both grown up.

♦　♦　♦

After the 4–0 derby victory, City went on to reach the League Cup final in 1976 playing against Newcastle United, but once again I wasn't there to enjoy it. I travelled to thirteen away games that season and had religiously gone to all the home games but I'd long since stopped collecting programmes. This proved to be a big mistake. The programmes contained vouchers that were pasted onto sheets and you needed a sheet with 20-odd vouchers to qualify for a final ticket. I had nowhere near this amount. I had found a few programmes lying around the house and the front covers from the away programmes could be cut off and used as vouchers, but I was still short, as was Steve Wadsworth and his younger brother Alan, who had also joined us at Chorlton. They were eventually both sorted out for tickets by an uncle and made it to Wembley. Unfortunatley I had no such benevolent relative.

I watched the cup final build-up on Granada TV's *Kick Off* programme the night before the match and I was in tears that I wasn't going. The coaches and cup final specials had departed for London without me on board. I pleaded with my dad to let me go down ticketless on my own, but I was fourteen and he was having none of it. Obviously wracked with guilt about his failure to come through with my dream ticket, my dad took me to see a live game that day: Bolton Wanderers v Wolves at Burnden Park. Some consolation! I was devastated that I wasn't at the Twin Towers, but dad thought that a short trip up the M62 might take my mind off this major disappointment. It only made matters worse.

To this day I couldn't tell you the final score at Bolton as I was totally disinterested. I stood in a paddock on the side of the pitch opposite the tunnel with my dad's cheap little transistor radio welded to my ear listening to live commentary of the League Cup final. I'd shout out 'come on City!' and conspicuously cheered with delight when former Chorltonian Peter Barnes scored City's first goal. It was 1–1 at half time and the second half sounded tense, until the decisive moment arrived. As the radio commentator described it, 'The ball arrives in from the left, headed on by Tommy Booth, knocked back by Hartford and what a goal, Dennis Tueart has scored with a 30-yard overhead kick!' In my excitement I grabbed my dad, forgetting all about the radio, which fell to the ground and shattered into several pieces. That was it. City were 2–1 up with plenty of time left for play, but I'd smashed the radio beyond repair. We immediately departed from the thrills of the Bolton v Wolves match and made the long hike to the car. My dad didn't have a car radio and it wasn't until almost an hour later when we'd got home that we found out the score from my mum. City had won 2–1 – although Tueart's overhead kick wasn't from 30 yards.

The following day I met Steve and Alan Wadsworth and we went on the 108 bus to the Town Hall to watch the victorious City team parade the League Cup. They kindly and thoughtfully brought me a City flag from Wembley and accompanied me to see City holding some silverware. But I didn't feel part of it. After the parade, walking past the Town Hall and back to the bus stop, I noticed a lonely City rosette floating limply, face-down in a puddle. It was symbolic of how I felt.

It still annoys me that I wasn't at Wembley, particularly as City haven't won anything since that final. This means that, at forty-eight years of age, I haven't seen them win a major trophy. My dad did purchase season tickets the following year and I've had one ever since. But it's been a case of shutting the dressing room door after the team has run off with the cup. Years later I was discussing this with my mate Bibby, who casually said, 'It's a shame I didn't know you back then. I had a couple of spare tickets, which I gave away on the day!'

14

The Final Stretch

The following year I graduated from the Lower School to the Upper School located on Corkland Road. Chorlton Lower School had little architectural merit and conformed to the standard concrete and glass combination of its day; Chorlton Upper School was no improvement. The main building was a nineteenth-century, predominantly wooden construction, with the not-so-subtle exception of the new red-brick wing which was built in the playground area and housed facilities for practical subjects such as domestic science. Today all that is left of the second tier of Chorlton High School are the iron railings which now surround a small housing estate. Those iron grilles once hemmed disaffected pupils like me into what was hardly a camp of concentration. Such was my negative nostalgia of Chorlton High School that I never went back to have a look at the Upper School until far later life when I discovered it had been demolished.

I had high hopes that the Upper School could give me a fresh start and a clean slate. As my sister – by now a sixth form prefect – had astutely informed me, 'At Upper School you will be treated like more of an adult, if you decide to act like one!' But I didn't, so I wasn't.

Those two final years at school were the most vital in shaping what sort of qualifications I *might* gain before I ventured out into the big wide world. Thankfully, I'd managed to shake off metalwork and the thug teacher with the 'Double Diamond' and elected to take on domestic science instead. Vinny Turner also decided to take this option and we both thought we might be in for a good laugh, and we were right. Both of us took serious stick for enrolling in cooking lessons from all our contemporary 'macho boys'. This was the 1970s and there were strict sexual divisions on who did what. Sewing, knitting, cooking and bringing up baby were for the girls, while drinking, smoking, gambling and farting were for the boys. Indeed, the only bloke to put on an apron in those days was *The Galloping Gourmet*, Graham Kerr, but his cooking programme was Canadian so he didn't count.

After our first cookery class, Vinny and I received serious grief. Our enemies presumed we'd been baking fairy cakes, but we'd actually been baking pasties which smelt great in our cute little Cadbury's Roses baking tins. It was all a bit girly, but once we showed our detractors the more than edible pastries that we'd produced, the merciless jibes began to subside. Not only that, but I was quick to point out that, 'while you lot have been knocking the crap out of a smelly piece of molten metal, making some daft-looking hinge that you'll never use, we've been enjoying a much less noisy pursuit with plenty of girls on hand to help us as we struggled to mix the pastry.' Domestic science wasn't such a bad idea after all.

We started baking a Christmas cake in October. I asked the teacher, 'Won't it go mouldy by the time Chrimbo arrives?' But I was reliably informed that it would be okay as the brandy in the cake would preserve the fruit. 'Brandy, what brandy? This just gets better and better.' At least it would have done if I'd remembered to bring the brandy by the time we made the cake mix! When Christmas arrived, I'd baked, marzipanned and iced that cake with great love and affection. I was proud that it was the centre-piece at our family Christmas table. Unfortunately, when my mum cut the first ceremonial slice, the brown mincemeat filling had – as predicted – turned to green mould. I was devastated as it was unceremoniously swallowed up in the lonely pedal bin, which occupied a dark corner of the kitchen.

When it came to the actual domestic science exams at the end of the fifth year, I did okay in my theory but I made a complete hash of the practical. As I wasn't supposed to be making hash, I was in big trouble. By totally ignoring the teacher's repeated advice of 'make sure you practice your recipes at home in advance,' my efforts did not result in a successful outcome. We'd been given the exam questions prior to the practical test. The question I got was something like, 'You are living in a caravan and your mum is an obese anorexic diabetic with early signs of beriberi. Prepare a suitable five-course meal on a portable gas lamp using a cardboard basin, a wax spatula, a chisel and a croquet mallet.' Perhaps not, but it might as well have been by the end result of the job I made of it.

In the exam itself, I attempted to make lemon curd. But mine mustn't have curded properly because the eventual spread I produced was a funny sort of yellowy-grey colour. It was runny in its consistency and had bits of lemon peel floating around in it. If that substance was thin, then my custard – to go on my overcooked bread and butter pudding, which resembled a dish of soggy toast – was the total opposite. I started mixing the custard in the pan, but no matter how much powder I put in, for some reason it just wouldn't thicken up. Then one of the girls whispered in my ear, 'Take it off the heat,' which I did. I think they had to throw the pan away it set so hard, with its little pockets of custard powder encased within yellow concrete. Needless to say I failed the exam, but I never regretted having a go at cooking. These days I'm a bit of a whiz in the kitchen and even my wonderful mother-in-law Joan – a dab hand who knows a thing or two about the art – is often moved to comment, 'He can certainly cook.' But that wasn't always the case.

◆   ◆   ◆

If my schoolwork was average at best, City meanwhile had been enjoying a humdinger of a season in 1976/77. Liverpool, City and Ipswich were all in contention for the title, but City's draw at home to Liverpool on Boxing Day proved to be costly. Dave Watson put through a late own-goal on an icy pitch in a game that City dominated and should have won. We were going well in the FA Cup as well. In the third round, City had seen off West Brom after a replay at the Hawthorns. We'd also recorded a fine 3–1 away win at Newcastle's St James' Park in the fourth round. This turned out to be a hairy experience, with Newcastle fans allowed into the City section to relieve congestion.

There was further trouble a few weeks later in the shape of the fifth-round tie away at Leeds. Joe Corrigan pulled off the best save I've seen live, but we were still beaten by a late Trevor Cherry goal. Joe's amazing stop from Allan Clarke should have been *Save of the Season*, but the BBC gave their coveted *Match of the Day* award to United's Alex Stepney instead for a shot that hit him on the backside. During this period, Corrigan was at his peak.

After the match there was fighting all the way back to the coach park and I stuck close to my dad. Despite the violence, the main observations in my diary were that, 'before the game, we had some great chips from the "*United Fisheries*" chippy at 11p a bag.' They received a top five-star rating on the Worthy 'Chippyometer' for price, presentation, temperature, taste and quantity; important stuff to a fourteen-year-old. Upon our return my dad went out for a pint to drown his sorrows and when he came back I was in bed watching *Match of the Day* on my oversized black-and-white telly that we'd acquired from the Scouts' jumble sale. Dad came into my room and was obviously worse for wear. Earlier in the season Jimmy Hill and City's supporters had fallen out due to derogatory comments Mr Hill had made regarding Brian Kidd. The following week, at Maine Road, the crowd sang, 'Jimmy Hill's a bastard!' This wasn't lost on the inimitable Mr Hill, who commented on TV, 'For those Manchester City supporters who were questioning my parentage earlier today, I can inform them that my mother and father are alive and well and living in London.' After the Leeds game, Mr Hill analysed the game with a big cheesy grin on his face and my dad exclaimed, 'Look at his face, he's loving this, the bashtard.' The reason I remember what my dad had said was because I was a few months shy of my fifteenth birthday and to his eternal credit, I'd never heard him swear before. Therefore I knew he was genuinely upset.

Consequently, City were out of the cup but we were still going well in the league. By the time we went to Liverpool on 9 April 1977, both clubs were neck and neck for the title. Anfield was the main ground I wanted to visit in my early travelling days. Dad took me on the supporters' club bus from Maine Road. It was a hot and sunny spring day and I was excited at the prospect of my first trip up the M62, but did have some reservations about going to Anfield. United supporters at school had told me horror stories, but on the day I overheard Helen Turner placating some of the younger lads as they sat outside the souvenir shop waiting to board the bus. She told them, 'not to worry. They're not a bad set of lads the Liverpool lot,' with a voice that reminded me of the great Les Dawson when dressed in drag. She always went to the front of the bus, picked up the mike and said in her gravelled tone, 'Right you lot at the back, when we get there I want you all to behave, and we'll have none of this (she'd demonstrated the 'V' sign) and we'll have none of that!' She'd then demonstrate the sign for the word that rhymes with tanker, whereupon – like clockwork – all us naughty boys at the rear would shout, 'What, like this Helen?' and we'd proceed to show her all the signs.

When we arrived at Liverpool, the charabanc pulled into the vast coach depot of Stanley Park. We didn't stay long as we were met by a welcoming committee of 200 Scousers ready for the fight. So much for Helen's words! The police found a parking spot somewhere near Goodison Park and we began the long walk through Stanley Park, where mobs in red scarves waited to pick off City fans as they walked by. My dad was totally oblivious to the obvious threat, as he always was, so much so that when we finally got to the ground, he went up to the biggest Scouser he could find and asked him, 'Can you tell me where the away end is, please pal?' I closed my eyes in trepidation, only to hear, 'Er, it's over dere mate,' as he pointed to the Anfield Road End about five yards behind us. Once in the ground there was no relief from the threat of impending death as both the home and away fans stood together in the same section. When Brian Kidd equalised an earlier strike from Liverpool's Kevin Keegan, there was a cheer from the City fans, but for safety reasons, it wasn't the unbridled exhibition of jubilation that usually greeted a goal. Not long after, Steve Heighway slammed home a Jimmy Case rebound off the bar and City lost 2–1 to give Liverpool the edge in the title race.

A few weeks later City were at Derby. My dad didn't go to this game, but he put me on 'A coach' on my own under Helen Turner's supervision. It was around about this time that I started to notice a tubby lad with a big mop of red hair and a white, freckled complexion. We always let on with the same economy of words, 'All right Blue.' We'd regularly say this to each other, without the faintest idea that within a couple of years, we'd become friends for life. That trip to Derby put paid to our title hopes. City lost 4–0 and I witnessed our title challenge fall apart from the upper-tier seats.

City finished a point behind Liverpool at the end of the season, and have failed to put in a sustained challenge for the title ever since. At least Jimmy Hill was happy.

15

Freedom

The following year was my last at school, probably the most important but eminently the most forgettable. This was season 1977/78 which saw City eventually finish fifth in the league. That Christmas, four mates and I went to Ayresome Park, Middlesbrough, on the day after Boxing Day. There were some really grim and nasty places to visit in those days and this was one of them. Unfortunately, we didn't know what we were letting ourselves in for. However, we were soon given a clue, as on the way up there, one of the lads on the trip, 'Turkey' Evans, spoke to a local in a North-East transport café. He told him how gruesome it could be at Ayresome and warned us all to be careful, while warning Turkey, 'If anyone asks you where you're from after the game, tell them Darlington. It isn't far from here and you might get off without a kicking!'

The coach parked next to a cemetery, a route march from the ground and within a stone's throw of the local hospital. This was a handy arrangement. After the match – which City won 2–0 – we split up and I was quick to realise that there was trouble in the air and behind me. This was confirmed when I was tapped on the shoulder by a shadowy Boro fan who asked, 'You're Morn Sidi, aren't ya?' I replied in my best North-Eastern accent, 'noah,' and was promptly punched on the back of the head before being chased by four of them. In those football violent days of the 1970s and '80s, it was always wise to have a well-versed set of regional dialects which you could call upon when approached by a would-be attacker trying to suss you out as an enemy Manc. Indeed, I had an extensive repertoire of finely honed Scouse, Brummie and Cockney accents at the ready for just such occasions. Unfortunately, my Geordie needed some extra work and, like everyone else, my Welsh accent never failed to sound more like that of an Indian waiter.

As I legged it down the side of their main stand, I grabbed a copper for assistance, but he pushed me away and I fell to the ground, only to be met by a volley of kicks from those in pursuit. While being treated like a football, I managed to crawl between two cars and, on seeing my plight, a Good Samaritan Boro fan came to my aid, dragging me into his car and driving me the mile or so back to the coach. By the time I got out I was shaken and a little bit stirred, but all in one piece.

I was one of the first back to the coach and witnessed its remaining occupants limp back covered in cuts and bruises, Turkey being no exception. Like mine, his eyes were somewhat less symmetrical than they had been when he left the coach.

'What happened to your big plan, Turkey?' I asked as he tenderly nursed his swollen shiner and fat lip. After a subtle pause he replied, 'They asked me where I came from and I couldn't remember that I was supposed to say Darlington, so I said Burnley instead and they battered me.' Even though I had a black eye and a swollen nose of my own, I couldn't stop laughing.

Graham Moore gave me a lesson on how to beat the mob. He went on the train to Boro and on his way back to the station he walked through a shopping centre where shaven-headed 'Ayresome Angels' waited in ambush. Graham told me he could see City fans being picked off and attacked. He put his plan into operation by popping into a greengrocer's, buying a 10lb bag of potatoes and walking past the mob with a grin and a bag of spuds under his arm. Nobody suspected he was an away fan.

I tried this ruse a few years later when I found myself in a similar situation at Chelsea. Our minibus was parked half-a-mile down the road and I had little choice but to walk through several hundred seething Chelsea 'nutters' in order to get back to the relative safety of the van. I remembered Graham's ploy and bought a Cox's Orange Pippin from a barrow boy and walked through the lot of them munching my apple. Nobody gave me a second glance!

A few days after Boro we faced Leeds away in the FA Cup once more. I was in a physics class when the draw was made for the third round and Steve Wadsworth and I had a radio under the bench to hear the commentator say, 'Number 17, Leeds United, will play number 23, Manchester City!' We both shouted 'yes!' in delight and promptly got detention. It was a great chance for revenge and one we were not going to miss. In order to claim a coveted match ticket, you needed voucher 'O' from your season ticket book and I came up with a simple method of getting more tickets for a couple of my mates. I took a black pen and changed the 'C' on a previous unused voucher to an 'O' and away we went, literally. City won at Elland Road with a great 2–1 victory, which was remembered for the Leeds fans' pitch invasion at 2–0 down with a few minutes to go.

The win *was* sweet revenge and I thought we were on our way that year. We were drawn against Brian Clough's resurgent Nottingham Forest at the City Ground, but the original game scheduled for the Saturday was postponed due to a frozen pitch. The postponement created problems. The new date was a Tuesday evening, which meant that I would have to cut school if I was going to get there. On that day we had a double games lesson, which meant that I was able to feign injury halfway through. It was freezing cold as I writhed about on the floor like the proverbial dying fly. The games teacher 'bought it' and told me go to the big, green, wooden pavilion, get changed and wait there until the session ended. I wasn't supposed to shoot off and meet my dad who was waiting across the road.

City lost 2–1. The following day I got up on time, as was the deal with my dad, despite the fact that we had arrived home in the early hours. As I walked towards the Upper School I spotted Mr Crofts, the school headmaster, waiting by the front door in his mortar board and batman cape. He only wore this outfit when he meant business. I would probably have been able to sneak past him undetected, but in my haste to meet my dad, I'd inadvertently left my school tie on a peg in the dressing room and approached school with a bare collar. This was a mistake! I was grabbed by the hair, thrust in the direction of the irate headmaster's office and ordered to await retribution. As I stood there shaking in my three-day-old smelly socks, I was joined by four others who had also skipped lessons in the afternoon to witness Forest's Peter Wythe and John Robertson end the latest quest to see City win a trophy.

As I was first by the door, I was first to cop for Crofts' rage as his imposing 6ft-plus frame bounded towards a rapidly shrinking me. I feared the worst and the worst materialised. He grabbed my arm and thrust me into his office. Once the door was slammed he gripped me once more, this time by the hair and gave me an almighty shove. I crashed against a table in his office, resulting in a lump on my forehead. 'Get up and listen to me!' he sternly ordered, 'I'm tired of you. I'm tired of the lot of you. You are a complete waster and you will never get anywhere and make anything of your life.' Then he gave me the strap and said, 'Now get out of my office. Your parents will be receiving a letter about your truancy.' That was the least of my worries, as my dad knew I'd wagged school, even if my mum didn't. The annoying thing about the whole incident was that this was only the second time in the five years I was at Chorlton that I'd deliberately absconded.

The first time I went AWOL occurred when my mum had gone to work and I was last one out of the house. But I didn't have my own key and once I'd shut the front door, I couldn't get back in. As I walked up the path on my way to the bus stop, I decided to sneak out a harmless little SBD (Silent But Deadly) fart, or so I thought. Unfortunately, it proved to be that crucial bit more and any notions of sitting down on the bus and going to school had just squirted straight into my underpants. I was forced to spend the whole day cowering by the back door in the freezing cold, bemoaning my bad luck and poor judgement. The highlight of the day was when the coal man arrived. He asked me what I was doing standing by the back door. When I explained he replied, 'Don't you just hate it when that happens?' As if following-through was an everyday occurrence in the coal-lugging game. With all that weight crashing onto their leather-shielded backs, perhaps it was. Relief finally arrived when, at around 4.30 p.m., my mum returned home to bring a belated conclusion to my sticky situation.

Years later when I was working at Manchester Town Hall, I saw Mr Crofts standing outside of one of the committee rooms, waiting to go into a meeting. I went over to him and said, 'You might not remember me. My name is Steven Worthington. I was one of your pupils at Chorlton. You once told me that I was a complete waster and would never make anything of my life. I've worked here now for the last seven years and I'm currently doing a degree. I have made something out of my life, but it is no thanks to you or your Chorlton High School.' There was no response. I have no doubt that Mr Crofts was an intellectual genius, who had had more than likely, had a bellyful of lackadaisical pupils like me in his school. Chorlton was formerly a high-achieving grammar school under his tutelage, but as a comprehensive, I only ever saw Crofts at assembly. I had the impression that he'd lost interest once the status of his school had changed. Nevertheless, it didn't give him licence to treat anyone the way had treated me.

Later that year I sat my mock exams and my last remaining school report confirms what Mr C.A. Crofts and most of his teachers thought of my efforts. The results revealed some abject scores and accompanying comments on my year's work. Geography, 37 per cent: 'He has good intentions not always enforced by hard work.' Woodwork, 34 per cent:

'With an all-out effort in the exams, he could succeed.' Physics, 28 per cent: 'He started the year well but has declined towards apathy recently, he must work consistently.' Domestic Science, 37 per cent: 'He must settle down to work if he is to succeed in GCE.' History, 52 per cent: 'Steven lacks concentration and maturity [my sister Julie could have written this]. It is a pity because he has the ability to do well.' English, 54 per cent: 'He appears to have matured slightly this year. His work is interesting but marks are lost because of his illegible handwriting.' Maths, 16 per cent: 'Only sheer determination and hard work will lead to success. Much time has been wasted in the past.'

As if they weren't bad enough, my form teacher commented: 'Unfortunately, he is not really pulling his weight. However, there is still time for success in some subjects with sheer hard work and determination.' My year teacher commented. 'I trust he has not wasted too much time to achieve anything worthwhile. He may regret the distractions he found so amusing.' Headmaster Crofts was far more reserved on paper than he was in his office, commenting: 'Regrettably, we haven't somehow managed to persuade Steven to work.' Except for Physical Activities. The report stated, 'A good term's work!'

When it came to the exams, it went from bad to worse. I've already described my domestic science disaster, which was soon to be joined by a woodwork catastrophe. The mitre joint I was making during the exam split in two, instantly ending my chances of success. It was ironic really as, later in life, I became rather proficient in building joints of a different variety.

I went into the maths exam in a total state of panic. Not for fear of my lack of knowledge but for the fact that my mum had loaned me her best Parker pen. I had managed to lose it about 20 minutes before the exam commenced, and it was weighing heavily on my mind. When I got into the main assembly hall to sit the 16-plus, which meant either CSE or GCE depending on the standard I might achieve, I soon noticed my lack of equipment. Most of the other pupils had impressive collections of protractors, compasses, calculators, set squares, etc. In short, all the tools needed to successfully embark on the exam. I hadn't even realised we were allowed to use calculators so I didn't bother bringing one. Perhaps just as well as I'd have probably spent most of the time working out how to spell 'SHELL OIL' or 'BOOBS' in upside-down digits, as you do (710 77345 & 58008 to save you bothering). In fact, all I was armed with was a pencil, a ruler and a realistic foreboding of impending failure.

Before commencement of the maths exam, the teacher warned the whole hall that, 'Under no circumstances are any of the candidates allowed to leave before the end of the examination [90 minutes later]. You can now turn over your papers.' I turned mine over, spent 5 minutes reading the questions and thought, nah! I then wrote my name at the top of the blank sheet of paper, yawned, had a nice long stretch, took one last look around the hall, got up and walked off into the sunset, never to be seen in Chorlton Upper School again. The way I saw it, what could they do about it? I was gone and never even bothered to go back to pick up the solitary CSE Grade 1 English certificate that I'd been awarded. This meant – technically at least – that from five years' study at Chorlton High School, I'd managed to come up with one O Level. It could have been worse; I might have ended up with none at all.

I had failed in every subject (getting an unclassified result in maths) except for English language, which was fair enough really as it was my mother tongue so I should have known something about it. Don't get me wrong, I'm not proud of my lack of qualifications and I realise that the blame rests squarely on my shoulders. However, I didn't want to go to Chorlton High School, and I'm sure the outcome would have been much better had I been allowed to attend Brookway High with most of my Button Lane mates. When my results finally arrived, my mother went ballistic. She screamed, 'Do you want to be a binman because that's just what you're going be?' I replied, 'What's wrong with being a binman? It's noble work and someone's got to do it!' There was a certain irony to my mum's comments, because I did end up working for the council, but in a subtly different capacity. Besides, she had it all wrong. My main ambition was to be an ice cream man, with all the associated benefits. Steady pay, company vehicle, out on the road everyday, meeting new people and all the free choc-ices I could eat. I had a plan all right and it would be put into action.

16

Losin' My Religion

It might not be evident, but up until the age of fifteen, I was a reasonably religious individual (or 'devoutish' as they might say in ecumenical circles). During the mid-1970s, the Worthington family attended the Protestant St Michael and All Angels Parish Church on Lawton Moor Road. My parents didn't force me kicking and screaming to go to church; getting our knees grubby from the well-trodden, wine-stained navy blue carpet at St Mike's altar was just something we did without question on Sunday mornings. Dad and sisters Julie and Joanne were in the choir and I got in on the act. I became an acolyte (or candle-carrier) and once I'd successfully negotiated Confirmation class, I became a cherubic-looking altar boy. This was quite a responsible position and I even got to say a couple of words at a certain point during the Sunday morning Communion Service. But more than once I lost concentration and forgot where my cue was and said, 'Almighty God' at the wrong moment at least three times during one morning service in front of the usually sparse but reverential congregation. The vicar must have rolled his eyes, looked up to the heavens and said those words in reverse order more than once or twice on my account.

Being an altar boy had its benefits, such as access to the leftover Communion wine in the 'dressing room'. More than once I helped 'clear up' the alcoholic Vimto-coloured nectar that had been temptingly stashed within the unlocked wine cupboard. This never failed to put an enigmatic smile on my face. It was a smile that was often confused for my apparent glow of contentment as a result of my morning confabulation with 'the big man upstairs'.

I went to church 'religiously' every week. But even at the height of my faith, I was never really sure what good, if any, church attendance did. It was sometimes only less than half-an-hour after a service that the Worthington family were in full-blown row mode once more. Our serene holier-than-thou masks were soon cast asunder as we quickly resumed our by-now usual in-family hostilities. One major thing or other – such as who had the most roast potatoes on their Sunday lunch – usually kicked it all off.

Apart from my sisters and I, there were several other younger people within the congregation, but they weren't exactly the most exciting or outgoing of individuals. The boys were of the greasy side-parting, specky-four-eyed nerd brigade and the girls were of the woolly tights, long dress and cable cardigan variety. However, I suspected that there were one or two fit, nubile bodies hidden underneath the dowdy clothing. This often sent my furtive imagination into complete overdrive. But in reality, there wouldn't be any opportunity for me to lose my cherry with some hot religious chick in a forbidden clandestine liaison at the back of the Harvest Festival display after Bible reading class. This was something I'd often fantasised about during many a long, dour, boring and predictably sanctimonious sermon. Of course, it never actually happened. Church birds were far too prim and proper for such carnal occurrences. Besides, perhaps it was just as well, what with Jesus gazing down below from His lofty crucifix, which dangled high above the altar, giving Him a panoramic view of all that went on within our vast, star-shaped church. The congregation could neither notice nor imagine my wicked and sinful aspirations within the middle of a church service. Like my large plastic briefcase, a baggy white cotton cassock could hide a multitude of sins.

On those Sunday mornings the majority of our congregation was made up from well-to-do elderly people who were always kind and polite, even though they always shouted like barrow boys at the old Smithfield Market due to their dicky hearing aids. But they always appeared genuinely happy to have an opportunity to mix with the younger element in the after-service coffee and biscuits.

In my early teens I took my faith seriously enough, in fact, so much so that the vicar and I once had a chat about the prospect of me becoming ordained. It was an offer I could refuse and I did there and then. The thought of me spending my life as part of the clergy wasn't something that excited or appealed to me. I still harboured ambitions of becoming an ice cream man.

By the time I'd got to the age of sixteen, I'd completely lost all interest in religion. I came to a perhaps unjust conclusion about

elderly people. I decided that the reason they made up the majority
of the congregation was that they were all 'coffin dodgers' putting in
some insurance time before their day of reckoning at the Pearly Gates.

Why did my faith diminish so rapidly? One reason was that that my
prayers were never answered, particularly with regard to football, the
alternative religion where the masses paid slightly more enthusiastic
weekly reverence. City had been going from bad to worse and I never
seemed to get the material things that I desired. As I got older, all I could
see were the negatives and injustices that went on all around me, and so
the concept of divine intervention became totally inconceivable.

Since then I have given life, death and religion a great deal of
thought. I now look at religion and God with an even greater deal
of cynicism than in my youth. Don't get me wrong, the concept of
life after death is a comforting one. However, as Burt Reynolds put it
in the classic 1978 movie *The End*, rather than going to heaven, it's
more a case of, 'shrivelling up, turning yellow and holding your breath
forever.' Besides and to quote Elaine May in *A New Leaf*, another of my
favourite 1970s comedy films, 'Isn't it presumptuous to expect eternal
life?'

Like most people, I live with the intimidating fear of death. It's not so
much the act of death itself I worry about, it's more that I will miss life's
rich tapestry and won't be around to witness how things pan out once
I'm out of the game. Things such as watching my offspring's lives unfold
into old age or City winning the quadruple, which is surely only a matter
of time.

17

Ch, Ch, Ch, Ch-Changes

During my years at Chorlton, my non-school mates had radically changed. By 1978, Billy Roddy and family had migrated to the upmarket houses in Sale Moor. They were too far away for me to be bothered to call for him. Besides, I was now a member of what could loosely be described as a 'gang' of lads who mostly congregated outside the 'Park Wine' off-licence on Moorcroft Road during cold dark nights. These included Button Lane School pal Terry Hyland and his foster brother 'Sly Andy'. We weren't a 'gang' in today's street parlance – our pursuits were of a far more innocent nature.

On winter evenings our gang would venture to Moston in North Manchester and back again for a 4p return bus fare. It was a round trip in the pitch black which would take the best part of three hours to complete. This meant that at least we could stay warm during our 'entertaining' nights out. But these trips were eventually curtailed when a bigger gang of lads gave us some verbal grief at the turning point at Moston Cemetery. It was a wise move not to go back there as it was miles from home and we were vulnerable to a good kicking with nowhere to run but North Manchester. This might as well have been on the other side of the world, given what little any of us knew about its geography.

My old pal Terry Stanton was still on the scene, but he didn't share my need to be out every night. I was always scared that if I wasn't always there, I'd be out of the sacred loop, although usually nothing ever happened worth missing. In fact, being in a gang was downright dull. The arrival of Bonfire Night gave us an opportunity to channel our entrepreneurial creativity. One of our better ideas was to dress up in rags and pretend to be a Guy Fawkes rather than being bothered to make one for 'a penny for the Guy' as the ruse never really paid off. It was harmless fun like many of the games. However, on one occasion things went drastically wrong when playing 'knock and run'. The routine was to knock on the door and then shoot behind the safety of the front gate. At the first sign of door movement we'd chuck eggs and run off. But one night I came a cropper. I knocked on a door, shot off without looking and ran straight into a front gate, which had shut. I lay on the floor with absolute agony in both legs, with a pungent combination of yolk and shell festering in my anorak pockets. I still had the cheek and yet quick presence of mind to ask the irate victim, 'Is Johnny playing out?' But the bloke was having none of it. The chastened old fella had taken enough and had wisely fitted a spring gate, which had shut without me noticing. The police were summoned and I was led by the ear to my home. Luckily my parents were out, but Mrs Steele the next-door neighbour 'bubbled' me when they returned. I copped for it after they were informed of the shame of the police appearing at our front door. The police had respect in those days. My mum took me round to the victim's house the next night to apologise for my actions. From then on that chap always waved to me as I went past his house on a regular basis.

Meanwhile, Terry Stanton was far too cool and indeed slow to play knock-and-run. He was far more preoccupied playing his increasing array of punk records in his 'parlour.' Terry had developed a fine taste for punk music and had a collection of records from bands of which I'd never heard (such as Wythenshawe's Ed Banger and the Nosebleeds whose 'Kinnel Tommy' was a punk/football classic). I didn't pay much attention, although I was intrigued to hear tracks from the Sex Pistols and the Stranglers that had been banned on the radio. I really got into punk after the Rock Against Racism event – organised in conjunction with the Anti-Nazi League – which was held in Moss Side, Manchester, in the summer of 1978 and attracted an audience of 25,000. It was the first live set I had attended. I'd seen Slade 'live' during a Christmas recording of 'Lift Off With Ayesha' at Granada TV studios courtesy of Mr Johnson. But they were miming.

I must have been so green in those days. Steel Pulse and punk poet John Cooper-Clarke supported headline act the Buzzcocks, none of whom I had the foggiest idea about. But once the Buzzcocks started knocking out some of their tracks like 'Orgasm Addict' and 'Ever Fallen in Love' I was hooked. I have several enduring images of that gloriously hot day, which include dodging the contributions bucket for the cause, as I was skint as usual and the crowd baying for 'Fast

Cars', which I didn't realise was a request for a number rather than a strange warning of a speeding vehicle coming my way. Finally, I was approached by a black bloke who resembled Bob Marley with his long dreadlocks and woolly hat predictably resplendent in the colours of the Jamaican flag. He offered me for sale what looked like a greeny-brown Oxo cube. This I later found out to be marijuana.

I asked if the Buzzcocks made records as I thought that all releases were the dirges that made it into the charts. But Terry assured me that he had the Buzzcocks' back catalogue and a lot more besides. Within a matter of weeks, I familiarised myself with his collection of punk records, particularly those of the Sex Pistols and the Stranglers – a band who quickly became our gang's favourite 'New Wave' outfit and one I still love to this day.

Although I was well into the music, I became a punk in spirit rather than in looks. I didn't bother tearing up my clothes and putting a pin through my nose. Indeed, my biggest rebellious gestures were to rip all the penny round collars off my shirts and adopt the granddad look while having all my flared jeans turned into 'ankle stranglers' by our Joanne on my mum's sewing machine. Besides, I had astutely recognised that music historians would go on to pronounce 1978–81 as technically the post-punk era and wisely decided against wearing the uniform, which was becoming somewhat passé, almost slightly embarrassing. My new allegiance to the punk movement did not sit well at all with my older sister Julie. She was used to dominating the lounge music centre without challenge, especially when my parents were out. Now she had some turntable competition.

It soon became a straight duel, a battle of wills. It was the Carpenters, Fleetwood Mac, Supertramp, Carly Simon and James Taylor versus The Clash, the Sex Pistols, The Stranglers, Buzzcocks, The Ramones and Stiff Little Fingers and there was to be only one winner. I was listening to the Pistols in the lounge one day with Terry Hyland. We were merrily pogo-ing away when my elder sister entered the room. As we headbutted the lampshade for the umpteenth time she issued her demands. In Julie's usual arms-folded, stern-faced domineering way she instructed that I 'take that rubbish off right now!' But I wouldn't concede to her demand. Julie took matters into her own hands grabbing the arm of the record player and ripping the stylus across my album, causing a great scratch right over the 'A' side of the punk classic *Never Mind the Bollocks*. I was incensed. I gave her a good, hard shove and the back of her head went crashing into the lounge's glass doors, leaving an ominous 'Our Julie'-

shaped hole gaping through the corrugated pane. My sister was okay but the door was history and so, I thought, was I. It had been a proper punk reaction, and my mum gave me one of her own when she got home. I received a 'clip round the ear' and all punk records were banned from the lounge, because they made me violent, according to my mum's psychology.

◆   ◆   ◆

There were even punks at football matches. An away game at St Andrews on 22 April 1978 became one of those seminal moments in life that we don't realise the significance of until later. I didn't have a good vibe at Birmingham City. The place looked like a desolate wasteland with an imposing set of featureless flats pushed up against the main stand. In order to gain access from the coach to the away section, you had to slip through a block of threatening abominations. It wasn't a comfortable manoeuvre.

On this particular day, I walked into the section reserved for visitors known as the Tilton End. There was a local welcoming committee, mostly made up of spiky-haired punk rockers mingled in with skinheads. They were waiting at the other side of the turnstiles and attacking innocent away fans as we entered. Just before kick-off there was a mob of about fifty or so City fans standing on the terrace looking at each other uncomfortably while fearing the worst as the Kool Kats' (a mob of City hooligans in the 1970s and early '80s – recognised as City's main and only fighting 'firm' of note at the time) clapped-out bus was yet to arrive to save the day. The Brummies took the higher ground behind us and shouted, 'Oh we're the barmy Tilton Army,' as they charged at us. With nowhere to go and heavily outnumbered, thirty of us ran onto the pitch still being chased by the marauding home fans. I got over the halfway line before cutting over to their main stand and diving in the lower tier seats.

The stewards came looking for uninvited guests such as me, but the fella in the seat next to me said, 'Just keep your head down mate and you'll be okay.' The lad dishing out the sound and benevolent advice ever so quietly was Graham Moore. He turned out to be a City fan from Sale Moor and lived on Sandford Road, home of the horny dog that had so often taken a fancy to my right leg. As City caned the Brummies 4–1, I had a good chat with Graham and he invited me to the Altrincham and Sale City Supporters' Club. This soon proved to be a home from home where I would meet many people whose friendships I retain.

♦   ♦   ♦

That summer, after finishing at Chorlton, I was in a serious dilemma. Should I go out into the big, wide world and look for a job and a quick 'buck' armed only with one CSE Grade 1 English qualification and a bronze medal in swimming? Or did I move to further education and have one last crack at gaining some worthwhile qualifications? Unfortunately there weren't many openings for grammatically correct lifeguards in Manchester, but somewhere along the way I'd bumped into my old Button Lane classmate Charlie McCormick. He told me that he'd enrolled at West Wythenshawe College for a course in horticulture. I took the brief walk to see what my local seat of further education had to offer my clueless mind. After much promising to my mum and dad that I'd pull my socks up (even though I was wearing flip-flops at the time) they kindly allowed me to enrol on a course. That meant that any financial contribution I should make to the running of the household would have to wait at least another year. It also meant that, if successful, it would give me five O Levels to add to my solitary English success at school.

On Monday 18 September 1978, I became an official layabout, also known as a full-time student. The first day began at 1.00 p.m. and ended at 7.30 in the evening, allowing me get up at a reasonable hour, do my mag round in morning, then embark on the 10-minute stroll to college. What bliss. No buses to board and a nice lie-in before having to study, this was my kind of learning. When I arrived at college as a 'fresher', there were a few familiar faces there, notably that of Steve 'George' Graham from Chorlton, the boy against whom I'd had my solitary fighting success. We'd long since let bygones be bygones. He soon became a good mate, along with Billy Callaghan from Button Lane School. But there were a few other new faces who became particularly good pals that year, including Lee Crewe and Ian 'Harry' Boyle, nicknamed after the character in the satirical cartoon of the day, *Wait 'Til Your Father Gets Home*. He was a lad who liked having and providing a laugh.

Having endured years of comparative misery at Chorlton High, 'West Wivvy College' – as it was known by the locals – was a joy to attend (when I could be bothered). Who was it who said, 'Youth is wasted on the young?' Contrary to Oscar Wilde's haughty assertion, I had a great time and made the most of it.

Although ultimately fairly unproductive once again, my year at college proved to be my most enjoyable so far. The advantage of college was that there were no uniforms, no bullies and no teachers. We now had lectures from people who were much more laidback amid classes full of students who were there because they wanted to be, rather than being forced into the building by the hair. If I didn't fancy a lecture, I didn't go. There were no repercussions, apart from at the results stage as I was to find out later.

I used to spend quite a lot of time going to Manchester and hanging around the New Wave Record Store in the Underground Market off Market Street, a cool place to see and be seen. It was entertainment in itself watching the great unwashed punk fraternity buying all sorts of multi-coloured vinyl records from *the* most obscure bands. These discs were always being played in the tiny shop. But music wasn't the type of study I should have been concentrating on.

In addition, there were further distractions. I soon discovered beer and despite my choirboy looks, I was able to drink to excess in the local pub – the Gardeners Arms – without being challenged by the landlord about my age. I'd been without a pint for sixteen years and so I had a lot of catching up to do, although not as much as I'd have liked. Beer was only about 40p a pint, but 40p was a lot to someone on £1.20 per week for a mag round. I didn't qualify for the £32 per term Government Further Education Grant and had no means of income other than what I earned at Tom McGarry's paper palace.

My daily diet consisted of the canteen's cheapest 'meal' of baked beans and chips, which I ate for the majority of the year. My jealousy at fellow students who'd secured grant funding was tangible and I totally resented the fact that they could comfortably afford to place sausages on their plates to accompany their beans and chips. But at least poverty had a positive effect on my waistline as, coupled with the lack of food, I'd enjoyed a growth spurt which had taken me to 5ft 10in as my cuddly, but unwanted, pot belly had stretched out to zero.

Food wasn't the only thing on the menu that was out of reach. I had developed a serious interest in girls. But without the means to pay to take a girl out, any aspirations on that front were doomed to failure. With no car, no money and Harold Steptoe's dress sense, I wasn't much of a prospect to the opposite sex. In those days, if you went out with a lass, the bloke was supposed to pick up the tab for the whole night out, unless you went Dutch. But Holland was totally out of the question on my budget. When I gained some success and asked *out* a college girl called Marilyn, when it actually came down to it, going *out* was not a regular option. That was unless she fancied standing outside the chip shop all night supping a carton of gravy with me and my mates while waiting for something to happen – which, of course, it never did. On the one occasion we did go to a nightclub I had no money left after I'd paid the admission fees and bought the first round.

The next time my new girlfriend wanted to go out, it became a straight choice between her and an EP by The Skids on 12in red vinyl entitled *Wide Open*. Foolishly, I let her know that I had a bit of spare cash but wanted to spend it on the record rather than female maintenance. However, I still have the EP up in mum's attic!

18

1979 . . .

. . . Was a pivotal year in my little world in many ways. *The Life of Brian* was released, Richard Beckinsale of *The Lovers*, *Porridge* and *Rising Damp* fame died prematurely and there was spine-chilling horror in the air in England. 'Tucker' was getting a raw deal in *Grange Hill* and scary movie *Halloween* was terrifying audiences up and down the land as the 'Yorkshire Ripper' was doing it for real a bit too close for comfort in the north of England. But perhaps, scariest of all, Thatcherism would soon begin. It was no wonder the vast majority of the female population was hooked on Valium.

Things were also getting a bit frightening on the football front. In the final year of the 1970s, City lost their greatest player, Colin Bell, who had succumbed to his debilitating knee injury. But at the beginning of the year, on 6 January, Malcolm Allison was appointed as 'coach' at City. There is an old adage that you should 'never go back to one who you've loved', and Mal should have listened and taken heed. It was no coincidence that it wasn't long before the wheels started to fall off City's wagon as later that month came the first of far too many 'shock' cup exits.

Shrewsbury Town were top of the Third Division and the small, snowbound pitch was in their favour as City took them on at Gay Meadow on 27 January. We had Corrigan, Donachie, Hartford, Barnes, Channon, Kidd and Deyna in the team – all internationals; I wasn't anticipating much of a problem. Before the game, a local told me that, 'City will win. You're far too strong for our little side.' City's fans were packed into the cramped but roofed Station End of the ground, which resembled a vandalised bus shelter, although not quite as luxurious. It was so jammed that many were hanging off the roof not daring to let go. However, the mood was jovial and there was even a mass snowball fight before the game.

This was my fiftieth away game, but it was marked with disaster. Channon, Power, Kidd and Barnes all missed great chances, and gave Shrewsbury the opportunity to score two goals, which TV presenter David Coleman took great delight in rubbing in on *Match of the Day* later. I always thought this game was the catalyst that made Allison's mind up to make radical changes. City had appeared more than lethargic that day and should have done much better with the team at Mal's 'disposal' (this being the operative word) although the adverse conditions hadn't helped our cause. Big Mal's reaction was way over the top. He soon embarked on a suicidal policy of selling tried and trusted internationals on the cheap and replacing them with unproven and over-priced youngsters. This brought the financial ruination of the club from which it took many a blue moon to finally recover. However, chairman Peter Swales' faith in Big Mal cost City more than just money.

Malcolm's first signing came just over a month later, when Barry Silkman joined from a well-known club named Obscurity. He made his debut at Portman Road against Ipswich Town and scored City's goal of the season during a 2–1 defeat. It was to prove a one-off and he only played 19 times for the Blues, with his socks slovenly rolled down to his ankles on each occasion (only Rodney Marsh could get away with such a sloppy look). It wasn't the only memorable thing about the day. Before the game and at half time, a film production company was filming a movie called *Yesterday's Hero* starring Ian McShane. The comical sight of twenty-two actors trying to contrive a goal for McShane to score at the City end was more entertaining than the match itself. Once he'd finally managed to 'score', McShane – his dad was a former United player and chief scout – came running over to us in a delirious celebration only to be met by fans who couldn't even be bothered to be apathetic about it. When the film was released I could be clearly seen in the crowd in my blue cagoule with a moody and disaffected expression, before Liam Gallagher came up with the same arrogant look many years later.

This wasn't my only claim to media fame in 1979. On 22 February, QPR sold their 'keeper Phil Parkes to West Ham for a record transfer fee. That night, there was a piece on the *ITN News* showing Parkes making a great save against City at Loftus Road. I was right behind the goal and you could see me clearly. When the clip was aired, I was eating my tea from a tray in front of the telly with my parents. Just as my mum said, 'Look Derek, there's our Steven behind the goal,' up went the 'V' sign from me on national TV. I got a telling off for that one and again later on, as it was shown once more on *News at 10*. My mum was not best pleased and optimistically commented, 'I hope nobody is watching this!'

♦   ♦   ♦

You have probably gathered that my limited budget didn't stop me travelling to City away games. Luckily for me, dad had been made redundant at the Kellogg's plant and had secured a pay-off, so he was temporarily loaded and he was generous in funding my pursuit of away grounds. The best league game I attended that season was at Tottenham on 3 February. City won 3–0 and I watched it among the Tottenham fans in their hallowed territory: The Shelf. After the match there was fierce fighting along Seven Sisters Road and as our bus pulled outside the main stand, a Tottenham fan took a 10-yard run up and punched my coach window as hard as he could. The podgy ginger-haired lad sitting in front of me turned around and said, 'Oooh, now that must have 'urt!' Hopefully it did.

During my college days, I went to every City game of the season, home and away, bar one. This was a rearranged fixture at Molineux against Wolves, but it clashed with a geography field trip to Castlefield, Derbyshire. I was compelled to attend or I couldn't take the exam, which turned out to be slightly ironic – City drew 1–1 and the field trip was a good laugh. Indeed, there were several good laughs at college, two of which came in successive day trips to London.

On Thursday 8 March, the government & politics class enjoyed a trip to both the Houses of Parliament: the Commons and Lords. Britain had just survived 'The Winter of Discontent' and we were met by local Wythenshawe politician Alf Morris and his young son Morris Minor, who took us into the House of Lords. Not being able to stand the excitement of it all, 'Harry' Boyle and I quickly sloped off to a pub in Whitehall for a few pints of flat, southern beer which contained mysterious floaty bits. After a decent lunchtime we queued for a seat in the public gallery for Prime Minister's Question Time during which the Tory Opposition leader Margaret Thatcher gave Labour Prime Minister James Callaghan a grilling. That was if he could hear her, as we (Harry was sat on the other side of the public gallery), communicated with each other through the juvenile medium of 'coughing tennis'. As the political heavyweights battled it out on the Commons floor down below,

Harry and I coughed out our lungs in a vain bid to gain infamy through *Hansard's* verbatim record of the debate.

This had been my first ever visit to London without watching football and my second came the next day as we were back in the capital once more. The college Students' Union branch had organised a coach to join their disaffected demonstration which started at Waterloo Bridge and finished at Hyde Park Corner. The demo was in support of overseas students' rights to full grants; not that I gave a toss about it as I hadn't seen anyone protesting against my lack of supplementary sausage funding. However, the coach fare was only a couple of quid and I took full advantage of this cheap day out. We were given banners and marched like true militants to the accompaniment of a Scottish Sex Pistols' tribute band, 'The Sax Pastles', who were playing on a lorry ahead of us. We got about 200 yards down the road. Then as the march went one way, we went the other and spent the rest of the day wandering around London on the razzle, frequenting some of the Soho boozers that we'd been supping in the night before.

A couple of weeks later – on Friday 23 March – I went to my first ever paid gig at the Russell Club in deepest darkest Hulme to see a proper Scottish band, The Skids. I paid £1.50 for a ticket, but such a high price was now of little consequence as my financial plight was about to change. One lunchtime, while craving other people's sausages in the college canteen, I overheard Charlie McCormick saying that he worked in the Brooklands Trades & Labour Club (BTLC) as a 'pot collector'. He cleared up empty pint pots from the ever-thirsty customers and it was lucrative (anything better than the £1.20 Tom McGarry paid me on a weekly basis was lucrative). Not only were they hiring, but my dad drank there on a regular basis. He had a word with the steward. The interview went something like, 'Can you pick up that pint pot over there?'

'Yes.'

'Okay, you've got the job.'

With the old song 'We're in the Money' playing in the background, my punk collection soon grew as did my list of away grounds. The pay averaged over £20 a week for three nights and a Sunday lunch session. This meant I could quit my mag round after five years of unreliable service, much to the relief of Tom McGarry.

Working in the local CIU-affiliated Labour Club – or Hammond organ land – was a great experience. There were all sorts of characters who made their own unique contributions to my early education. The BTLC was always an amusing place in which to work. Whenever I dropped a pint pot – which was frequently – somebody would shout out, 'I name this ship,' or, 'Sack the juggler!' The Reds would often comment, 'Hey Steve, it's a shame City haven't collected as many pots as you have!'

There was also the bloke in the off-white, vinegar-stained Kershaw's Sea Products' coat. He appeared on Sunday nights peddling his basket of crustaceans. He was rather effeminate and also had a speech impediment, with the result that he tempted his would-be customers with 'thee food, thee food!' in a high-pitched camp voice. The reply was always, 'Have you got any crabs on yer, cock?' or 'Have yer got any muscles? Yes? Well go and lift that table up then, fish fingers!'

One of the great characters was my dad's drinking partner Alf Hillary, a self-educated man who completed the *Guardian* crossword each day. He'd have been in his early sixties and regularly entertained me with his crap jokes and anecdotes. On Monday nights, the older ladies and gentlemen enjoyed traditional Scottish dance lessons in the concert room and Alf once told me about the sad tale of their dance tutor, Mr Dunstable. He was captured by the Japanese in Burma and was tortured. But bravely and courageously he wouldn't spill the beans. That was until, as Alf put it, 'One day they nailed his feet to the floor and played Jimmy Shand records!'

Alf was no stranger to pain. He suffered a debilitating open shrapnel war-wound in his right leg which rendered it useless. In the Second World War he was stationed in North Africa fighting the combined forces of the German and Italian armies. One night he went on routine patrol and got lost behind enemy lines. Even though there was an officer present, the others looked to Alf (or Hil' as he was nicknamed) for advice as the only non-conscript in the party. As Alf's mob had no idea where they were, it was decided they'd rest up for the night on the high ground to try and get back to their position in the morning. Hours later, Alf and his patrol were sternly woken up to the sound of an Italian officer down in the valley below. He shouted on his megaphone in Joe Dolce-like broken English, 'We now dat you ara upadare, coma downa nowa and surrender to de Italiano Army.' Alf and his boys had strayed to the edge of an enemy camp which was over a hundred strong and in position at the bottom of the hill. Alf and his mob of ten were hidden behind bushes at the top. Alf's response was to take aim and shoot the announcer in the chest. Alf and his patrol frantically ran one way, and the Italians 'scarpered' the other. Once Alf and his men had stopped running, the officer shouted, 'Who fired that shot?'

Alf tentatively put his hand up and the officer continued, 'well done then Hillary,' and they soon found their way back to safety. I mention this anecdote because, as far as I'm aware, Alf is the only person I've ever met who actually killed someone. When I quizzed him about any conscience he might have had afterwards, he told me, 'You don't think about such things when your life is on the line. When it's you or them, it's much better if it's them.'

My regular chats with Alf, particularly in his later life, gave me a healthy appreciation and respect for older people and some of the miserable things they've had to endure to reach a ripe old age. He was a grandfather-type figure to me. I respected him and took heed of the nuggets of wisdom on life he'd often throw my way. Towards the end of Alf's life, he was housebound and my dad became his diligent carer. I regularly visited the old boy, but watched him struggle to move around without the aid of a Zimmer frame or read his trusty *Guardian* without the help of a magnifying glass. He was a proud man. I asked him if the thought of dying gave him any relief, given that his body had virtually given up on him. I was looking for a reply which could be comforting should I ever reach such a magnificent old age.

'Nah Steve,' he said, 'there's no future in the bloody cemetery: I'll hang on here as long as I can.' Alf died aged eighty-four. I placed a copy of his beloved *Guardian* on his coffin as it was gently lowered into his perceived oblivion.

◆　◆　◆

The 'club' had a reputation for up-and-coming comedians such as Jim Bowen and Chubby Brown. It was an era that coincided with me being at my thinnest; I was down to a 28in waist, an excessively vain reaction to the constant jibes I got at school for being tubby. One night Chubby Brown appeared on stage in front of a packed concert room while I was wearing a bright yellow top. Every time I had to walk along the front of the room to collect the empties he had a pop with 'classics' such as, 'Fook me, a seven stone canary', or, 'Fook me, there's an anorexic chip!' There was nowhere to hide as I had to carry on doing my job like the consummate professional that I wasn't. Near the end of his act and after yet another pop, I remember him saying, 'I'll bet he's thinking: will yer just fook off, ya fat bastad,' and I exaggeratedly nodded my head with a big incredulous smile to bring a great big cheer from the audience.

It wasn't just the comics that packed them in on Sunday nights. The cheesy covers band Civvy Street usually meant a mad night. The place would be packed and jumpin' with local middle-aged jivers trying in vain to recapture their youth. Sometimes the club would be jumpin' for a different reason . . . when football reared its belligerent head. One night the compère – a likeable United fan – made one joke too many about the Blues and their increasing problems. Tony Dean – a big, hard local City fan – had had enough of this baiting and got up on the stage and launched the compère into the tables below, kicking off a mass brawl. There were glasses flying, tables and chairs being smashed over heads and plenty of indiscriminate hand-to-hand scrapping, with fifteen to twenty drunken club members of opposing football persuasions. It was brilliant entertainment! My only concern over the incident was that I had to sweep up the mess at the end.

The Labour Club was usually a great place to be – apart from the thick clouds of toxic blue smoke that enshrouded us pot collectors. On Sunday lunchtimes I literally had to cut my way through the fumes into the concert room as my bloodshot eyes witnessed the ladies enjoying their weekend fix of ciggies, bingo and milk stout, as they compared their respective Sat'day mornin' 'hairdos'. Apart from the severe coughing, the smelly, smoke-ridden clothes and the headaches, the money was good and there were side benefits.

One of my colleagues in the pot department was a buxom young lass called Carolyn Ruttledge. She became my first official girlfriend in a tempestuous and fickle relationship which ultimately failed the searching test of one week happy, then six weeks totally fed-up. Give us a subject and we'd have an argument. We often had arguments about how many actual arguments we'd had (as opposed to fiery debates, heated discussions or red-hot exchanges of views – which didn't count as arguments). In the end we mutually sacked each other while maturely deciding that it just wasn't worth the hassle or the throat lozenges. Breaking up was the one thing we didn't contest.

A further benefit of the Labour Club was the free ale. Once they'd had one too many, club members would regularly treat me to a few beers, but not through their generosity. Along with the other pot collectors, I went on the prowl for a spot of 'mine sweeping'. This was our glutinous way of clearing the ale that had been bought and paid for by punters, whose eyes were bigger than their bloated stomachs. With so much ale to be drunk in so little time, I soon mastered the art of downing someone else's pint in one. At the 'club' I had everything a young man could want: free booze, a good wedge of cash and a bit of slap and tickle on the way home.

♦   ♦   ♦

It was after one of these 'mine sweeping' Sunday night sessions that Terry Hyland and I came across one of the strangest things I've ever seen. We were walking back home when we were confronted by something totally bizarre. About 20 yards in front of us and about 30ft in the air, two fluorescent orange hoops were suspended in the clear night sky. I asked Terry to confirm what he saw.

'There are two bright orange circles hovering in the air,' he said.
The circles were both symmetrical in size and shape, about 3ft in diameter, about 10in thick and a foot apart. They looked a bit like two outsized Fruit Polos which appeared to be observing us. After a minute or so, the circles simultaneously turned on their sides and swooped away over a field. It was a bit like the effect used in the arrival of the Mysterons in *Captain Scarlet*. We both issued a two-word expletive. As we looked up, it happened again. They hovered in the same spot then shot off over the fields. We stayed for another 15 minutes hoping for another sighting. The episode was a total mystery.

Terry came round to our house the next morning. He described perfectly everything I'd remembered which meant that drink couldn't have played a part. Neither of us reported the incident but, as much as I'd have liked to, I couldn't shrug the episode off easily.

♦   ♦   ♦

The constant late-night working at the Labour Club, plus the other distractions, took a detrimental effect on my college studies which – surprise, surprise – weren't really coming along too well. My lack of discipline in attendance with no worry of recrimination or retribution meant that by the time the exams arrived, it was all starting to go in a familiar downward spiral. For the history exam, I should have been answering questions on Samuel Pepys and the Haddock Wars, together with the Staffordshire Lettuce Famine of 1568. But when I had a look at the questions I thought they were way too difficult. Instead I started weighing up the sections of questions that I hadn't studied and found one entitled 'The Second World War, 1939–1945'. I'd seen the film

Kelly's Heroes and a couple of episodes of *World at War* so I decided to answer this section instead.

Geography was worse. 'Harry' Boyle had told me that the exam was in the afternoon, so I was in bed at 10.30 a.m. on the day of the test when the phone rang. The caller was one of the lecturers, who asked me, 'Where are you?'

'Why do you ask?' was my incredulous reply.

'Because the exam is this morning and they're all 30 minutes into it!'

I ran to college and the first person I saw in the foyer was Harry and he was laughing his head off. He'd taken his own duff advice and missed the exam as well, which they wouldn't let us re-sit. A whole year's work had gone down the drain. It also meant I'd missed the away game at Wolves for nothing!

At the end of my college year, I'd managed to pass government & politics and – don't ask me how – economics as well. I now had three O Levels with which to tempt prospective employers into giving me a job. The summer turned out to be successful in the employment stakes. My mum worked at Wythenshawe Hospital and she'd managed to put in a word on my behalf. In effect, she secured me a temporary contract as a hospital porter, wheeling the sick and the wounded. The interview was as tough as ever.

'Can you push that wheelchair over there?'

'Yes.'

'Okay, you've got the job.'

I started at 8.00 a.m., which was like getting up in the middle of the night. But I soon found that I could catch up on my much-needed sleep in the wheelchair storeroom when the head porter wasn't looking. Although the job only lasted a few months, it provided me with life experience. Within the first hour, I witnessed my first naked woman, but it wasn't quite the experience I had imagined. The porter's office had received a call to send two lads up to Ward 11 to take a female patient to X-ray.

Another more experienced porter and I wheeled up a trolley with due haste and diligence. We were requested to gently and carefully lift her ailing body onto our trolley. She was as naked as the day she was born, but, unfortunately, this birth had been delivered some ninety-odd years earlier and the poor old dear had just soiled her bed. Ward 11 turned out to be the geriatric ward. I remember commenting with great compassion and humanity, 'Aaaaaaw no, I'm not touchin' that!'

Luckily the old girl was oblivious to my immature outburst, but the nurses weren't and made sure I was the one who had to lift her up from the feet end and receive the appropriate ticking off when I finally returned to base.

I quickly acquired a sound understanding of how being in good health is everything. The affable Bill Taylor, formerly the City and England coach, was in one of the wards at this time, and I regularly had the pleasant task of wheeling him down to the X-ray department. Unfortunately it wasn't long before he succumbed to his illness.

With this portering job in tandem with the job I enjoyed at the Labour Club, I was earning a lot of money, which allowed me to buy my first music centre (a Pye 1062) to crank up in my box-room, much to the chagrin of the neighbours. When I wasn't playing new wave music at anti-socially high volumes, I had Derek and Clive waxing lyrically with their abusive but hilarious comedy. I could recite their third album, *Ad Nauseum*, off by heart. In fact, at one point, I played Pete and Dud's abusive patter so much that Mrs Steele, the next-door neighbour, must have thought I shared my room with a couple of foul-mouthed Cockneys.

◆   ◆   ◆

It was my best summer to date and the icing on the cake duly arrived on FA Cup final day when Manchester United met Arsenal. As usual my dad and I watched the annual event on our 'trusty' rented colour telly. The Gunners were cruising to victory at 2–0 with 5 minutes to go. Good news as far as we were concerned. As my dad and I relaxed on the couch grinning contentedly, United managed to pull it back to 2–2. Disaster! But all was not lost. Liam Brady – socks around his ankles – prodded a tired but accurate pass in the direction of Graham Rix's loosely coiled 'afro' hairstyle. He clipped a tantalising cross into the box. It was a centre that eluded goalkeeper Gary Bailey as Alan Sunderland appeared like a moustachioed Yorkshire angel and smacked home the winner. As the former Wolves man ran off in unrestrained celebration, my dad reciprocated by throwing his freshly made, steaming hot cuppa into the air. We both danced around the living room showered in the tea – it was like a scene from a Grand Prix podium. My mum also went ballistic when she saw the mess.

The summer also afforded me the opportunity for a couple of holidays, one of which included my first foreign City trip, to watch the Blues take on Bruges and Beerschot in a four-team tournament in the Flemish region of Belgium. I'd only been abroad once before and that was to Ostende when I was three – coincidently where we were staying for this trip. It was a measure of how naïve I was that, after our first night out on the town, I hadn't realised that our hotel was in the middle of the red light area. As I walked back to our temporary residence with an equally clueless companion, we wondered who the scantily-clad ladies were who were sitting in shop windows reading magazines or knitting.

The trip to Belgium was indeed enlightening, and I realised that there was a big wide world waiting to be experienced, a world full of new people and new opportunities. Six weeks later, my gang of mates led by Sly Andy, broke into my house and stole some of my Stranglers and Gary Numan LPs and a few cans of my dad's beer. It wasn't the crime of the century, but I quickly found out who was responsible. Once the many recriminations were over, I had lost a whole set of so-called friends.

However, the theft proved to be a blessing in disguise. The college people had proved to be a sound bunch and I took up Graham Moore's offer and started attending the Altrincham & Sale City Supporters' Club, which proved to be a great source of higher quality buddies. The first night I walked into the clubhouse I couldn't miss Phil Knowles, all 6ft 5in of him. But it wasn't his height and imposing size that made me think he'd be a good bloke to know; it was the Stranglers' *Rattus Norvegicus* patch on the back of his Wrangler jacket that told me we were going to be pals. Phil, John Eaton and Graham were all keen on travelling to away games and we teamed up to go on many an adventure to watch the lacklustre Blues. In addition, Terry Hyland nailed his colours to my mast as his foster brother Sly Andy was kicked out for his part in the heist of the century. Neither Terry Hyland nor Terry Stanton had been involved in any way and consequently remained my only local pals. This made my life uncomfortable, if only for a short while.

♦   ♦   ♦

After college had finished and before the hunt for a full-time job had begun, there was still the small matter of the leaving party to attend. This was held later than scheduled on Friday 28 September at the

Hunting Lodge on Oxford Road. The place wasn't exactly rocking so one of the lads there asked me if I fancied going to the Factory (AKA the Russell Club) to see a local band. We set off for the long walk into deepest, darkest Hulme, which reminds me of the sinister and supposedly futuristic backdrop during the scene in *A Clockwork Orange* when the tramp gets battered.

This turned out to be one the best gigs I've witnessed, even though it was only my third at the time! About halfway through their playlist, local band Joy Division had the crowd in the palm of their hands. It was about this time that a punk rocker – who must have been well over 6ft tall with a Mohican Spike – started a fight in the crowd. The band immediately went off stage, prompting a crescendo of boos from the floor. A few minutes later they came back on, and almost immediately, bass player Peter Hook, leapt off the stage and creamed the Mohican over the head with his guitar. They dragged him out by his feet and the band played on.

Peter Hook later told me that he saw a lad head-butt an innocent fan from behind. The victim – whose jacket was peppered with Joy Division badges – was at the front of the stage. Hooky took exception to this attack and ran to assist but forgot his guitar was plugged in. The flex yanked him back which made him fall and, as he did so, he inadvertently lamped the attacker with his guitar!

◆   ◆   ◆

The year still had a few more changes in store. I decided not to return to college and become a full-time layabout instead. However, my dad had other ideas in respect of my future, and any impending bedsores. He put his foot down and marched me to the careers office at Civic Centre, Wythenshawe. It was a good move on his part, but I wished he'd at least have let me change out of my pyjamas. The careers officer looked at my qualifications and set about finding my new career. Unfortunately, the posts of bra-fitter at Marks & Spencer's or beer-taster at Boddington's Brewery were unavailable.

Within 24 hours I had an appointment for an interview at Manchester Town Hall for the post of clerical officer, despite me holding out for a job with Mr Whippy. The careers officer phoned me at 9.00 a.m. and asked if I could go for interview at 10.30 a.m. I threw on my Sunday best suit with one of my dad's nylon ties. The only time I'd ever been to the Town Hall was to see City bring back the League Cup in

1976, but this was three years on and I didn't know what to expect. My preconceived idea of the Town Hall was that of an old building with one office and the mayor sitting at one end in all his regalia and a few people sitting in suits at the other. When I arrived there my vision couldn't have been more oblique.

The mayor was nowhere in sight and the place was a veritable maze of corridors and offices full of moustachioed men. The moustachioed women arrived a few years later in the mid-1980s when the Lefties were elected into power. What did impress me was that everyone I met seemed really friendly and happy, including my interrogator – Mrs Muriel Pearson – a kindly lady who virtually walked me through the interview. Obviously impressed with my dad's natty brown kipper tie, she helped me on my way.

'Can you brew tea and carry a piece of paper around all day?'

'Yes.'

'Great, you're in!'

The following day I was sent for another interview at the DHSS and, on the day after that, for the position as trainee warehouse manager. The next week I was miraculously – as far as I was concerned – offered all three jobs. But the warehouse position was out, because they'd said they wouldn't be prepared to let me have time off in midweek in the event of a City away game. It became a straight choice: take up employment in boring old Sale at the DHSS or work in the city with all the opportunities to 'admire' the girls once the sun came out. I chose the latter.

On Monday 15 October 1979, I began my first full-time job, located within the ornate but soot-covered Victorian building that was Manchester Town Hall. In those days, the dark and gloomy neo-Gothic structure was tucked into a dreary city centre worlds apart from today's bright and modern expanse. The first thing I noticed as I got off the bus in Piccadilly, was the burnt-out shell of the Woolworth's building on Oldham Street. It had recently been gutted by fire, tragically killing ten people in its rage. However, this charred mausoleum perversely complimented the rest of the bleak, dank surroundings of what at the time was a tired, old industrial city in decline.

I walked into the main committee office to be greeted by my new colleagues. The first thing I noticed was that they were speaking into walky-talkies, or so I thought. They were actually talking into Dictaphones, which recorded speech for secretaries to turn into banal local government jargonised text. I only mention it as this machine gave rise to the greatest in-office joke of its time, 'Here mate, can I borrow your Dictaphone?'

'No, use your bloody finger like everybody else!'

Yes indeed, paraphrasing the words of Edmund Blackadder, 'those dark winter nights would simply fly by.'

During those first few weeks walking around the cool, semi-illuminated, mosaic-patterned Town Hall corridors with my trusty piece of paper in hand, I noticed a familiar podgy chap with his flaming mop of red hair and generous smattering of freckles. He turned out to be the same young lad, whose dad – like mine – had regularly dumped him on 'A' Coach, and picked him up once we'd returned. During these initial encounters we never stopped to chat, simply exchanging a nod and the mutual greeting, 'All right Blue.' This was until one morning when I stopped and said, 'I've had enough of this bollocks. What's your name?' He replied, 'it's Mark Bowden, or "Bibby" to my mates.'

'Bibby it is then. D'ya fancy a pint at lunchtime?'

It was the official beginning of another friendship which still lasts to this day.

◆　◆　◆

Other key moments in 1979 were undoubtedly seeing my heroes, The Stranglers, for the first time, (at the Apollo on Thursday 25 October). 1979 was also the year my sister Julie tied the knot at the tender age of nineteen, thus leaving our house to live in Sheffield with her student husband, David. My mum was up in arms, repeatedly telling Julie that she was way too young and that she was throwing away both her life and a prospective career. Mothers, eh? Julie and her husband David – now a professor at Surrey University – remain happily married today and both have highly successful careers and a large and loving family. Even so, I was with my mum on this one at the time: I didn't want them to get married either. It meant me missing the Tottenham away game on 1 September, which ruined another complete season, as it turned out to be the only game I missed. We lost 2–1. However, I didn't see the bigger picture. With Julie gone and with only my little sister Joanne to compete with, the roost was mine to rule – well at least theoretically.

19

England v Scotland

I t is the most ancient international football fixture known to mankind, beginning as it did on Hamilton Crescent Cricket Field, Partick, in 1872. My first real awareness of the world's oldest international came when I was thirteen. This was the classic match in which Colin Bell helped England destroy their northern neighbours 5–1 at Wembley. The action was accompanied on the live BBC coverage by classic David Coleman 1970s commentary with his unique and spontaneous description and flat, monotone, but clinical voice. I adored his comments such as, 'The defence knew nothing about it and the goalkeeper even less,' 'Goals pay the rent and Keegan does his share,' or 'Clemence was left holding the air.' However, my dad and I had our own commentary that day. In between the laughter, we came out with the usual classics which accompany poor goalkeeping displays such as, 'That 'keeper couldn't catch a cold,' 'They call that 'keeper Dracula 'cos he hates crosses,' and, 'He'll have bloody backache by the time this game finishes if he keeps having to pick the ball out of the net every 5 minutes.' Our house was a veritable hive of inventive comic one-liners.

My Button Lane schoolmate John Laing originated from Glasgow and I slaughtered him after the match. This led to a punch-up, with me being victorious for once. I wasn't much of a scrapper and only came out on top because I was first to draw blood. Besides, 'Lango' had a dodgy blood vessel in his nose which bled at the slightest hint of a sneeze, let alone a punch. My victory made it technically 6–1 in England's favour as far as I was concerned. *We'd* sent *them* homewards 'tae think again'.

Scotland's next trip to Wembley was a couple of years later in 1977 and they triumphed 2–1. The fans invaded the pitch and dug up the hallowed turf while swinging on and collapsing the goalposts, without an England supporter in sight. My previously dormant patriotism had been stirred into action and I vowed that, given the opportunity, I'd go to an England v Scotland match so that I could personally help to redress the balance of 99,945 to 55 (as it appeared to be when I arrived there a couple of years later).

My big chance came with the next scheduled England v Scotland match at Wembley in 1979. The City travel club had organised a trip which left Maine Road on the Friday lunchtime on City's executive team coach, which meant soft seats, a couple of bolted-down tables and windows with curtains. I went on this trip with Graham Moore and Ian 'Greeny' Greenwood and we had a two-night stay in room 802 of the Royal Lancaster Hotel. This was a swanky gaff that had featured in the Michael Caine film *The Italian Job* several years earlier. The trip also included a match ticket and transfers to and from the game all for the princely sum of £25 (call girls were an optional 50p extra!).

My first taste of forthcoming events came on the mid-afternoon journey down the M6 motorway. We were overtaken by great masses of coaches which, with all the tartan on view, resembled huge tins of shortbread on wheels. Once in London, the Scotland supporters were even more prevalent and the capital was like a sea of extras from the film *Braveheart*. Everywhere I looked there were groups of 'Jocks' looking like they had just survived a Bay City Rollers convention and had taken copious amounts of alcohol in order to try and forget such a dubious experience. The enemy's splendid national costume consisted of Tam-o'-shanter on 'heed', tartan scarf around neck, flag draped around shoulders and a sporran (a small handbag made out of a dead badger's posterior) dangling from the front of a kilt. But the outfit was incomplete without a Bannockburn banner in one hand and a bottle of whisky in the other (or perhaps one of those highly amusing cans of Tennent's Lager that used to come with a picture of a scantily clad 'Lassie' on the side?). All that tartan was the attire of the day, the next day and, in all probability, the day after that.

The old saying goes that London's streets are paved with gold, but that particular Saturday they were paved with drunks from each and every clan in Caledonia. Although the tartan tribe was imposing, it wasn't frightening. I soon realised that the vast majority were there to enjoy themselves rather than cause trouble. They had tried to dismantle the stadium and take it home with them on their last visit, but I think this was due to high spirits having just beaten the 'Auld Enemy'.

The game was a cracker, with three City players on the pitch. But Barnes, Watson and Hartford were all on Malcolm Allison's transfer list.

John Wark, 'the tackling 'tache' gave Scotland the lead and – although I was peeved at the time – it wasn't a bad thing. It was an experience in itself to witness around 98,000 Celts roar with delight at the first strike of the game and it was a fine spectacle even for my extremely biased self. It was at this time that a huge Scotsman – who looked like a cross between Billy Connelly's nastier brother and the shot-putter on the front of the Scott's Porridge Oats box – slapped me on my back and said, 'Get a dram o' that doon ye son.' He handed me a consolatory full-sized bottle of whisky which he had easily smuggled into the ground (as there was none of that pre-match-frisking-for-missiles nonsense in those days).

To the delight of our small but enthusiastic band of City and England fans, we equalised thanks to young Peter Barnes's effort. His scuffed shot somehow crept through a mass of players and into the left-hand corner of George Wood's net. Chorlton High School 1 Scotland 1! England went into the lead after the break thanks to future City manager Steve Coppell, and then another future City boss, Kevin Keegan, wrapped up a 3–1 victory. He scored a third goal following a neat 'one-two' on the edge of the box with Trevor Brooking. To be fair, and to my admiration and pleasure, the huge clansman thrust me what had now become *his* consolatory bottle after every goal. It had the same insistent instruction of, 'Och, get that down ye son.' It's always a great sign when the mass cry of, 'Bonnie Skirtland, Bonnie Skirtland, we'll support ye evermore,' goes up, because that's when you know Scotland have lost. Later on, an unforgettable weekend was completed with celebrations on a moored boat bar on the River Thames, appropriately named *The Old Caledonian*.

♦ ♦ ♦

After such a fabulous spectacle, the England v Scotland experience became compulsive viewing. The following year, the corresponding fixture was played in Escotia, home of culinary delights such as that wee timorous beastie . . . the haggis. Other Scottish delicacies included fried Mars bars, 'cock-a-leekie' soup and those never-to-be-forgotten sallow mutton pies, lovingly lobbed into the deep fat fryer.

Unfortunately, my Hampden debut got off to a somewhat troubled start. Having befriended a great bunch of Hearts supporters during the 1979 pre-season Skol Festival of Football in Edinburgh (which starred City, Hearts, Hibs and Coventry) I now had access to Hampden tickets. Having had too many 'sherbets' the night before, I overslept and missed the early train my mates had boarded. After a mad rush to Victoria station I managed to hop on a later departure. On arrival at the pre-Cultural City of Glasgow, I boarded a local train to Mount Florida: the stop for Hampden Park. My somewhat naïve policy of wearing my England scarf while on my own, was not a good one. As the train arrived at its destination and before you could say, 'D'ya fancy a game of dot-to-dot zit-face?' a small group of spotty youths punched and spat at my equally spotty face as they made their not-so-heroic departure from the train. It may sound a bit drastic, but it didn't really hurt.

The exterior facade of Hampden Park was as aesthetically pleasing to the eye as an eighteenth-century prison, although I'm sure Archibald Leitch would defend his national stadium if he was still alive today. The ground itself was set in a sort of battlefield-like terrain, which in turn was surrounded by imposing red-stone tenement buildings which arched over my head and frowned at my impertinent English presence. This setting – mixed with hostile locals – formed a frightening welcome. The England team also suffered as they struggled towards the players' entrance, greeted by numerous flashes of Scottish manhood from beneath the tartan skirts. It was noticeable that there were still plenty of drinks at-hand and in-hand, but the intensity and atmosphere wasn't quite the same on their own doorstep.

I was still on my own as I pushed my way through the clanking turnstiles. But my luck was changed for the better as virtually the first person I spotted amid the cast of thousands was 'Football' Tony. He was accompanied by my other City pals, together with our hosts from the Heart of Midlothian.

The teams were greeted by the 'Hampden Roar' and by all manner of flags and anti-England banners. It was truly an awesome sight and must have been even more impressive during those pre-crowd safety days of 140,000 plus. As usual, the Scots were full of song and verse, with their traditional ballads such as that Rab C. Nesbit ditty of 'Flower of Scotland' and that other classic, 'Tae dye an English bastard', although they are never kind enough to tell us which colour we are going to be dyed. Indeed, whenever Scotland played against the English in those days, you always heard my old favourite, 'We hate Jammy Hall [Jimmy Hill] he's a poof, he's a poof!' But the one song they always got their teeth into, to the tune of 'Those Were the Days', was a gentle little number that went, 'We forkin' hate England, we forkin' hate England, we hate, we forkin' hate England,' which is why, for 90 minutes at least, I hated them.

England won 2–0 with goals from Trevor Brooking and Steve Coppell, which put us in good heart for the journey to Edinburgh on an open-top double-decker bus. When we arrived at the Ardmillan Club, we were treated to numerous drinks from very magnanimous and sporting losers. No wonder I love Edinburgh and its people.

My only other spot of bother in an England v Scotland game came at Hampden four years later when Bibby and I had a knife pulled on us after over-enthusiastically celebrating a Tony Woodcock equaliser. While we were taking a leak at the back of the stand, a less than friendly nutcase threatened us, 'If ye cheer like that again, I'll cut ye forkin' cokes off,' as he brandished a knife in our direction. Bib and I could each have both done with a 'woodcock' at the time and I've never re-holstered my willy more quickly.

After that match Bibby and I took our lives into our hands again. We were standing in a huge snake of hundreds of kilted Edinburghers at Glasgow Central when they all started singing 'Tae dye an English bastard'. After a few renditions we'd taken enough. We put on our lilywhite hats and scarves and started singing, 'Engerland, Engerland, Engerland,' at the top of our voices. This was met with a deafening riposte of, 'Spot the loonies, spot, spot, spot the loonies.' I'm still here to tell the tale thanks to the commendable Scottish sense of fair play.

In fact, my worst and most frightening memory of the various trips to Scotland was of a culinary rather than violent nature as guests of Barry Gibson, one of the Hearts lads. Terry Hyland, Bibby, Dom Cosseron and I had to face and consume mutton pie, chips and beans for *breakfast* while suffering with woeful hangovers the morning after the victory before. As turning down any sort of hospitality was not the done thing, it was a challenge we had to meet. Somehow we were up to the task as Barry inexplicably disappeared that morning leaving us in his flat to lock up and join the other Hearts lads in the Ardmillan.

When Barry arrived later, he wouldn't tell us where he'd been. This became apparent a few days later when an envelope arrived on my doorstep containing the 1955 FA Cup final Manchester City v Newcastle programme. I'd mentioned I needed it for my collection during the previous night's entertainment and Barry had sneaked off to a programme fair to acquire it. The fact that someone who didn't really know me would go out of his way, and at great expense, was one of the most impressive gifts I've received. No matter what the myth may be about Scotsmen being tight, take it from me that it is as insulting as it is inaccurate. In my experience, they are the most generous and hospitable people I've ever had the good fortune to meet.

20

Into the 1980s

My third decade on the planet had finally arrived, this despite me only being aged seventeen when the Rabbie Burns Five piped the highly predictable 'Auld Land Syne' into the Brooklands Trades & Labour Club concert room for its customary raucous reception on New Year's Eve.

The 1980s were to prove radically different from the '70s in terms of style, music and football, and not necessarily for the better. The charts were full of the usual middle-of-the-road pop pulp which compulsively pervaded the testosterone-fuelled, plastic teenybopper-inhabited 'fizz palaces' which I willingly frequented at the time. Indeed my toes are starting to curl as I recall the early '80s and that 'cringe-worthy' Dexy's Midnight Runners record, which seemed to haunt me wherever I went. I couldn't work out whether 'Come On Eileen' was a message of encouragement or a sexual instruction. Either way, I hated it with perhaps a slightly over-venomous passion.

Any optimistic hopes I might have harboured for the new decade in terms of success for my football team were quickly dashed. Things were starting to go wrong for City and it was a trend soon to be confirmed. Within the first week of the 1980s, my beloved Blues suffered what was arguably the most humiliating defeat of the club's history. The date was 5 January 1980 and City had been drawn at Halifax Town in the FA Cup third round. I visited this fine bastion of Yorkshire in Graham Moore's trusty Ford Escort with Football Tony, John Eaton and Phil Knowles. Given the previous season's ignominious knockout at the hands of Shrewsbury Town, we were all somewhat paranoid before the game. City had Big Mal at the helm and he'd seen to it that we had the country's record signings in the team, Steve Daley, and the dynamic million-pound striker Kevin Reeves.

At the time, Halifax were rock bottom of the Fourth Division and they hadn't won for weeks. Before the game we stopped off for a pint and a chippy lunch in Elland, just outside our destination.

Once inside the rustic White Rose pub, we settled into cosy seats beside a crackling open coke fire, its flames licking the back of the brass-dimpled chimney breast plate while warming our perished feet and equally cold demeanour. All was fine and dandy until a wizened old bloke offered his 'individual' slant on things. He was suitably attired in his locally made, but grubby, Gannex overcoat, a flat cap, and a lapel badge which said, 'I'm a stereotypical Yorkshireman, please buy me a pint 'cos I'm a tight git,' while holding a whippet under his arm. Without a word of introduction, he leaned over our table and uttered the words I'd been dreading since the draw, 'Ee lad, ah saw Town play last week, tha'll beat 'em today, tha's *crap* tha nus?' I became totally immersed in the fresh déjà vu of the Shropshire nightmare flashing up so vividly in the memory.

These were indeed famous last words. It was a cold, damp and dreary day; it had been raining all week and the pitch looked like a waterlogged battlefield. The conditions were not suited to our *slack* passing game. The venue, The Shay, was appalling and remains *the* worst professional football ground that I've ever been to, and I've been to a few (some weeks later I saw Hearts play at Alloa, and that ran it a close second). City fans were spread all over the ground and we were hard-pushed to spot a Halifax Town supporter until 13 minutes to go as disaster struck when Paul Hendrie squeezed in the only goal past Joe Corrigan. It went in at the end where I was struggling to keep my feet from sliding down the muddy bank. Within seconds I was on my backside, both literally and metaphorically.

Before you could say, 'Oh bugger I think I've left the hosepipe running in my allotment,' we were out of the cup. It was a 'giant killing' and the score reverberated around the country. The early 2.00 p.m. kick-off made matters worse as we were the first major cup exit of the day. Consequently, it was quite early when Football Tony and I were dropped off, drowning our sorrows in the Railway Clubs of both Victoria and Piccadilly before making our way to the Labour Club and my Saturday shift as a pot collector.

When I arrived the United supporters gave me merciless stick. In fact, I almost lost my job when I 'playfully' lobbed a snooker ball at one of them and 'accidentally' knocked a table full of glasses over another. It could have been double disaster, but my boss, the club steward, gave me the benefit of what little doubt there was and I got a reprieve. The following Monday I had some measure of revenge when Ossie Ardiles' solitary Spurs goal knocked United out, but it was small comfort.

♦   ♦   ♦

Meanwhile I'd been getting to grips with my full-time job at the Town Hall. I'd got the hang of photocopying and walking around the table collating council agendas as was a junior clerical officer's role. Not only that, but I could now easily brew tea for twenty-eight people in one go. I'd also learnt how to play Space Invaders and I was in the pub every lunchtime for a pie and a pint and endless on-screen games trying to beat my personal best of 36,330 (according to my trusty diary).

One of the boys in the office was a focused individual called Chris Hulme, a respectable bespectacled lad to whom I looked up (not that he was any taller than me). Chris was a few years older and proved that through dedicated hard work, you could rise up the ranks in local government. He'd also started at the bottom, but had already gained a couple of impressive promotions and was waltzing through his high-level college qualifications with a conscientious and studious approach which was totally alien in my world. In short, he was everything that I wasn't, except that he was also a big Blue, from a big Blue family.

Chris Hulme must be one of the top five United-haters that I've met (and I've met a few candidates in my time) so he was not a difficult bloke to like or appreciate. I spotted Chris in the Kippax during a home game against Leeds. As I made my way towards him, the crowd surged forward and I inadvertently clattered into a big bloke, who took immediate exception. He grabbed the top of the hood of my duffle coat and thumped me in the face twice. It was a slight overreaction on his part and my upper lip split wide open. The cops were soon on the scene and arrested my over-zealous assailant on a serious charge of 'lamping a spotty teenager without a licence.' Chris and I spent the rest of the afternoon in St Mary's Hospital waiting to have my lip stitched as Paul Power equalised in what finished a 1–1 draw. The bloke who attacked me turned out to be a nightclub bouncer who was fined £30 for his troubles. I later received £504 from the Criminal Injuries Compensation Board for the scar I still carry. A strange monetary imbalance there, but not one I was complaining about – £504 was a tidy sum in those days and I blew the lot within a few months.

With my new-found wealth, I soon bought numerous pairs of pleated trousers, brushed cotton shirts, thin leather ties and box jackets to pose in at night. I even had a pair of white 'Bally' leather shoes, in which I strutted around with one hand strategically placed in my right pocket, thinking I looked a cool dude (but in reality I must have looked a bit of a dick). By day my 'cool' image changed to that of an urban wise guy, or one of 'De boys' as Football Tony would say. At first I adopted the 'Perry Boy' look, complete with 'flick' hairstyle (later taken to the extreme by Phil Oakey), Slazenger jumpers with jumbo cords and boater shoes. But this smart image was to be taken further with the introduction of expensive tennis gear as endorsed by McEnroe, Borg and Connors, with outrageously expensive brands such as Sergio Tacchini, Fila and Lacoste. All such overpriced drip-dry cotton took pride of place in my wardrobe, promoting the regular parental catch phrase of, 'You must have more bloody money than sense.' At the time, of that there was no doubt.

The 1980s saw the dawning of the 'New Romantics'. As I hadn't been an old romantic, or any sort of romantic for that matter, I steered well clear, although I did find some of the music appealing. 'New Wave' was alive and kicking and the post-punk/nu-electro era was upon us and I was well up for all of it. The start of the new decade saw David Bowie *Heroes* and *Low* derivatives, Gary Numan and John Foxx's Ultravox, grab my initial attention. However, it was David Sylvian's Japan that had me hooked to near obsession. I loved the music and adored and tried to emulate their chic style; but failed miserably.

I also embarked on my brief career as a 'clubber' with fellow pot-lad Darren Hendley. This didn't involve harming seals, but instead it was more to do with tripping the light fantastic at Manchester's hottest night spots of the time: Tiffany's, Smarty's, Rotters, De Villes, Cellar V, Rafters and Placemate 7. However, these nightclubs paled into insignificance when compared to Pips on Fennel Street. Pips was to Manchester what Studio 54 was to New York and it was the Holy Grail for Darren and I, as we tried in vain to gain admittance each week. The joint reeked of the acrid stench of dry-ice and sizzling burger fat and it was always rammed with an eclectic mix of enthusiastic revellers. But, due to our cherubic looks, we both had obvious problems in gaining access. We never stood together in the queue: either he got in and I didn't or I got in and he didn't. It was a nightmare. It wasn't until I came of age at eighteen that they allowed both of us in simultaneously and I had to prove my legitimacy with my passport. Looking way younger than I was had some disadvantages, but as I was to discover later, it also had some advantages as well.

We weren't disappointed with Pips; it had numerous rooms to cater for all musical tastes. Once we'd finally got our memberships, we spent most of our time prancing around in our 'cool' leather Bryan Ferry box jackets (Darren's red, mine luminescent yellow) in the Bowie room, soaking up Fad Gadget, Bauhaus, Kraftwerk, Simple Minds and David Bowie. These were great nights in my carefree youth, topped off with life-threatening chips, peas and salmonella pie from the infamous Oxford Road Chippy and the equally life-threatening journey home on the all-nighter to Wythenshawe. Everyone who boarded that bus behaved like St Trinian's kids on a blue Smarties-fest, much to the annoyance of the chastened and underpaid driver.

It was after one of these full and varied nights out that I ended up sharing a bunk bed with Darren having crashed at his parents' house, only to be woken up abruptly early in the morning by his mum, Shirley. She had burst into our bedroom screaming at Darren, as she had discovered a 'Richard the Third' lying guiltily in the middle of her new kitchen floor and just a couple of yards from the downstairs loo. Darren had been known to go walkabouts after a heavy night on the ale, peeing in the wardrobe, etc. Even though he had two younger brothers, it was a fair bet that Daz was to blame. He hotly denied the crime, blaming it on the new puppy. His mum bought this and marched downstairs to bollock the dog. We heard nothing more; well for 10 minutes at least. That was until she thundered up the stairs once more and burst into our room shouting, 'You filthy liar!' Darren lay cowering in the foetal position under his quilt still protesting, 'It was the dog, it was the dog!' To this Shirley replied, 'Is the dog turning off the lights now? There's some shit on the light switch, you dirty little get!'

♦   ♦   ♦

I gave your average lush a run for his money in the drinking stakes and looked to get fit again by expressing an interest in turning out for the Brooklands Trades & Labour Club Football Club. I hadn't played a proper game of 11-a-side since the third year of school. However, my knee had temporarily stopped giving me gyp, so I started pounding the streets in a grey hooded sweat top with the *Rocky* theme tune playing incessantly in my head.

Nobody at the Labour Club had seen me play and I'd told the team manager that I was a right-winger, even though I wasn't. I thought I'd try to get forward for once and see how it developed. I had to wait until 10 minutes to go before I got my chance. I hadn't played open-age football before and as a 10 stone wet-through seventeen-year-old weed, I must have looked like lean and easy meat to my opponent – a fat, baldy full-back. Within a couple of minutes the ball came my way and I miscontrolled, it but in doing so, the ball inadvertently went through the defender's legs. I seized the opportunity to send in a beautiful right-foot cross which was converted for the winner. Just after the re-start the burly defender said, 'If you do that again, you'll be going home in an ambulance,' to which I replied, 'If I do that again I'll be floating home on a cloud.' Needless to say, I went home on the bus. This turned out to be the Labour Club's last game of the season and I didn't turn out for them again. I managed to dine out on that moment as word got around the BTLC about what a great tricky winger I was!

♦   ♦   ♦

2 May 1980 was my eighteenth birthday. To celebrate, Darren and I journeyed out to the Russell Club to see Martha and the Muffins of 'Echo Beach' fame. Martha Ladley – the fitter of the two Marthas in the band – responded to my cheeky wave and blew me a kiss about which I bored poor old Daz at the end of the set.

The following day, City were at home to Ipswich and I was joined by a coach load of Ardmillan Hearts fans who were watching the Blues for the first time, while helping me celebrate my new-found status as a *legal* drinker. We spent most of that weekend drinking in the City Social Club, which meant having to endure the disgusting Greenall's keg bitter or equally awful Grünhalle Lager. But the Hearts fans seemed to enjoy themselves, particularly as City managed to win 2–1 and they all got well 'pished'. On the Sunday they were treated to an organised trip around Maine Road for a quick look in the 'bored' room and a longing fawn at the empty trophy cabinet before running onto the hallowed turf for a quick game with an invisible ball, which I'm sure made groundsman Stan Gibson very happy indeed.

Missing Magazine playing live at the Russell Club on Saturday 3 May – the day after my birthday – was regrettable. However, I wasn't complaining; it was a great weekend and it gave me a chance to reciprocate the many generosities I'd received back in *Auld Reekie*, not that I could ever come close as the Hearts lads were in a class of their own in that regard. But I was really into Magazine and would loved to have seen the now sadly departed and legendary Scottish lead guitarist John McGeogh in that great original line-up along with Howard Devoto, Barry Adamson and Dave Formula.

This was just the start of summer 1980. Less than a couple of weeks later I was at Wembley for an England international against the then World Champions, Argentina. I had a ringside bench on the lower side of the ground and sat there open-mouthed as I watched the seventeen-year-old Diego Armando Maradona warming-up with sublime ball-juggling tricks. The lad arrived at Wembley with a big reputation and, although he wasn't one of their 1978 World Cup-winning team, it was clear that he was class. England won 3–1 and Maradona failed to score. But what the statistics hide is the moment of pure genius when he dummied England defenders Phil Thompson, Kenny Sansom and Phil Neal. It appeared that there was nothing he couldn't do with a ball.

England were on their way to the European Championships in Italy in style . . . that was until four days later I saw them hammered 4–1 by Wales on a hot, sunny day in Wrexham. But a 2–0 win over Scotland at Hampden put us back on track and we were off to Italy with all guns blazing.

I was also on my way to an *Azzuri* adventure. On Sunday 8 June, I flew from Heathrow to Turin with Tony Whitley and Nigel Crossley, a couple of amiable City fans from Chester. It was my first flying experience and it was exciting. Scottish goalkeeper Bob Wilson sat in front of me, but I didn't ask him why he was on his way to Italy as the Scots hadn't qualified. Our first excursion in Turin was to an English pub accompanied by a number of Ipswich fans. On the way we managed to take a wrong turning and stumbled upon the red light area. I quickly realised that the saucy slapper approaching us was a lady-of-the-night, even though it was 12.30 in the afternoon. She had a cleavage in which you could have buried a bread van and we all walked past her with our eyes popping out and our tongues unravelling by our feet in true cartoon style. But none of us had the money or the bottle to do anything about it so we went to a nearby bar for a beer and a game of cards instead.

Playing cards in Italy was brilliant, especially the currency which was around 2,000 lira to the pound. You could raise the pot by 4,000 and sound big. In reality it was only a couple of quid. It gave you the feeling that you were playing for really high stakes, particularly as the pile of notes stacked up. On the downside, the winner could usually only buy one round! After a few beers the Italian 'lady' strolled past the bar in her stiletto heels with a seductive smile. It was then that one of the Ipswich lads came up with a bright idea. We'd all put in 5,000 lira and cut cards for a ride on the local Ducati. I got a two of hearts and so I was out of the humping stakes. Neither Nige nor Tony fared much better, but the Ipswich lad who suggested it came up with an ace of spades!

After a couple more drinks, the 'Tractor Boy' – as Ipswich fans are known – raised enough courage. About 20 minutes later he returned ashen-faced and almost in tears. He wouldn't tell us what had happened until a few more drinks had loosened his tongue. As he put it in his Ipswich drawl, 'We got in the room and she took her top off to reveal a fabulous pair of boobies and we started kissing and getting down to it. But when I put my hand down below, I quickly realised that Francesca wasn't in fact Francesca after all . . . she was actually Franco!'

Later that afternoon, we visited the Britannia Pub, the usual 'authentic' English boozer that appears compulsory in most major Continental cities. It wasn't long before the north/south divide had taken a detrimental effect on the general mood of the collective England supporters present. Leeds and West Ham fans started arguing and it almost came to the point of a brawl. This wasn't surprising really as the argument was about the usual important emotive subjects such as why flat beer is better than ale with a head and why a wash-house is far superior to a lock-up for the storage of various goods, both perishable and otherwise.

The row gained momentum as a gang of thirty smartly dressed young Italians arrived. They calmly dismounted their Vespa scooters and parked outside the front of the pub. With military planning they walked quietly into the bar, ordered a pint or a bottle of beer and walked back to the front of the pub. A few minutes later, a volley of pint pots and bottles were hurled through the front windows and we were showered in glass and ale. Within seconds the high-pitched scream of the Italian police sirens burst on the scene. We expected to fight our way at the front of the building but the Italians were also in the process of fleeing. I legged it around the nearest corner, quickly spotting a newsagent's and grabbed a copy of *La Gazzetta Dello Sport* from the outside rack. I watched as the cops chased both the English and Italians as I stood outside the shop hiding behind my newspaper trying desperately to look like a local, although I may have had the paper upside down for all I knew.

Nobody in our party was rounded up, but we were all shaken by the time we met up back at the hotel. The best thing to do now was for everyone to stick together, so the next day we went down to a local park for a game of 50-a-side football before the England game against Belgium at the Stadio Comunale (formally the Stadio Mussolini, now revamped as the Stadio Olimpico di Torino). Things were going well when Ray Wilkins gave England the lead after 25 minutes. When Jan Ceulemans equalised for Belgium 3 minutes later, the fun began. We were in an open end behind the goal with about 10,000 England supporters in a crowd of 15,186. In the corner to our left were several hundred Italians who cheered when Belgium equalised. Within seconds England fans decided to 'have a look' at the locals. There was a bit of pushing and shoving. The carabinieri had moved over to the perimeter of the stand and fired canisters into the crowd. One landed a few feet from me as I shouted, 'It's okay, it's only a smoke bomb.' But as I stood there rubbing Chlorobenzylidene Malonitrile into my eyes, I inexplicably started blubbering and crying for my mummy. Then the penny dropped: it was tear gas. Needless to say the rest of the game was a bit of a blur. There was more trouble on the way back to the hotel as local mobs of youths, who had watched events on the television, came out to see if they could stir it up.

When we arrived back at the hotel, my travelling companions, Tony and Nige, decided to phone home to tell their parents they were okay. I thought I'd better ring mine, imagining they would be concerned. My dad answered. I said, 'I'm okay. I'm fine. I only got hit by tear gas.' He replied, 'What tear gas? Don't be soft, I haven't even watched the match, I've told you before, my team is City not England. Are you having a nice time son?'

In fact I wasn't. I was on holiday and didn't need the constant hassle whenever we wandered into Turin. The next day we packed up our bags and headed off to the peaceful town of Vercelli, located on the train line between Turin and Milan. It was a good move as we were treated to a couple of calm relaxing days before we ventured back into Turin for the big one – Italia v Inghilterra.

Whether it was down to the trouble or lack of tickets, England's support went down from 10,000 to about 1,500. The word had gone round to meet at the station for Sunday's game and when we arrived back at Stazione Porta Nuova, there was a tangible unease.

Turin city centre traffic was at a complete standstill as the English mob was marched along the main street in glorious sunshine fronted by armoured cars all the way to the Stadio Comunale. The outcome would decide whether or not England would progress in the tournament. All the England fans were located in a corner area behind a goal, the ideal target for missiles hurled by the Italians who were located directly above. It wasn't until the teams were on the pitch and the national anthems were in progress that we burst into the ground and took up our positions in the first segregated football match held in Italy. The combination of trepidation and excitement meant I enjoyed every minute of its electric atmosphere, including the deafening roar of the 59,646 crowd when Italy's Marco Tardelli scored the winner with 11 minutes to go.

We had booked and paid for a room back in Vercelli that night, but the streets of Turin were at a standstill with horn-blowing, flag-waving Italians who had clambered on to the tops of their Fiats to celebrate their victory. We wisely decided to stay in our old hotel in Turin, avoiding what would have been a precarious journey back to the railway station. We were under siege, but it was an enjoyable experience in a perverse sort of way. The defeat meant that England were out of the tournament after only four days, but we still went on to the final game against Spain in Naples.

The heat was off, but not literally as we travelled down the boot of Italy via Milan and Rome, before staying in Sorrento where we had a somewhat more sedate final week, taking in the sights of Capri and Pompeii (or 'Pompey' as it says in my 1980 diary).

The summer had been disappointing and when City's pre-season programme commenced, I was desperately in need of a tangible indication that things were going to get better. In pursuit of the dream, I was on my travels once more. In early August I hopped over to Holland on a trip to see those Dutch maestros, FC Breda. Here I witnessed the mighty Steve Daley and the even mightier former Newport County idol, Paul Sugrue, score for the Blues on foreign soil as we swept to a majestic 3–2 victory. But any false dawn was soon washed away in a shower of reality which hit Maine Road in the shape of the now sadly departed Kaziu Deyna's former team Legia Warsaw. They hammered City 5–1 at Maine Road. It was a warning shot for the season ahead, starting at Southampton where Mike Channon's double was enough to beat us 2–0. Days later Sunderland promptly thumped us 4–0 at Maine Road. Less than a week into the new season we were already in turmoil and it was clear that this was not going to be a championship term for Malcolm Allison and his expensive team of young misfits.

It was all very distressing to watch. In addition to Channon, former players such as Doyle, Watson, Barnes and Kidd all scored against City for their various teams. The only thing I could do was to drown my sorrows with other people's beer in the Labour Club. The October visit of champions Liverpool showed us all just how far City had regressed. Kenny Dalglish took advantage of a City defence which had more cracks than a patio that had just staged the final of the world fat blokes' pogo-stick championships as Liverpool wiped the floor with us, winning 3–0. Things then came to a head in a cold, dark night match at Elland Road. If City lost we would end up bottom of the league. It was a position that chairman Peter Swales had publicly stated, 'mustn't happen'. It did, and Big Mal and Tony Book were sacked. It was all very harsh on my mate Book, a man who was clearly in love with the club, as I'm sure was Big Mal but not as much as he was with himself. Bookie did resurface at regular intervals in later years. He was usually wheeled out to temporarily take up the reins when City were between managers.

City were now managerless and bottom of the league, and a first-class replacement was needed and quickly. This turned out to be John Bond from Norwich City. With some astute signings from the footballers' retirement homes throughout the country, 'Bondy' went for experience rather than youth. He signed players such as Gerry Gow, Tommy Hutchison, and Phil Boyer while getting rid of Allison's expensive flop Steve Daley, along with Paul Sugrue and Kaziu Deyna. The Blues started climbing up the league and began a couple of promising cup runs, one of which was to take us all the way to Wembley and possibly my first chance to see City actually win something.

21

Wemberlee!

ity were still in the League Cup when John Bond took over in 1980. Victories over Notts County and West Brom with what were predominantly Allison's players (as Bond's new signings were cup-tied) had brought City to a two-legged semi-final with Liverpool. In the home game Kevin Reeves scored after just 3 minutes, but the ref disallowed it. To this day I don't know why. The Blues went on to lose 1–0 to a late goal and, despite a valiant effort, went out at Anfield with the soon-to-be-forgotten Gary Buckley being City's star of the show. The Blues took great support to Liverpool that night, and once more our coach windows were bricked on the way out. I could never work out whether the Scousers didn't like us or our windows. Bricking the coaches had become a traditional pastime on 'Murkeyside' whether visiting Anfield or Goodison. So much so, that when the bus reached a certain point by the local cemetery, I always tied my scarf around my face and ducked down in anticipation of the brick or broken piece of headstone being propelled through the window.

It was tough to accept, given the referee's decision in the first game and the rousing display in the second. In consolation, both performances had illustrated how far the team had come in such a short space of time under Bond. We were still in the FA Cup which began on 3 January 1981 with a home game against Crystal Palace, who had their latest manager Malcolm Allison in charge. Since his fall from the wobbly stool that supports all City's managers, Big Mal had flown back to the Eagles' nest.

♦　♦　♦

By now I was back in the saddle and in pursuit of further educational qualifications having started a one-year BEC General Certificate day release course at Fielden Park College in West Didsbury. The Town Clerk's Department staff officer had sent me to middle class suburbia in an attempt to boost both my limited qualifications and knowledge. I joined several other 'remedials' from various council departments who had to start on the bottom course through lack of O Levels.

BEC Gen was supposed to be the equivalent of four O Levels and provided the gateway to the BEC National and BEC Higher National certificates. They brought with them the welcome incentive of pay grade increments which were not to be sniffed at. I now took college seriously. The most worrying aspect about the initial BEC course was that it included a subject known as 'Bookkeeping' – one skill I couldn't get my head around. With my lack of mathematical gumption, I had more chance of mastering Egyptian hieroglyphics from a Swedish textbook than tackling basic accountancy successfully. To make matters worse, it was the last lesson and it ended at 6.30 p.m., so the temptation to cut the lecture was often too great to resist.

I was halfway through the BEC course by the time City took on Palace in the FA Cup on a cold, dark winter's afternoon at Maine Road. Big Mal turned up with his lowly Palace side, 'desperate for a win,' as he put it. Typically, Big Mal had the temerity to run onto the pitch in a Palace tracksuit – partially obscured by his Burberry-style raincoat – to try to take the acclaim of the Kippax before the match began. Although some responded warmly, the majority sang the praises of Johnny Bond instead. I have no doubt of Malcolm's allegiance to the Blues and never underestimate what he achieved with Joe Mercer during City's halcyon days. However, as far as I was concerned, he totally messed up at Maine Road when he managed us for the second time and I wasn't sympathetic when he returned as manager of Palace. I was delighted that City won the game with four second-half goals.

It was late in the following evening that the police reported that they had arrested a suspect in connection with 'The Yorkshire Ripper' murders. The day after his capture, City were drawn at home against Norwich City, Bond's old club whose team contained his son Kevin or 'Spesh' as he was sarcastically named by City supporters. If every club capitulated like Norwich used to do against the Blues we would have been the best team in the land. City always beat the Canaries and won 6–0 on this occasion. At the end of the game, Bond was so concerned about his son's disappointment that he jumped down from the directors' box into the players' tunnel and broke his ankle.

1. *Above:* Humble beginnings at 239 Wythenshawe Road.

2. *Above right:* Just checking. Male paranoia, aged two and a bit.

3. *Right:* Attitude at Anglesey with our Joanne and Julie.

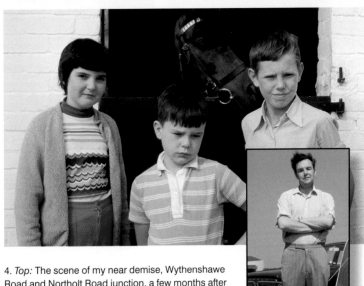

4. *Top:* The scene of my near demise, Wythenshawe Road and Northolt Road junction, a few months after splatteration in 1971. *(Courtesy of the Manchester Archive)*

5. *Above:* Not best pleased at Auchenlarie, with Julie, Billy Roddy and Mr Ed (background).

6. *Right:* Dad proudly displays his huge Zephyr 6 next to his equally massive tent.

7. Sunday Best nylons.

8. Chorlton High School (Lower). *(Courtesy of the Manchester Archive)*

9. 1970s Button Lane shops with McGarry's newsagents hiding under its canopy. *(Courtesy of the Manchester Archive)*

10. Happy families in the mid-1970s.

11. Cherubic fanatic.

12. A dormant Brooklands Trades & Labour Club after closing down in 2008.

13. What the … (p*ss artist's impression of the invasion of the Fruit Polos).

14. Tension mounts prior to England's clash with Italy, 12 June 1980.

15. With Geoff Garrett, David Sylvian and Lynn Garrett's right eye at the Oxford Road Show, 20 January 1981.

16. The Blue Army outside Wembley prior to the centenary FA Cup final with Spurs, 9 May 1981.

17. Meet the players. Inside the San Siro with John Eaton, Gary Birkett and Dom Cosseron, 24 August 1981.

18. Phil Knowles (white T-shirt) relaxes with the boys at the camp site bar on the outskirts of Madrid at the World Cup in Spain, 1982.

19. The Likely Lads. Me and Terry Hyland on our return from my 21st birthday booze-up on 2 May 1983.

20. Brighton Trip I, fancy dress and fancy jumpers, 10 March 1984.

21. Charlie, Gilly, Bibby and Bugsy enjoy a beer at Brighton Trip II (Gilly went as a striking miner), 3 November 1984.

22. Gilly shares a joke on the back row of a Lee Athletic team photo, 21 January 1990. Back row: Mark Bowden (manager), Rob Taylor, Jim Grant, Mike Orr, Steve Worthington, Paul Gilsenan, Terry Doyle, Martin Burns, Mark Taylor, Jock Brocklehurst. Front row: Carl Taylor, Darren McCauley, Alex Murray, Andy Smith, Stewart Freeman and Dave Lydon.

23. A small degree of success.

24. Where true love begins: the Jolly Angler!

25. My gorgeous 1980s Christmas chick.

26. Wedding belles. The cast: Dad, Darren Hendley, Tony Morehead, Steve Annette, Pete Moore, Jerry Sweeney, Johnny Copper, Terry Hyland, John Eaton, Steve Worthington, Phil Knowles, Paul Flynn, Ian Greenwood, Neil Burrows, Mark Bowden, Paul Gilsenan, Andy Mills, Stewart Freeman, Jim Grant, Paul Conlan.

27. Lee Athletic 1993/94. Back row: Steve Worthington (manager), Russell Bell, Simon Foster, Jim Grant, Terry Hyland, Phil Knowles, Richard Holland, Dai Hughes, Mark Taylor, Pete Moore (secretary). Front row: Stewart Freeman, John Gillespie, Dave Hickman, Dave Wadsworth, Mike Mitchell, Arch Stanton.

28. Touchline reaction to another Lee Athletic disaster (with Mark Taylor and Jim Grant).

29. Lee Athletic 1995/96. Back row: Johnny Copper, Phil Knowles (assistant manager) Mark Taylor, Pete Gillespie, Jim Grant, Richard Rogers, Lee Jenkins, Simon Foster, Jimmy Loftus, Pete Moore (secretary). Front row: Derek Fisher, John Gillespie, Ian Salt, David Beech, Steve Worthington (manager), Mark Whittaker.

30. The flat of fun (top left).

31. At Maine Road with Noel Bayley and Flynny during the summer of Euro 96.

32. With King Colin Bell, 7 January 1994.

33. Leaving the Maine Road pitch for the second and last time.

34. The Beehive prior to the last game at Maine Road on 11 May 2003.

35. Preparing to stuff the Germans in the Olympiastadion Munich, 1 September 2001.

36. With Alex the German City fan, Gary Tipper and Cliff Doyle prior to England v Sweden in Cologne, 20 June 2006.

37. Lee Athletic 1999/2000. Back row: Pete Moore (secretary), Sean Durden, Jim Grant, Colin Baker, Pete Gillespie, Terry Hyland, John Colligan, Lee Jenkins, Phil Knowles. Front row: Steve Worthington (manager), John Gillespie, Kevin Garvey, Steve Sharrett, Carl Taylor, Paul McCole, Andy Smith.

38. With Sam Gilsenan, 'Mary Ds', Eastlands, 2008.

Next it was Peterborough United away and yet another potential banana skin to worry about. Thankfully, City didn't slip on a real or metaphorical one thanks to Tommy Booth's solitary strike. After the match I witnessed a vicious punch-up on the bridge located near the London Road ground. Two equal gangs of thirty set about each other. In such a cramped and confined space it was tight-fitting, toe-to-toe fighting which the police had a tough job in quelling as they waded in with their flailing truncheons. In those days there was always likely to be trouble no matter whom or where City were playing. Not because City's fans were any more belligerent, but because football violence was just part of the times.

The next round was the quarter-final at Everton. The day before the match I bumped into City players Steve Mackenzie and Dave Bennett during my lunch break. They were in a sports shop in the Arndale Centre. Stevie Mac told me to be careful as it could, 'go right off temorrah', as he put it in his Cockney twang, and he wasn't wrong. But he continued, 'By the way, do you think a lock-up is better at storing both perishable and non-perishable goods than a wash-house?' I made a deep sigh and said, 'Just leave it Macca. You've got more to worry about, such as an important FA Cup quarter-final tomorrow.'

Having had enough of dodging flying bricks and glass on the coach, I went to this game in the car with my dad with the strains of Echo and the Bunnymen and The Teardrop Explodes playing in the cassette player. 'Rescue' and 'Reward' provided an appropriate background 'Merseybeat' as we ventured into Liverpool.

The match remains one of the best away games I've witnessed. I've still got rare *Match of the Day* highlights of a game which had everything; well everything except a winner and an alien spaceship landing on the pitch midway through the second half. But in addition to Steve McMahon sporting an unlikely full head of hair, this match also had a penalty, a sending-off and a dramatic late equaliser. This came courtesy of a late lob from Paul Power that sent all 18,000 City fans into delirium earning a 2–2 draw and a replay at Maine Road.

When the game ended, my dad didn't hang around. We left the ground hastily trying to get back to the car, parked behind Everton's Gwladys Street End. Perversely, this was possibly the safest place to be as it was the opposite end of the ground from the away supporters. As usual, my old fella was totally oblivious to the carnage going on outside the ground. Meanwhile, Bibby and his mate Paul 'Gilly' Gilsenan went on the train that day. On their way back to Lime Street station Bibby was approached by a gang of Scallies, one of whom asked him the time. My quick-thinking mate promptly pointed to his mouth and made 'urrrrgh, urrrrgh' noises, to which one Scally said, 'Ah, let's leave him alone lads. He's a 'kin mute.'

The following Wednesday, City beat Everton 3–1 in the replay at Maine Road in front of 52,532. I'm sure retribution was taken out on the visiting Scousers within the dark and unforgiving labyrinth of cobbled alleyways which surrounded our old ground. It was a great victory and one my dad and I celebrated in the local boozer, the Park, late into the night (well until 10.30 p.m. actually, as it was early closing in those days with 10 minutes' drinking-up time).

The draw for the semis pitched City with high-flying Ipswich Town, while other semi-finalists Spurs were paired with the Wolves. My own personal build-up to the Ipswich semi-final came the day after we'd beaten Everton. This was the furthest the Blues had ever been in the FA Cup since we last won it in 1969.

The semi-final was held on a boiling hot spring day on 11 April 1981 at Villa Park. I could hardly contain my excitement at the prospect of the Blues making it all the way to the 100th FA Cup final. But this was far from certain as Ipswich were challenging for the league title – by the end of the season they were runners-up to Aston Villa. In my diarised version of events, I described this as, '*The* best day of my life so far.' I went to Birmingham on the train and missed the fun in the traffic jam on the motorway. United were away at Coventry and a minibus load of Reds were on their way to Highfield Road on the M6 when they got marooned between two City coaches as the traffic jammed to a standstill. The two coachloads of City fans got out and started rocking the minibus, almost tipping it over.

The atmosphere inside Villa Park was amazing and I was standing in the Holte End with Football Tony. At the end of 90 minutes there was no score, but in extra time City got a free-kick right on the edge of their box. Just as I shouted out, 'Don't let Power take it,' City's moustachioed captain thankfully took no notice and unleashed a tremendous shot which flew past Paul Cooper and into the Ipswich net. But as all around me went delirious, I just stood there crying like a great big baby. It is the only time I've ever cried inside a football ground, except perhaps with the aid of the tear gas in Italy. But these were the tears of unbridled and delirious joy that only football can bring. City held on to win. By way of more than adequate consolation, Ipswich won the UEFA Cup later that year.

Despite his heroics, I always gave City's captain Paul Power a lot of stick. Perhaps this was because of the hunched-up way in which he ran, or maybe I was influenced by my dad's dislike of the way he played. Whatever it was I always used to shout out, 'I hate you Power', on a regular basis. This was usually when he was within earshot at away games just to make sure that he could hear me. But on reflection, I was out of order. Paul drove City in to the cup final with some sterling performances. He also proved himself to be a winner when he joined Everton near the end of his career and won a championship medal with them, playing a full part in their success. I was extremely impressed with him when he arrived at Maine Road on 29 November 1986 in Everton's ranks. He didn't smile or raise his arms in celebration despite his goal in their 3–1 victory. Instead he showed his class by simply running back to the halfway line with his head bowed, like a proper Blue. City were relegated that year and I didn't resent him. In fact, he now has so much respect in our house that Power has become rhyming slang for shower, which is now abbreviated to, 'I'm just off upstairs for a Paul,' and my wife knows exactly what I mean. It's a good job his surname wasn't Crank.

Almost a month after the Ipswich victory came the centenary FA Cup final. Spurs had seen off Wolves in their semi-final and had also won the battle of pre-cup final publicity, which placed the general public firmly on their side. This was largely through the smash hit Tottenham club song 'Ossie's Dream' which had been released by those musical 'genii' that were Chas & Dave. The song featured the immortal line from Ossie Ardiles, 'In de Cup for Totting-ham.' A year later when the Falklands War began, the diminutive Argentinian had to scurry back to his homeland.

Indeed it was Spurs' Argentine 1978 World Cup-winning duo of Ardiles and Villa that made all the pre-match publicity. This was slightly ironic given that, years later, it came to light that City had first refusal on the pair before they signed for Spurs. But as usual, Peter Swales thought he knew better and City didn't make a move. World Cup winners or not, I always thought that the media were biased towards the Londoners throughout the build-up and on the day. It seemed to me as if City had spoilt the FA's party by gate-crashing the 100th FA Cup final.

I journeyed to Wembley on an official supporters' club coach trip on the day of the match with all the usual suspects, plus Chris 'I waved my flag when Tommy Hutch scored' Hulme from work. Although we were staying overnight in a hotel in Bayswater, our coach cut a Sky Blue swathe straight up Wembley Way in the pouring rain. City took to the pitch to the usual pomp and ceremony and set about winning the cup.

We soon went the right way about it when Tommy Hutchison's diving header gave City the lead, which we held until there were only 10 minutes to go. The rest is history. Glen Hoddle's late free-kick was deflected off Tommy Hutch's shoulder and wrongfooted big Joe Corrigan as it flew into the opposite corner of the net at the end where we were standing. The unfortunate Scotsman had scored both goals in a 1–1 draw and I must have been one of the few people in the ground who knew how he felt. Although my *faux pas* in a high school game wasn't exactly of the magnitude of the 100th FA Cup final, at least Tommy didn't have to go on stage on the Monday to tell his whole school about it. Besides, the own goal would have been academic had Steve MacKenzie converted his late chance from point-blank range at the other end. He hit the post.

Despite City being the stronger side in extra time, we couldn't find a winner. So we all went back to the hotel in Bayswater, knowing we'd have to do it all again the following Thursday.

◆ ◆ ◆

The next night I was on my travels once more, but this time in pursuit of musical entertainment. When I arrived back from Wembley I met up with Terry Hyland, Geoff Garrett and his sister Lynn and we took a train to Leeds to see Japan for the first time. The gig was held at Tiffany's. It was a small venue and standing only which made the experience more intimate and enjoyable, with the iconic David Sylvian on stage, with blonde hair at the front and brown at the back, knocking out a medley of cool and mesmerising songs. We stayed so late at the gig that we missed the last train. Terry, Geoff, Lynn and I spent the night on the platform waiting for the first train back to Manchester at 6.00 a.m. After the excesses of the cup final, it was not what I needed, but still I made it into work that morning. This wasn't due to my conscientious attitude I might add, but because I needed to conserve my leave for the replay and for a few other things I had up my sleeve for later that summer.

◆ ◆ ◆

Despite the replay being on a Thursday night, City took more support to Wembley than we had done on the Saturday. Although I went on a coach from Maine Road, Terry Hyland went in his mate's dad's black cab and they left the meter running just to see how much it would have cost from London to Manchester. I remember being told that it came to over £100 just to get there! These days you'd probably only get as far as Knutsford for that amount.

As for the game, Spurs took an early lead with a scrappy goal from Ricky Villa. MacKenzie equalised with one of the best goals ever scored at the old Wembley. It was a goal which never got the credit it deserved, and it was one I failed to see live – I was too busy watching Spurs fans being attacked with flagpoles (or flagsticks in reality) in the City end at the time.

In the second half, City took the lead with a penalty from Reeves when Paul Miller and Chris Hughton contrived to bring down Dave Bennett in the box. But the lead was not decisive. Garth Crooks equalised and everyone in the world has seen Villa's winner as the BBC screen it at every opportunity they can to this day. Joe Corrigan must have nightmares about that goal. Ray Ranson – now owner of Coventry City – Nicky Reid and Tommy Caton looked like rabbits in the headlights of a chugging van as the bearded Argentine skipped around them all and planted the winner past our hapless 'keeper. It was ironic in a way, because Villa had been substituted in the first game and received a more than generous ovation from the City fans as he dejectedly walked back to the Spurs dressing room. Spurs won the cup and on my way back to the coach I saw a Tottenham fan covered in blood with a hole in the belly region of his yellow Spurs away shirt having had an altercation with City's bunch of baddies, the Kool Kats.

22

Hungary for Success?

I was nineteen when City lost that cup final and my dad put a consoling arm around me saying, 'Never mind son, there'll be other finals in other years to come.' I had no idea how wrong he would be. Since then, success for City has been about as rare as sightings of the lesser spotted cross-eyed Cyclops. Despite the disappointment, however, it was a measure of my voracious appetite for football that City played no less than 57 competitive fixtures that season, and I went to every one of them. But I wasn't finished there, by a long shot.

The England v Scotland match was at Wembley nine days after the cup final, and England lost 1–0 to a John Robertson penalty. We whizzed back home in Graham Moore's trusty Ford Escort and met John Eaton and Phil Knowles. We were off to Manchester Polytechnic to see Bill Nelson's Red Noise, ably supported by A Flock of Seagulls (or A Flock of Haircuts as they were also known). After the gig we tried to get into the John Bull nightclub, but the bouncers stopped me, saying I wasn't old enough. I took out my Wembley ticket stub and told him that if, 'I was old enough to stand among eighty-odd thousand England-hating Jocks all afternoon, I think I'm old enough to get into your nightclub.' To my amazement, the slack-jawed doormen said, 'Fair enough, mate,' and let me in!

A week later I was on my travels again. I'd befriended a like-minded City fan Dominic Cosseron. Dom was the son of a French dental repairman who now lived in Gorton, and we'd planned to follow England across the Continent as they attempted to qualify for the 1982 World Cup. Things had not gone according to plan in the other qualifying matches and England needed to beat either Switzerland or Hungary in their own back yards, if they wanted to progress.

Dom and I had bought tickets on the Orient Express, which would take us through to Hungary. The first stop was supposed to be Basle, but we didn't get that far. We'd loaded up with wine at Calais and boarded the train to Switzerland. There were no vacant seats in second class so, instead, we decided to join several other England fans in the first class compartments. All was well at first, but a ticket inspector took exception to our occupation. He told us that we had to move into the standing room only located in the packed second class carriages. By now the cheap plonk had taken effect, and he got short shrift to that suggestion; 20 minutes later Inspector Clueless returned and, as we hadn't budged, he gave us the ultimatum that, 'If you do not vacate zee seats by Lille, you will be arrested by zee police.' Lille came and went and we thought we'd got away with it. But the train made an unscheduled stop at Charleville-Mézières, where the police were waiting in force on the platform. I nearly lost Dom at this point, which would have been a disaster, not least because he could speak French and I was hoping he could talk us out of the corner we were in. They loaded twenty of us into the French police's version of the Black Maria (*la porc van noir?*) and carted us off for interrogation and charging.

I told Dom to explain that there were no second class seats and that we'd gone into first class as they were the only seats available for what was to be a long overnight journey through to Basle. Dom started pleading our case to the desk *gendarme*. I thought Dom was doing okay as the officer was smiling and nodding his head in a positive manner. That was until I heard amid the conversation, names like St Etienne and Paris St Germain. I quickly pulled Dom to one side and said, 'How's the explanation going, Dom?' He replied, 'We're knackered. We're just talking football.'

As luck would have it, the police didn't have enough room in the cells, so they took our details and kicked us out into the street. It couldn't have been better really, because we found a hospitable bar and a B&B for the night. The next morning we left the hotel oblivious to the fact that I'd left my loaded wallet in the hotel room. Luckily, the French owner found it and successfully chased me down the street to return it. His honesty meant that my trip could continue. I didn't have a credit card or carry traveller's cheques, so I would have been right up '*Rue de la Merde*' minus the requisite propulsion implement. I was suitably grateful.

During the shenanigans the night before, Dom and I had been ordered to report back to the police station at 8.30 a.m., but there was a through train to Basle leaving Charleville-Mézières at 8.00. We boarded that and were not surprised to see the beaming faces of the rest of the England lads! The train got us into Basle by mid-day and it all worked out rather well in the end.

When I returned home I conveyed the whole story to my younger sister Joanne. I warned her to be on the lookout for any SNCF train guards dressed in navy uniforms with round peaked caps that might knock on looking for me. She wouldn't answer our front door for six months! In fact, it turned out that my giving a false address to the French police of 1 Mickey Mouse Walk, Liverpool, was the right move as, a few weeks later, Dom got a bill from French Railways for £25, which he paid.

The England v Switzerland game wasn't one to write home about – mainly because I couldn't be bothered with postcards, but also because we lost 2–1. It was shameful both on and off the pitch. Before the match Dom and I had mixed-in with the Swiss locals who had an impressive knowledge of English football and most of whom had heard of Manchester City, which I always found endearing. They were dressed from head-to-toe in red and white, and were waving flags and clanking cowbells, but this didn't stop England's thugs laying into them both outside and inside the ground. It was sickening to watch. There was little Dom and I could do to stop it. We watched helplessly as those friendly-looking Swiss people received a kicking just for having the audacity to support their own country at home.

The English tabloids were full of pictures of the trouble the next day, one of which included a snap of a man being stabbed on the terraces not far from where I had stood. I'm not sure whether the victim was Swiss or English. Much of the aggression was not just aimed at the Swiss, but it was also in-house between Chelsea, West Ham and Millwall. We'd brought our social disease over to the Continent and it was the first time in my life that I was ashamed to be English.

After a night of wailing police sirens in the background, Dom and I embarked on the next leg of our journey to Hungary, stopping off en route for a quick look around Zurich. Then it was back on the train to Munich. The journey was long and the weather was boiling, so by the time we'd found our hotel we were ready for a drink, which wasn't a problem in Bavaria. Somehow we stumbled into what we were told was the biggest beer keller in the world and had been the venue for many of Hitler's speeches. The beer was strong and my legs were weak. On the way back to the hotel, Dom jumped on me for a piggy-back without warning and we crashed to the floor, my face taking the brunt of the impact. We had one more day and night in Munich, with me nursing severe cuts and grazes on my hands and face. We then moved on to Vienna on a train that would have made British Rail look rapid.

After a couple of days in Austria's historic capital, the only thing of culture we managed to locate (in a city full to the brim with it), was a statue of some long-haired bloke in eighteenth-century clothing. We both presumed it was an old, but successful, manager of the local team Rapid Vienna. It turned out to be Mozart. In reality, we weren't such heathens, but to our shame didn't exactly go out of our way to immerse ourselves in the vast array of history.

On Thursday 4 June, we set off from Wien's Westbahnhof station to meet their Hungarian communist neighbours. Dom and I were lucky to be allowed into Russian-occupied Hungary. When we reached the Austro-Hungarian frontier, the train stopped and the Communist border guards inspected our documentation. The first thing my stern-looking inquisitor noticed was the severe gravel marks on my face and hands. Not surprisingly, he wanted to know how I'd acquired them. The first thing he said was 'how?' Although I wanted to hold up my right hand and reply with a similar Red Indian greeting, I thought better of it. Instead I made the universal sign of beer and went cross-eyed as I moved my head from side to side and pointed at the floor. He gave me a knowing look, nodded his head and walked off apparently satisfied.

On arrival at Budapest, we were instructed to visit the nearest police station to get our visas stamped. By this time I only had around sixty quid left and Dom didn't have much more. We were worried that our money wasn't going to last, particularly as we had to pay for two nights' food and accommodation and we didn't have any match tickets. We'd been warned not to change any money with anyone but the banks, but a Leeds fan chose to ignore this sound advice. Instead, he swapped some of his cash with a local 'Arthur Daley' type who was lurking behind the back of the 'cop shop'. This cash turned out to be a pile of newspaper sandwiched between two Hungarian *forint* notes! Leeds were second behind United in my list of detestables and I couldn't help but laugh at his stupidity. He'd swapped £100 for about £4-worth of *forints*.

Dom and I were more careful, but to my dismay, we were charged a fiver each for the privilege of a stamp on our visa and we were also given an address at 24 Endrodi Sandor. As we stood staring at a bit of paper with puzzled expressions, one of the Chelsea lads advised us, 'That's where your digs are, mate.' The fiver we'd paid was for two nights at this address. Off we went on the chain bridge across the River Danube and over to the posher Buda side of the city. We were delighted to find that we had been allocated a plush villa overlooking the side of a stunningly picturesque tree-covered mountainside. We lodged with a little old lady and her attractive young granddaughter.

That evening we met up with the Chelsea lads to sample the local brew. Most of them were complaining at having been put into total dives over on the Pest side of the city. Some had even got out and booked hotels at further expense but Dom and I had really landed on our feet and stayed in the lap of luxury for a pittance. We soon realised that our money was going to last and later that evening we went to a top city hotel restaurant and ordered the local goulash for starters (which surprisingly turned out to be a soup rather than the homogenised stew to which we were accustomed). This was followed by a couple of big fat juicy steaks, and the bill came to only £3 each.

Later in the evening, we were sitting outside a bar with the Chelsea lads, when television presenter Jim Rosenthal strolled past. Having been informed that none of us had tickets for the game, he smugly commented that we had, 'no chance of getting in, as over 800,000 Hungarians have applied for tickets. It's the biggest thing in their recent football history' (even bigger than Puskas' belly as it turned out). However, the Cockney lads had a plan and told us to meet them at the Intercontinental Hotel the next morning.

It soon became clear why. The England players were staying at the hotel, but more to the point, the match tickets were being despatched to the foresighted supporters who'd acquired them through official means. There were a couple of officious-looking English blokes sat at a desk in the hotel foyer, with a large register in front of them. One of the Chelsea lads took a bit of a survey from behind the back of the desk and sashayed out again, saying to one of his mates, 'Robinson, eight.' Off went his mate who nonchalantly mooched over to the official at the desk and said, 'Robinson. Eight tickets, mate.' These were handed over as he ticked poor old Robinson off the list.

It just so happened that there were six Chelsea and two City fans and we were all happy as we made our way to the Budapest funfair for the morning's entertainment with 'our' match tickets safely in our pockets. Over at the funfair, it was time for a North v South challenge. In the middle of the park was a huge rickety old wooden rollercoaster which had claimed the lives of a couple of unfortunate riders a few weeks earlier. This had led to the temporary closure (or so we were told by a smiling, shifty-looking local who was rubbing his hands at the prospect of further disaster). The complex game we invented was to each down four pints in quick succession then get straight onto the rollercoaster and the first team member to throw-up was the loser and had to buy the beers. By the third straight ride, Dom was whiter than his tee-shirt, but was determined not to yield. Luckily as the car pulled into the finish, one of the Chelsea lads chucked up and, against all the odds, City had recorded a victory against Chelsea on foreign soil. The daft thing was, the whole round of eight pints only cost around 75 pence, but it was worth it for the pride of winning such a prestigious competition.

The following day we managed to tap City goalkeeper Joe Corrigan for two more tickets and we gave them to a couple of grateful England fans. Dom and I made our way to the home of the 'Mighty Magyars' (the Nep Stadium) in good time. But even outside the ground I could sense that the atmosphere was tense: an ominous portent of impending danger if ever there was one. This became apparent when one of the local thugs tapped Dom on the shoulder and asked him if he wanted some of this? He pointed down to the heaviest and most sinister-looking brass knuckle-duster I'd ever seen. Dom declined his generous offer of a certain broken skull.

England had to win this game to retain any hope of qualifying for the 1982 World Cup finals. However, before the match got underway, the ageing Ferenc Puskás played in an exhibition match to the delight of the packed 70,000 crowd. Even though the great man was on the large size, he was still revered like a footballing god (the Nep Stadium was eventually renamed in his honour). After the fun came the serious stuff. There were only about 300 England fans in the Nep, with the vast majority of the trouble-causers from Switzerland having long since departed. The stadium was a huge, single-tiered, open bowl except for a roof which partially covered the stand from which the players emerged. Many of the locals had banners exclaiming previous famous 6–3 and 7–1 victories of the 1950s and one end was largely full of uniformed Russian soldiers who added to the intimidating mood. However, we were to have the last laugh as England won 3–1, thanks to a brace from Trevor Brooking – one of which lodged in the stanchion of the goal after it had rifled past the Hungarian goalkeeper's ear. Kevin Keegan scored the other from the penalty spot and later described this as, 'the one [England game] I most enjoyed.'

After the match, the locals were slow to leave and clearly wanted to take out a spot of retribution. The irony wasn't lost on me that this was arguably at the peak of the Cold War and the English football supporters were relying on Brezhnev's Boys – the Russian soldiers – to give us safe passage from the stadium. Behind the stand was like being in a bear pit as the locals tried to have a go. But the good old 'Ruskis' surrounded us, with their rifles at the ready.

Once it had all settled down, Dom and I left the vicinity of the stadium for the city centre, draped in our flags. Suddenly we heard the sound of a dark and eerie siren. It was similar to those advertising imminent air raids over English industrial cities during the Second World War. We soon learnt that it was giving notice to the locals to evacuate the streets. As all Hungarians around us hastily departed, Dom and I stood our ground. Within minutes we could hear the deep droning of what turned out to be Russian tank engines. It was an impressive and compelling show of force from the Russian occupants in the form of a column of heavy artillery. The parade trundled through Budapest's main thoroughfare and seemed to last for hours, but was in reality a matter of minutes. As the tanks rumbled past, I exchanged incredulous glances with a Russian tank commander of about my age who was peering from his turret at little old me draped in a Union Flag. His life and mine were literally worlds apart and it was a brief encounter I'll never forget. Given their previous efforts to protect us, I was almost tempted to salute him, but thought better of it, remembering the old adage, 'Never mimic a Russian soldier while he's sitting on top of a great big 26-ton killing machine.'

As midnight approached, most of the England fans met up at the Royal Hotel and we celebrated late into the night. Before we left Budapest (one of the most beautiful cities I've ever visited), we tipped our hosts at the villa a fiver each, which made the old lady's eyes well up in happiness – it was such a vast amount of money to her. Dom and I then caught the train back home following three days and two nights in Hungary having only spent the equivalent of £35 each in total. What a place and what a trip.

♦　　♦　　♦

We left Hungary on the Sunday morning and arrived back in Manchester late on the Monday evening after our twelve-day excursion. The next day my BEC General exams commenced. There's nothing like a bit of preparation to ensure success, and I had had nothing like a bit of preparation. I sat the first exam almost cold, with about an hour's revision stored in the memory bank. Over the years people have told me of their recurring nightmares that they come to exams completely unprepared, having skipped many of the lectures. They wake up in a cold sweat thinking they have surely failed. That year I actually lived the dream.

I waffled my way through the various written examinations over the next three days. The results came out a few weeks later and I got a phone call from the staff officer, Alan Jones, to go to his office. My heart wasn't literally in my mouth as I trudged up the stairs like a man on his way to the gallows, but in builder's parlance, I was ab-so-lute-ly bricking it. I already knew they'd received a poor report from the college about my year's performance. But, to my amazement, I was told I'd passed the exams and could have my incremental pay award and move on to the BEC National Certificate if I so wished. I could just about accept that I'd scraped through most of the subjects by the skin of my teeth. I could not believe I'd managed to pass bookkeeping.

On congratulating me on my unlikely achievement, Mr Jones said, 'You're a bit of a dark horse, aren't you Steven? That must have taken some bottle for a young lad like you to learn typing!' I looked down at the result sheet and there it was, 'Typing – Pass!' I hadn't even done typing and there was no mention of bookkeeping on the sheet. I just said, 'You've gotta do what it takes to get nearer to the girlies, Mr Jones,' having quickly remembered the domestic science benefits of my schooldays. I smiled and walked out of his office totally puzzled. Typing had been the alternative choice to bookkeeping, but neither I nor any of the other lads on the course had even taken it. At first I presumed that some poor lass had probably passed typing but ended up failing bookkeeping. I made a few phone calls to a couple of female students I'd become acquainted with. But it turned out that nobody had failed. I kept my head down and my mouth shut and moved on to BEC National at St John's College in the city centre a few months later.

The summer was still not over and there were a couple more foreign trips to be had, courtesy of the Criminal Injuries compensation. City's pre-season included a trip to Glasgow where I saw City lose 2–0 to Rangers at an enthusiastic Ibrox, and I managed to re-acquaint myself with the Hearts lads and watch them lose to Sunderland at Tynecastle. A few days later City were scheduled to play in Germany and Holland, and I went with the Piccadilly Supporters' Club Branch. It was a much-needed holiday after the draining mental exertions I'd used in my exams!

The first game was in northern Germany where City took on Werder Bremen, as part of the transfer deal that took Dave Watson to foreign soil. City had played them at Maine Road in the previous close season and won 4–0, and Watson had since moved back to England to play for Southampton. All the easier to beat them was the theory, but how wrong can you be? This proved to be *the* biggest defeat I've seen City suffer . . . 8–0! Although we were 3–0 down at half time, nobody expected the Germans to score another five in the second half. At the end of the game, Paul Power led the team over and apologised to the fans for the performance.

On the following Saturday City took on PSV Eindhoven in Holland and got a far more respectable 1–1 draw, courtesy of Dennis Tueart's strike. We were based in Amsterdam and, after the match, a couple of fans told us that they'd heard City would be playing at AC Milan in two weeks' time. In our 'tired and emotional' state, it seemed like a good idea to organise another wee excursion. I didn't feel at all well that night and noticed a sinister looking cluster of spots ingrained in my tummy region, but thought no more of it.

Dom, John Eaton and I planned for the trip and the three of us plus Howard Jones, Gary Griffiths and a couple of others set off for Italia on Saturday 22 August 1981. The journey over was memorable, with Dom encouraging us to drink Black Russians on the ferry, resulting in Eaton almost going for an unscheduled swim in the Channel and me falling off a train platform and landing on one of the live tracks at the Gare du Nord in Paris a few hours later. Thankfully, no train was approaching as I was unceremoniously hauled back onto the platform by my drunken buddies.

In Milan, we found a suitable flea-ridden hotel, where I secured us a three-night tenure using the advanced Italian I had leaned there in 1980, which consisted of two words, *'Quanta costa?'* Like true ambassadors of England, the first job was to dump our bags and find a suitable watering hole. By now well-oiled and armed with a bottle of wine in each hand, we strolled into the local municipal park for a quiet afternoon's relaxation. This consisted of diving into the large concrete fountain and blasting little Italian children's radio-controlled boats out of the pond with the fountain's jet of water. It was wildly amusing to us, but not too popular with the locals. On hearing police sirens, we made a hasty exit and walked briskly back to the hotel, where we discovered that the room Dom, Eaton and I were sharing had been flooded as one of us had left the tap on with the plug still in!

During the ensuing drunken, but friendly, argument and recriminations, a 'butty fight' broke out, with large amounts of sweaty ham sandwiches, cheese barms, pork pies and cakes (left over from the journey) flying out of the window and into the street below. The rank of dormant Fiat taxis parked directly underneath our window started to move as the food continued to rain down.

The commotion had caused a small crowd to gather on the street. However, they weren't 100 per cent sure from which open window the missiles had been launched once things had gone quiet and we'd run out of ammo. That was until Dom popped his head up at the wrong moment and the crowd all pointed upwards at our window while shouting 'Arrrrrrgh!' in Italian. Within minutes the hotel manager was banging on our door, and we reluctantly let him in to find a flooded room and a plethora of dead sandwiches stuck to the ceiling.

He 'politely' asked us to 'Clear up ada mess and vacate-a da room by da morning or I'lla cutta offa alla ya cocksa.' The next day I woke up with a wicked hangover. To make things worse, I was wracked with guilt and remorse, particularly at my role in the model boat-blasting sketch in the park. There was no solace as we slowly put together the full story of what had happened. Like true diplomats, we went down to the reception desk and apologised to the hotel manager. Much to our surprise, he said we could stay if we promised not to, 'Flooda da rooma no-a-more-a and not throwa no-a-more-a fooda froma da window.'

This was Monday, the day before the game which we still weren't totally sure was taking place and so we decided to take a trip down to the San Siro stadium to check things out. At the ground, we were unable to purchase tickets and so we looked for an opportunity to gain entry to the stadium. At the main gate we were greeted by a military looking security guard who said it was not possible to go inside. No problem. We simply produced our MCFC Travel Club cards and told him that we were the players, there to inspect the pitch for tomorrow's game. He accepted the explanation with no qualms at all, which was surprising given that we were each in possession of a partly-consumed bottle of wine. You can perhaps picture the amusing sight of six half-cut Mancunians strolling around AC Milan's hallowed turf and inspecting the pitch in true FA Cup final day style.

The next evening we made our way to the stadium for the match. We waited expectantly outside the players' entrance and the team looked pleased to see us. I tapped Nicky Reid for tickets by using the Old Chorltonian card, and physiotherapist Roy Bailey also emerged with 'freebies'. We took up our positions in the most expensive seats in the ground. The match was attended by 25,000 supporters and it just so happened to be Joe Jordan's first game in Milan's colours following his recent transfer from Manchester United. He looked up with a bemused expression as the teams were paraded onto the pitch while the eight (our six plus two more) City fans present sang in unison, 'Jordan is a . . . [rhymes with banker]!'

The game itself was entertaining and was notable for a fine performance from my favourite City player, Dennis Tueart, who was described by a Milan fan sitting next to me as '*magnifico*'. Needless to say, City lost 1–0.

On the way back home both Dom and Eaton had contracted chicken pox and suffered badly. Not only was it the icing on the cake, it gave me the answer to the mystery cluster of spots I'd noticed back in Amsterdam a few weeks earlier. Apparently, I was the carrier of the disease!

23

Cricket!

I was introduced to the great summer game in the early 1970s. My dad was mostly an armchair fan, but occasionally took me to Old Trafford to watch Lancashire CCC. The team consisted of great stars of the day such as Clive Lloyd, Barry Wood, David Hughes, Frank Hayes, David 'Bumble' Lloyd, Peter Lever, Peter Lee, Ken Shuttleworth, Jack Simmons and Harry Pilling.

The Red Rose line-up also included Farokh Engineer. He was a big, powerful wicketkeeper who once accidentally stood on my foot on his way off the pitch as I sought his autograph. The spikes on his boot went through my left plimsoll into the fleshy bit between my big toe and the next one along. I returned to my dad in floods of tears. He must have thought it was because I hadn't managed to get the famous Indian wicketkeeper's signature saying, 'Never mind son, you'll get him next time.' But I never went near him again just in case! The incident left a big hole in my pumps until my feet burst out of them several months later after a sudden growth spurt.

As I got older my dad allowed me to OT with my school mates. We spent many a summer's afternoon watching that great Lancs side during the six-week school holidays. We would sit just behind the boundary rope admiring the gladiatorial batsmen as they went about their business; innocent days for an innocent boy.

By the time I went to my first Lord's final in 1984, I was twenty-two and no longer wet behind the ears – having finally managed to successfully master the difficult technique of drying the back of my head with a towel. Lancs had made it to the Benson & Hedges showpiece having beaten Nottinghamshire in the semi-final at Trent Bridge. That day out sticks in the memory because our car was pulled over just off the A610 by the police checking for 'Flying Pickets' at the height of the miners strike.

The final was a great experience. Bibby, Jerry Sweeney and I went to Lord's. Jerry was a good mate from the Town Hall who supported United, which was a rare thing on two counts. I don't have many mates who are United fans and, secondly, they normally don't like cricket as they find the rules just that bit too difficult to understand. We set off on the Friday night, boarding the last train from Piccadilly station each armed with a couple of flagons of cider and a pocket full of money. By the time we reached Euston station, I had neither cider nor a pocket full of money; I'd lost the lot playing three-card brag with a bunch of Burnley fans. So much so that I'd already secured a loan from the ever dependable 'Bank of Bibby' to keep me in the game. As we drew into the station, beads of sweat gathered on my brow as my eyes fixed on the pot that might return all my money with interest. A final tentative turnover saw me literally come up trumps, and I left the table with a relieved smile.

We queued amid the haze of a hot summer's morning. I was hit by the unique aura and sanctity of the place. Lord's had the atmosphere of a cathedral, and we paid due reverence by standing at the altar of the Lord's Tavern, praying for victory while getting suitably and contentedly inebriated. The game was against Warwickshire. Their supporters provided great entertainment arguing among themselves with Aston Villa supporters on one side and Birmingham City on the other.

Our arduous journey down had taken its toll on the three of us and by the time Warwickshire were bowled out for 139 in 50.4 overs, Bibby, Jerry and I were asleep. Eventually the crowd noise woke me with Lancashire needing only 15 runs to win with overs and wickets in hand. It was the first time I'd seen a team I supported actually win something. The laughs we had that day ensured that given the opportunity, I would be back for more.

I didn't have to wait long. A couple of years later, Lancs made it to Lord's again, this time facing Sussex in the Nat West Trophy final. This was the game where Bibby made a name for himself on the London comedy circuit when the good-natured spirit of banter was lost on him as Lancashire were losing. An obnoxious supporter of Sussex, located about six or seven rows down from us in the old Nursery Stand, was really getting on everybody's nerves with his Lancashire-baiting. After a few hours, Bibby had taken enough. Without warning, he coolly and calmly arose from his throne, serenely walked down six or seven rows, politely eased his way along the row of spectators sat alongside the Sussex fan, and promptly, and unceremoniously, poured a full pint of beer on his head. Bibby received a standing ovation from the hundreds of surrounding Lancastrians on his triumphant but nonchalant walk back to his seat. It was indeed a great moment. Lancs lost the game, but Bibby's behaviour provided some small consolation.

♦ ♦ ♦

Cricket has given me many other great moments over the years. There's nothing better than watching a game with the sun beating down on your neck and your cooler box nestled lovingly against your knee, containing as much alcohol as you can reasonably consume during play. This usually lasts around six hours a day, with the addition of lunch, tea and drinks breaks. Cricket affords the opportunity to get steadily but properly and utterly bladdered while enjoying the spectacle of two teams trying to outplay and outwit each other. And there you have it in a nutshell. Cricket: a civilised game, played by gentlemen, followed by complete 'piss-artists' (with the notable exception of the noble gentry and the temperant sober).

Since the heady, rowdy, but good-natured days of the 1980s and '90s, the cricket authorities have become a bit stuffy about fans bringing their own beers into the ground and we had to get cuter. As restrictions took a firm grip, burly bouncers and stewards began the weary practice of searching all bags and boxes for illicit hooch as you emerged from the turnstiles. The hypocritical aspect on the part of the cricketing authorities was that you were still allowed to buy as much beer as you wanted once in the ground. But as the queues and the prices were enormous, the best option was to sneak your own ale in.

Consequently, my mates' collective ingenuity was put to the test and we put into practice all sorts of methods. One idea – born from Bibby's interpretation of *Escape from Colditz* – was to hollow out large French sticks and put cans into the resulting shell. This, however, was too bulky.

An alternative was to fill up empty sparkling water bottles with gin & tonic or orange squash bottles with vodka & orange. One particular Friday afternoon at the Old Trafford test against the Aussies sticks in the memory. Just after the highly publicised ban on bringing in your own alcohol had been announced, everybody must have had the same idea. Normally, the rowdy behaviour started at about 4.00 p.m. once the effects of the beer kicked in. But on this day it was about 1.00 p.m. when the raucous antics commenced. None of the stewards present could understand why there were so many drunken people staggering around at lunchtime with a drinks ban in force. That was until everyone started merrily singing, 'We're all having a party; vodka, whisky and Bacardi!' These days, the stewards can even check your 'soft drink' bottles to see if the seal has been broken in order to foil smugglers.

Other schemes included injecting vodka into fruit and we even had the idea of putting alcohol in the shells of ice-packs used for keeping your cooler box cold. That was until we discovered that the ice-packs contained toxic substances and could have caused even graver effects than the alcohol itself. A few years ago I stumbled on a failsafe way of getting beer undetected into a cricket ground. You take two cans and place a thick slice of bread on top. Then wrap the package in tin foil. With the outline of the bread on view, it looks like a pack of sandwiches! Make six of these for the day and this will keep you going, until tea at least. Then you can always get in the queue at the bar for the official beer if you're still capable.

Food is just as important for a good day at the cricket. There are many great sights, and one is certainly of suave gentlemen resplendent in white linen suits, cravats and cream Panama hats. They carry extravagant basket hampers, complete with sets of best china crockery, sterling silver cutlery while crammed to bursting with salmon, strawberries and champagne (before the ban spoilt it for us all). Then there are the less sophisticated chaps who buy pie and chips from the pavilion or who'd slum it from the greasy refreshment points. My cooler box usually contains enough sandwiches to feed an army, although my favourite food story at the cricket does not include bread. It came at an England v India one day match at Old Trafford in the mid-1990s. Bibby and I found ourselves located among a large group of Indians. Once the eating began (which is usually even before a ball has been bowled) out came our bland-looking sandwiches, much to the horror of the engulfing guests.

'You don't want to be eating that crap,' said my Asian neighbour. 'You should get your teeth into this lot.' He and his friends then proceeded to ply Bibby and I with all number of Indian savoury and sweet delights. Our 'butties' were later consigned to the bin for the birds to enjoy once we had gone. There is camaraderie in cricket among supporters that is seldom seen in football.

In fact, cricket supporters can be a different class, but they can also be extremely partisan, hostile and vocal, but never really threatening. Particular fanatics are the Pakistanis and worse still the Aussies, especially back home in their barren upside-down world. Not unsurprisingly it was the Australians who invented the term 'sledging'. To Scandinavians, this probably means sliding down a snow covered hill on a wooden tray with a rifle on their back while in pursuit of some poor unsuspecting cuddly animal. But in cricketing parlance 'sledging' means giving verbal abuse to the opposition in order to distract and disrupt their performance. Both players and supporters are practitioners of the art of sledging and not many are better at it than Bibby. He once 'slaughtered' Surrey's affable former England captain Alec Stewart who was within earshot at a Lancashire away game at the Oval having returned from a miserable tour of the Caribbean. Bibby hit him with a tirade of one-liners which included, 'I'll bet you didn't get that sun tan out in the middle at the West Indies!' and, 'You were only there 'cos your dad picked you!' A couple of weeks later, in the return fixture at Old Trafford, poor old Alec was on the boundary within range of Bibby's acerbic tongue once more. As he came over Bibby shouted, 'Hey Alec, it's me again,' to which Mr Stewart turned round, smiled and put both hands over his ears!

Another fine exponent of sledging was Gilly. On a corporate visit to OT for an Ashes match, Gilly was introduced to the touring Australian team. He proceeded to hold court with a number of the Aussies. After a while, they were joined by the team manager, former test batsman Bobby Simpson. Before he could enter the conversation, Gilly asked, 'Are you the coach driver mate? Go and load those bags on the bus, there's a good lad.' The Aussie players fell about laughing as Gilly sat there dead-pan knowing exactly who Mr Simpson was!

You might think that all this banter could lead to trouble, but cricket violence is virtually unheard of, although Bibby almost started a new phenomenon in the late 1990s. He spent the day slagging-off two Yorkshiremen during a key cup semi-final at Old Trafford. Both these rather large lads also turned out to be out-of-town Manchester United supporters (what a dreadful combination, Yorkshire *and* United). Unfortunately I was sober, as I had an important job interview the next day. I was only too aware of how close Bibby came to starting a huge brawl, as other people slowly but surely began to join in the 'mass debate'. I suppose that an impromptu 'War of the Roses' battle would have been unique, but I was ultimately glad that it didn't progress that far.

♦   ♦   ♦

In my limited cricket-watching career, I've been lucky enough to have had the pleasure of watching many of the world's great batsmen. At their peak, the top batsmen can be as graceful as prima ballerinas and can produce a performance of cathartic effect. I've enjoyed a range of players from the raw batting power of Viv Richards and Ian Botham, to the grace and splendour of David Gower, Brian Lara and Sachin Tendulkar. I've also been privileged to see many of the modern game's best bowlers, ranging from the devastating pace bowling of the late great Malcolm Marshall, Michael Holding, Wasim Akram and Glenn McGrath, to the subtle spin bowling of Shane Warne, Muttiah Muralitharan and Terry Hyland. All these players are household names in the world of cricket, except for Terry, who was a decent spin bowler in our Lee Athletic cricket team and at Button Lane Juniors! Speaking of which, when I was a nipper, Button Lane had a school cricket team, but much the same as footballing XI it was a bit 'cliquey' getting into the side. Despite the fact that I once hit 23 in an internal practice match – the highest score of the session – I still failed to get picked. However, a few days later I travelled the short journey up Moorcroft Road to Rackhouse Juniors as part of the Button Lane squad in the first game of the 1971/72 school cricket season. I sat behind the boundary watching my team make the daunting and somewhat ironical total of 23 all out. As it only took the home side a mere 15 minutes to knock off the runs required, the two teachers in charge decided to hold another game. This time I was given a chance and came in at number 3. I managed to top score 19 out of a total of 43, but still wasn't picked for the side again.

Perhaps my future omission was due to my woefully poor fielding. I got underneath a skyer in that game and lost it in the sun as it bounced straight off my forehead leaving a nasty gash. It might also have been because we were hammered again, but after those debacles, the games teacher was reluctant to agree to any more friendlies.

It wasn't until my twenties when I resumed my belated batting career. I began playing for the Town Clerk's team at Manchester Town Hall and also turned out for Lee Athletic. My skills would surely come in handy when the Town Clerk's team made it all the way to the Manchester City Council Inter-departmental Cup final – 'The Town Clerk's Cup'. The match was played against 'Social Services' on a gloriously hot and sunny summer's evening. We made 153 for 3 in our twenty overs and as I was in at number 6, I didn't get a bat. I didn't bowl either nor keep wicket as I had done in previous matches. I spent the whole of the contest stood out on the boundary with my hands in my tracky bottoms playing pocket billiards.

When we were in the pub after the game, everyone was congratulating each other on 'our' great victory, until the captain soon realised that I was looking a bit fed up.

'What's up Worthy lad?' he asked with a smile.

'It was alright for you lot, but I didn't get a bat, I didn't get a bowl and I never once touched the ball in the field. I might as well have been the light meter, the amount of use I was in this game.' Needless to say, I didn't get the 'Man of the Match' award, but I did receive a nice oversized gold plastic statue of a cricketer to place on top of the telly.

The following week, the town clerk invited his victorious team into his office. This room was so spacious, you could have held a first-class game of cricket. He handed out to each of us a celebratory glass of port and commenced the usual polite chit-chat on such occasions. It was like having an audience with the king such was our reverence for Manchester's wily old chief executive. As he went around the team each in turn asking for a brief line on the match, he finally came to me, the youngest in the room.

'What was your contribution young Steven?' he asked. While it was tempting to reply, 'Er, nothing really, I spent the whole match with my hands down my pants playing with my bollocks,' I managed instead to come up with some diplomatic baloney statement about providing batting support should it have been needed.

We won the Town Clerk's Cup a couple more times before I left Manchester in 1989 for Cheshire County Council, and after that my playing days were restricted to opening the batting for Lee Athletic.

24

Marathon Man gets the World Cup Willies

After the Moss Side riots had taken their course and my bus had been re-routed back past the now-demolished Alexandra pub (AKA the Big Alex), the 1981/82 football season brought a first day home 2–1 victory against West Brom. Despite the FA Cup final defeat, it appeared that City were on the up and were now fit for purpose.

My own personal fitness was also on the up, as the barmaids at the Labour Club had persuaded me to enter the Manchester Charities' Marathon at the last minute. In fact it was only three weeks away and I was forced to embark on a crash course in jogging. I soon managed to master the complex technicalities of putting one foot in front of the other in a running motion by legging it back and forth to work, from Northern Moor to the Town Hall: a round trip of about 14 miles. At first I ran in my iconic but flat-soled Adidas Samba trainers, and then wondered why I had a sore back. But I soon bought a pair of Hi-Tec running shoes which had a spongy sole to absorb the shock and relieve my pain. I ended up completing the 26-mile 385-yard slog with Darren Hendley's mates, Mark Jives and Geoff Holte, at a sedate pace in 4 hours, 20 minutes.

After that I caught the jogging bug and started training properly. My running partner was a lean fella called Terry Davies from the Labour Club, who was arguably in his peak for the sport at the age of twenty-eight. We were running between 40 and 50 miles a week at decent pace, and had the amateur's target of 2:59 in mind for the next Manchester Marathon. Long-distance running was right up my street, and indeed most of the streets of South Manchester! I found a measure of inner peace as I jogged around the district collating and settling all sorts of personal issues in my mind, such as why did the women I'd tried chatting up in the pub always disappear to the ladies in pairs, only to emerge 5 minutes later in fits of laughter?

I was now focusing on my running and, although I hadn't quite sacrificed the demon brew, I had cut down and I was watching my diet, even restricting my pie-on-barm intake to just six a week. After a few months, the training was progressing well and my speed and stamina indicated that I was more than capable of beating my previous laboured time by some considerable distance. By way of testing our fitness levels, Terry entered the Stockport 'Daffodil' Marathon which was held in April 1982. I didn't fancy it as two marathons within a few months seemed a bit excessive for my slender frame. But shortly before the race my running partner was forced to pull out with an injury, so I ran in his name.

As my training routes in Manchester were mostly on the flatter ground I hadn't done any hill running. To my horror, the course was up and down like the dodgy Hungarian rollercoaster. This took an unexpected toll on my legs, particularly going downhill. I managed to complete the course in 3:29, which I thought wasn't too bad given that I'd started at the back and had paced myself poorly. By the time the flatter Manchester Marathon came around, both Terry and I would have a 2:59 time in the bag, or so I thought.

A week later I went on my first training run from the Town Hall to home, a gentle 7-miler that would ease me back in. Stupidly, I failed to warm up and stretch properly before I set off. I had got within a few yards of Central Library when there was a sharp cracking sound in my right knee. Within hours, my leg was in a plaster-cast and my jogging career was out of the window. Almost a year later an exploratory operation revealed a partially torn ligament. The NHS weren't prepared to operate further on this as it wasn't life-threatening and they didn't have the resources, and so that was that. At the tender age of twenty-one, I was forced to retire from marathon running.

♦   ♦   ♦

During this time, John Bond remained manager at Maine Road, and pulled a master-stroke when he made his most expensive purchase. The value of a truly gifted player cannot be underestimated. Millions of pounds have been spent by top clubs searching for a genius in football boots. In 1981 we acquired the services of a real-live genius in Trevor Francis. During his one incomplete season, Francis was *the* team as he ran the show virtually on his own. The man was a superstar, so much so that he had his own advert on Piccadilly Radio, where he would say, 'Hi, my name's Trevor Francis. City are at home this week, so why not come down to Maine Road and support the Blues?' He should have said, 'Why not come down to Maine Road and watch me take on the opposition on my own in *The Trevor Francis Show?*' Unfortunately Trevor was plagued by injuries that restricted his total number of games to just 29. I savoured all of them.

Our star player didn't play against United that season and the failure of his colleagues to maintain results during his numerous absences meant that the presence of the million-pound-man could not be sustained. However, during one of his absences, City did manage an away win against a struggling Liverpool. It was the first of only two City victories we've had at Anfield since I was born, and I'm happy to have seen them both. Despite Liverpool's poor form they went on to take the title after winning virtually every game for the rest of the season. John Eaton and I had done our 'get-in-for-junior-price-in-the-home-end' sketch, which happened to be the Kop – the revered home end of the Liverpool fans. But it proved to be a bad move when Asa Hartford 'scored' a disallowed goal. I jumped up and a Scouser punched me in the face. Without thinking, I hit him back with a cracking upper cut and expected to get hit from all angles by the surrounding Liverpool supporters. But only one person reacted and he simply said, 'Well done dere mate, 'ee deserved dah!' It was an amazing let-off and, just as I was standing there thinking the Kop is such a fair-minded football-loving place, an half-empty bottle of whisky came flying out of nowhere and hit Joe Corrigan on the head.

Although we won that day, the Blues paid the price for Tricky Trev's many injuries. Potentially, Francis could have turned the club around single-handedly. But the money he was being paid put a strain on the coffers and City's financial plight went deeper and deeper into the red. Trevor was sold after the 1982 World Cup and gates plummeted, as did City's fortunes.

◆   ◆   ◆

The World Cup was held in Spain. Phil Knowles, John Eaton, Andy Mills, Dom Cosseron and I planned to stay as long as England remained in the tournament. Graham Moore went on an official trip instead. We knew Graham's travel details including the camp site on which he would be staying so we arrived at Igueldo Camp Site on a hill that overlooked the Basque town of San Sebastian on Saturday 12 June, looking for a suitable spot upon which to pitch our wigwams. The tents provided for patrons of the official trip were already erected on the bottom field and we selected a spot on the higher ground. Once we were pegged-out we all took the two-hour bus journey to Bilbao in search of tournament tickets. One of the reasons for Graham paying £220 for his two-week trip was that it ensured match tickets. However, our train and camp site fees were half that, and we had a surplus of cash should the touts prove expensive. But they didn't. There were plenty of official tickets available, as the tournament was nowhere near sold out. Back then, mass international football travel was still in its comparative infancy and we paid £30 for all three England group games.

A day later, refreshed and feeling rather chuffed with ourselves, we were all on San Sebastian's golden sand displaying our samba skills during a game of beach football. But the peace and tranquillity was soon erased by a convoy of dirty and rusty, old and knackered charabancs snaking towards us. On one of the coaches we noticed an exhausted-looking Graham Moore sitting at the back, looking like he'd aged ten years. As we all stood there laughing and pointing at his pale and furrowed brow, he could barely raise a 'Harvey Smith' as his coach crawled past us shrouded in poisonous blue smoke.

Once the new arrivals had settled in, the first thing we noticed was the sharp rise in the price of the camp site sangria. We soon found out that the official organisers had different packages for their customers. These included various combinations of breakfast, lunch and evening meals, which had all been paid for, but not by us. It wasn't long before we were eating for 'nowt', as we'd wangled a few free meal tickets and got our faces known; so much so that nobody bothered to check whether we were entitled to eat their meals or not.

In addition, there were a number of outings, such as trips to a local fishing village, which was full of bars and topless beaches, as well as to the group games in Valladolid not involving England. Most of my mates were well aware that Valladolid was a 300-plus mile arid journey and wasn't a wise move on a clapped-out coach. When John Eaton told us he'd managed to blag his way onto the France v Kuwait trip for free, we a kept our mouths shut and let him wander off into the desert like a modern-day Biblical character. Late that night we were sitting in a circle outside our tents drinking frosty cold beer when John's sand-coated coach limped back in from Valladolid. We saw him slowly get off before trudging towards us, sporting a sun-parched face that was redder than a neon beetroot. All he could mumble was, 'You bastards!' as he slumped into his tent. We didn't see John for two days after that. However, at least he'd witnessed a small piece of World Cup history on his long, dry trip. During the match, the French scored a goal after some of the Kuwaiti players had stopped playing, having heard a whistle. The goal was initially awarded by the referee, who hadn't actually blown. This gave the Kuwait team a mass strop-on and they walked off the pitch in protest taking their ball with them. They eventually resumed play but only after the intervention of Prince Fahd. The referee had changed his mind to disallow the French goal, but they still won 4–1. At the end of the day, was such an historic match enough consolation for all the pain and trauma?

A few days later Sir Bobby Moore, an ambassador for the organising company, made an appearance at the camp site. I did meet him, but didn't manage to ask him much as I was in total awe of England's greatest captain. What a great gentleman and what a great loss to England as a nation when he succumbed to illness just over ten years later. Class is a quality which eludes so many of its coveters, but oozes unwittingly from the chosen few.

In the sweltering heat, England started off their challenge in Bilbao like the proverbial house on fire, with Bryan Robson scoring after just 27 seconds. The 10,000 or so England fans were heavily outnumbered by the French, who had pinned their national flags onto the fences behind each goal. But within minutes the English fans had unceremoniously ripped them down and replaced them with their own Union flags. There was little protest from the French and the only thing that kicked off was the match itself.

Afterwards we celebrated our 3–1 victory in the camp site bar with the mass of other England fans and a donkey. This poor, innocent animal hadn't even watched the match, but was led into the proceedings from the farmer's field next door for a few beers and a nosebag. It seemed to be having a nice time until one idiot decided to stub his fag out on the ass's arse. Naturally it went berserk, running up and down the bar, wrecking the place. The next evening, Eaton and Millsy decided to bring the donkey indoors once more. They crept into the field and opened the barn door only to have a double-barrelled shotgun pointed up their noses by the perturbed farmer. He looked at them with a stern expression and said, 'No' in a loud and gruff Spanish voice. Unfortunately, that was the last we ever saw of the partying donkey with the sore buttock.

It proved to be a unique trip and my transport to the next game provided me with a priceless piece of education. I travelled back to Bilbao for England's second game riding pillion on a powerful 1,000cc motorbike on the 50-odd mile journey, which felt like 10 minutes at 120mph. This was also the first trip I'd been on where I noticed people smoking 'weed' (marijuana). There were a few lads wandering around our camp site with contented expressions who couldn't have been happier had England won the World Cup the night before. There were a couple of Dutch lads staying in the tent next door and they were only too happy to show me how to roll joints, from the conventional three-skinners to cricket bat handle-sized twelve-skinners. After failing my woodwork exam due to my inability to build a joint properly, I now wished that my teacher had been from Holland . . . I'd have passed with flying colours. From there on in, my holiday became even more relaxed.

England managed to win the group, beating Czechoslovakia 2–0 and Kuwait 1–0 in games that featured goals from City's Trevor Francis. This success meant that we'd qualified for the next phase out in Madrid. We all said a fond farewell to Graham, packed up our tent and bags, rubbed out 'San Sebastian' and inserted 'Madrid' on our train tickets and off we went. During the journey to Madrid, Spain were playing Northern Ireland and the losers would be in England's group. We were desperate to avoid the hosts, but Gerry Armstrong's 47th minute goal gave the Irish an unlikely win. It was a victory that focused our attempts to get tickets from the Bernabeu the following day. But much to our surprise, there were no problems getting tickets for that phase either. We even got to see Northern Ireland in a group match against Austria which they drew 2–2 at Atlético Madrid's Vicente Calderón Stadium.

Except for the two superb football grounds, in those days Madrid was a dreary place to a twenty-year-old. There was little to do except cruise the tapas bars in search of entertainment and small plates of food. One night we were in such a bar when, unknown to us, the waiters had started a book running on which one of us would throw up first. They'd been plying us with all sorts of weird fish dishes and a casualty was imminent. Eaton finally obliged. A big cheer went up as money changed hands all over the bar.

The best night on the trip came on 4 July. We'd pitched up on a camp site on the outskirts of the Spanish capital and our field was located about 20 minutes walk from a United States Army base. The night before, a couple of American soldiers had marched into our camp site issuing an invitation to all England supporters to attend their Independence Day celebrations. The following day we waded through several cornfields and were welcomed into the barracks. It looked like the set from the brilliant 1950s series *Bilko*, with huge wooden huts and truckloads of soldiers who, in turn, looked like extras from another American TV comedy series, *Mash*. Everyone wanted to talk to us as the British were in high esteem due to the Falklands War and the way in which, 'Maggie Thatcher was kickin' ass.'

I thought that, at 6ft 5in, Phil Knowles was a big lad, but these guys were the tallest blokes I'd ever seen. The base was buzzing with activity, mostly focused on drinking. However there was also an abundance of food; ribs, hot dogs and burgers. At the end of the night, the Yanks were rounded up by their own Military Police after some in-house brawling. It didn't detract from a great night and a brief insight to the life of a 1980s American GI.

The following morning I woke Phil Knowles prematurely. I'd heard a suspicious rustling noise and noticed a huge green and orange insect at the foot of my sleeping bag, which looked far too big for me to tackle. This was no daddy long legs. I reckoned that, as Phil was bigger than me, he'd be braver, but this did not turn out to be the case. We both lay there with a severe dose of the World Cup 'willies', cowering in fear and not knowing what to do. But we had to do something, so I bravely picked up a shoe and threw it firmly at the 4-inch tent monster. It was a direct hit, but the bugger didn't flinch. In fact the shoe bounced straight off him! We were now in panic mode as the alien super-bug had the only door covered. Being the tough Mancunians that we were, we decided to use my pen-knife to cut a new door into the rear of the tent and bravely make our escape. When we got out, we kicked down the poles at either end and stamped up and down on the tent for about 5 minutes. The commotion led to the Germans in the tent opposite poking out their heads to enquire, 'Vot are you doink, Eeenglish pigdogs?' Phil replied, 'We're doing a rain-dance on our tent mate. We're absolutely sick of all this dry, hot weather.' They soon retreated back into their tent scratching their heads wearing puzzled expressions. The weird thing was that, after we'd finished our frantic foxtrot and put the thing back up, there was no sign whatsoever of the scary-looking alien and we now had a gaping hole in the tent I'd borrowed.

This lack of luxury proved too much for Eaton and Millsy who'd by now had more than enough of camping and they went into Madrid and spent the rest of the trip in a cheap hotel. However, Phil and I toughed it out with Dom and the rest in order to conserve money. We thought unbeaten England might go all the way to the semi-final in Seville, particularly as we'd managed a 0–0 bore draw with the Germans who, in turn, had only come up with a 2–1 win against their Spanish hosts. This meant that a 2–0 victory would be enough for England to progress. England could only muster a 0–0 draw against Spain, with the injured Kevin Keegan and Trevor Brooking coming on as late substitutes and both missing chances that might have gone in on a better night.

We all went home the next day. Phil and I left the tent pitched up on site. It might even be there today for all I know – but probably not as it was so shredded. The bloke from the Labour Club asked me where his tent was when we got back. He wasn't too chuffed when I told him it was flapping about in a field in Madrid! The Spanish World Cup trip proved to signal a temporary halt to my foreign jaunts.

♦   ♦   ♦

The summer of 1982 also coincided with the opening of Manchester's eventual iconic nightclub the Haçienda. Within weeks of its introduction to Manchester night life I watched Simple Minds and Echo and the Bunnymen in the same hectic and glorious July week. Not the best for acoustics or viewing, but certainly great for attracting headline acts, I was also lucky enough to see joint-owners New Order on numerous occasions as they drummed up enough funds to keep the place alive.

Even at the tender age of twenty, my single-man boogie nights were in recession and, within a year, I was dating my first steady girlfriend. She was a lass I'd met at work and had finally plucked up the courage to ask out. Unfortunately, not only did she have to contend with my passion for watching football, but playing was back on the agenda too.

25

We Are Lee!

I had no real intentions of getting involved in Sunday League football. As Dirty Harry had succinctly put it, 'A man's gotta know his limitations,' and I knew that I had many on the playing front. The guise of the Sunday morning sporting monster varies from the prehistoric thug at the one extreme to the languid, clueless, club-footed carthorse at the other. Unfortunately, I was simultaneously at both ends of the scale, but Phil Knowles, Graham Moore and John Eaton had bored me so much at City away games with their constant monologues about their exploits on the field of play that I had little choice.

It came to pass that Terry Hyland and I signed up together to play for Lee Athletic in the Altrincham & District Sunday League Division Two. The team intentionally played in sky blue and originated from the Altrincham & Sale City Supporters' Club. The club's name was borrowed from that of City favourite Francis Lee. Had it been a United Supporters' Club, the team might have been named after one of their heroes. However, Charlton Athletic wouldn't have been very original. We were Blues, so Lee Athletic it was. This led to the proud club motto, 'Lee Athletic FC – we don't come from Lee and we're not Athletic.'

My Athletic career began on 31 October in the 1982/83 season. The club was in a healthy position in the league when Terry and I arrived. Although I had briefly played for the conservatively named Brooklands Trades & Labour Club Football Club, the standard transfer fee of four pints of bitter and twenty B&H wasn't required, as my registration had lapsed and I wasn't worth such an astronomical amount.

It took a number of weeks for either of us 'new boys' (as we were then known) to get a sniff of a match, even though most players were rather pungent on Sunday mornings. Initially, we had to be content with entertaining ourselves by invading the pitch to celebrate striker

John Gillespie's regular long-range goals. The first game in which either of us got to play on the 'field of weeds' was a cup tie at 'The Fortress' against Premier League team Stretfordians. At 2–2, the game had gone into extra-time and our manager Colin Johnson (also known as 'Mass' because his 1970s beard made him look like a mass murderer) decided to give me a run-out. I couldn't have impressed because I received the 'curly finger' after just 10 minutes for showing the 'subtle' touch of a bailiff's knock. 'Sub subbed' was an ignominious start and hard to excuse. Back in the pub I gave it a go when I explained, 'I was a bit rusty,' to which Eaton replied, 'Rusty? You looked like you'd totally seized up!' I could take some consolation that our winning goal had been scored while I was on the pitch, but not much more. Consequently I didn't feature in the side for the rest of that season. However, Terry did better and had a few more run-outs.

The following season, 1983/84, saw a lot of changes. Mass quit his post as manager following a stark ultimatum from his wife that, 'If you don't quit that useless team of yours, I'll set fire to your underpants with you still in them.' Being allergic to fire, Colin took the hint and left pronto. He was quickly replaced by John, Pete and Simon Gillespie's dad, John Senior. As our new manager smoked like a beagle on piece-rate he was affectionately known as 'Menotti' after the famous Argentine chain-smoking manager César Luis Menotti.

Mr Gillespie took an instant dislike to me, probably because I usually turned up still inebriated from the night before and was often outspoken about his team selections which, in hindsight, justifiably didn't involve me. I didn't like his training methods either. We spent most of his evening practice sessions aimlessly running around the park in hopeless pursuit of that most illusive of commodities: fitness. Unfortunately, these training sessions lacked any scientific football practice. Having run ourselves ragged, we then spent the rest of the time practising 30-yard shots on 'keeper Phil, who was hardly troubled by our efforts. In fact, we were all so knackered from the running that hardly any of the shots had the power to reach him. I was to spend most of Mr Gillespie's solitary season in charge on the touchline following regular attacks of uncoordinated limb syndrome. I'd have been better staying in bed with my stuffed panda. That was until the day he decided to give me a shock run-out.

I had no idea of my impending opportunity. By now I was so disillusioned I didn't even bother taking part in the pre-match kick-ins. But before the home game against the mighty Hereford Rangers, and with a hangover of 8.9 on the Worthy scale, I reluctantly got my act together and started the game on the right side of midfield. After 20 minutes of running up and down the pitch a minute or so after the ball had gone the other way, I found myself so far offside in the opposition penalty box from a previous fruitless attack that the ref failed to spot me. The goalkeeper parried a John Gillespie rocket-shot and the ball fell into my path, with the goal gaping from 12 yards out. I didn't even bother controlling it before confidently slotting the ball home. I celebrated, not with cartwheels and knee-slides, but instead by staggering off towards the touchline and throwing-up. It should have been the turning point of my career with the critical but fair-minded manager, but he saw I'd gone a funny shade of green and was not pleased.

There was more fun to follow. I was in trouble with the referee for committing a bad foul which was, in reality, due to poor judgement rather than any malice on my part. This was only worth a booking. But when he asked for my name, I replied, 'Alfie Noakes' (a Derek and Clive character from one of their old LPs). This was met with much laughter from my team-mates and the referee inquired as to my real name. Once I had told him, he replied, 'Well then Steve Worthington, get off my field at once.' It was like being back at school, although the ref didn't actually bother to hit me when we got back in the dressing rooms.

The consequent ban and the disgrace of being sent off while under the 'affluence of incohol' – among other things – meant that I didn't play many more games that term either. This might explain why the team had done so well in my absence. They'd got into a position where they needed to win the last game of the season against Park Villa to be promoted but, unfortunately, so did Park Villa. Lee Athletic lost 2–0 to goals from Paul Sproston and Col Baker (both of whom later starred at Lee).

The following year, Mr Gillespie quit his post. I don't suppose the inordinate amount of whingeing from me helped things, so club secretary Pete Moore scoured the Northern Hemisphere to find a suitable replacement. Vernon Park was a man (not a recreational area) located in deepest, darkest Wythenshawe and he took over the reins. What Vernon knew about football you could have chiselled onto a stiletto heel – he proved to be the ideal choice for Lee Athletic. Although Big Vern knew little about the game, he did know enough to see that I was crap. Once again I spent the majority of my time standing on the touchline trying to clear my head or, in one case away at Carrington, helping to clear horses from the pitch before the game.

Speaking of animals, that season we were drawn away against Mobberley Rangers in the League Cup – a game in which I did get a start. It was a hot day and we were all looking forward to playing on the daisy-covered pitch in the serene and picturesque surroundings of the Cheshire countryside. The only problem we could foresee tainting our potential enjoyment of the event was that daisies were not the only thing covering the field. The pitch was also freckled with huge, steaming cow-pats, which the local cattle had kindly bequeathed us prior to their nonchalant departure.

Most of our players had one eye on the ball and one eye on the cow-pats, daintily skipping past and weaving in and out of these odorous landmines which were patiently waiting to explode underfoot. But once the game had slipped into full-blown ferocity, the dung-heaps became incidental until one of Mobberley's players went in with a slide tackle. In doing so, his right armpit plunged straight into the fly-covered sludge which flipped straight into his mouth! It was one of the most horrific moments I witnessed in my football career. Stewart Freeman summed it up in the dressing room after the match when he said, 'I think I'd rather suffer a broken leg than have had to eat crap like that!' Having experienced something similar on my Scout camp at Mevagissey, I could empathise with the victim.

By the end of the game, most of us had cow dung all over our strip and I was more than happy that it wasn't my turn to wash the kit; that task was Paul 'Woody' Wood's honour. The result gave the local paper a great headline opportunity of 'Home Team Eats Crap as Lee Tip Toe around Wibberley Wobberley Mobberley'. But it was an opportunity the press chose to ignore. Another spurned opportunity that day came to neutral spectator Paul Power. I remember Phil saying after the match, 'Wouldn't it have been funny if Paul Power had got his own back on you and shouted "I hate you Worthington!" from the sideline?' Luckily, Mr Power proved far more of a gentleman.

The following week we were away at Dane Road in Sale and we were all standing outside the dressing rooms patiently waiting for Woody to turn up with the kit. It was raining heavily. Belatedly, Woody arrived in his classy Ford Capri, complete with furry dice.

'All right lads. Why are you all waiting outside?' asked Woody.

'You've got the kit, that's why,' we collectively replied.

But Woody protested that he hadn't got the kit and we all feared the worst; Woody already knew the worst. He did have the kit and that it had been left in his car for a week, comprehensively splattered in cow poo. With only 10 minutes to go before kick-off, there was nothing else for it but to get changed into a filthy football strip. The whole team refused to put it on and we almost took to the field with a bare XI. Indeed, being bare would have been far more comfortable, but it didn't bother me. I happily put mine on first, having realised the inevitable and also having realised that the first to root in the bag was sure to get the best kit. We stank worse than a fishmonger's apron during a heatwave and we were certainly the dirtiest team in the league, at least for one game.

Seven days later the hapless Woody was at it again. As punishment, he'd been given a lesser responsibility of minding the goal nets for the week. Once more we found ourselves waiting on the striker. When he did arrive he proudly held up two bin bags containing the nets, saying, 'See lads, I didn't let you down this week!' We all trudged off to the goalposts to put them up. But the bags didn't contain the nets. They were two bags of leaves his dad had swept up from the garden and left in the garage before disposal. To quote an expression of James Finlayson and Homer Simpson it sure was a case of 'd'oh!' Pegging out the leaves was not an option and we had to wait a further 20 minutes for him to return with the right bin bags. Woody left the club not long afterwards for the sunny shores of Malta; he'd suffered a driving ban after taking one whisky too many after a Lee Athletic match. It meant the loss of a great striker and an even better 'cock-up' merchant.

The following season Terry and I briefly left Lee Athletic. Terry had been told that a team called Moss Villa – in one of the Manchester leagues – were looking for players – they were so desperate they took us both on. It was to be the only season Terry and I spent with them before returning to Lee, but we learned a lot. Both of us played every week and I ended up in goal during a cup run that took us to the semi-final, which we lost. I missed the experience, an evening meeting at work taking preference.

The previous game, the quarter-final, was against a rough working mans' pub side from Rusholme called Birch Villa. On our touchline we had a solitary shivering substitute and our manager. But they'd brought sixty Rusholme ruffians armed with numerous cans of beer and belligerent attitudes. I was grateful I was in goal as most of the action took place in their half; I have never played against such dirty and violent opposition. There is the well-versed term in football of 'putting it about a bit' but these lads put it about a *lot* that night. We had the cheek to take a quick two-goal lead and the fun began.

Our players were being smacked off the ball as knee-high tackles flew in from all directions. As the night drew in, it all got a lot darker in both senses as their supporters got in on the act and started attacking our team from the touchline. It wasn't long before it all descended into anarchy as we went 3–0 up midway through the second half. The match was marshalled by a solitary referee, with no linesmen, and he did his best to keep order until he, in turn, was punched by the player he'd sent off for 16 dirty tackles too many. The assault signalled a premature end to the game. The opposition took the opportunity to fight among themselves on the way back to the dressing rooms, strategically located close to the exit of the vast fields. Although nobody was seriously hurt, it remains the most sickening display of misbehaviour I've witnessed in amateur football.

The next season, Terry and I were persuaded to go back to Lee Athletic. We'd continued to play five-a-side on Tuesday nights with our former team-mates and our stories of comparative cup glory, coupled with Terry's ability and the obvious improvements to my game, meant that we were in reasonable demand. Not only that, but Lee were also in decline and it would seem that anyone who could fit into the kit would do.

Terry and I had been brought in to replace a number of the old guard who had moved on in search of greener pastures. This wasn't difficult given that our home pitch had less grass than a hippy commune that had just been raided. Key men such as the Gillespie brothers and my future flatmate Paul 'Flynny' Flynn had departed for a spot of 'pot hunting' at the Buck Inn – a local pub side that regularly won trophies. Flynny was Lee's number one 'keeper at the time, but we had more than adequate back-up in Phil Knowles who was a good goalie at our level, but he was always prone to make the odd cock-up. After a slow start to the 1985/86 season we lost our first five games. The draw for the first round of the Altrincham Senior Cup paired us with the Wythenshawe League's Shell works team. A large crowd of fifty turned up to watch the game, hoping to be entertained. They were not disappointed.

Athletic took an early two-goal lead, but late in the second half, Shell scored. Then the supporters were treated to a comical scene. John Eaton, a former Lee player who worked for Shell and followed their team's matches, commented to fellow touchline spectators, 'Last week, Shell's centre-half scored from a huge clearance from behind his own halfway line.' Right on cue the same guy launched a clearance from his half, which jettisoned the ball 200ft into the air. Phil looked alarmed as he soon realised that the snow-covered ball was likely to reach his goal. He sprinted off his line to take it before it bounced. The ball hit the deck 5 yards in front of him and bounced over his head and sailed another 20ft into the air. Next, we were all treated to the hilarious sight of Phil scrambling to get back to his goal as the ball came down for the second time. As Phil stumbled, landing flat on his face, he could only watch from a worm's eye view in a patch of dirt as the ball dropped perfectly into his net for the equaliser. The game went into extra time and we scored twice to record our first victory of the season. It was an impressive result given that Terry and I were declared unfit due to mystery injuries we'd sustained at Eaton's pre-match party the night before!

This victory gave us much confidence and we managed a few wins before we had to face Tavistock, the majority of whose players were from the 'warm and hospitable' Manchester overspill estate of Partington. This team was full of local 'hard-nuts' and they were the most feared team in the league. The side contained the Grimshawe brothers, and rumour had it that one of them had kidnapped a referee after one match! Apparently, they issued demands to have their respective dismissals revoked or they'd cut the referee's whistle off and shove his flag into such a position that it would take a 14-hour operation to have it successfully removed. They also had a player called 'Pick Axe' Pete whose shaven head revealed a lobotomy scar that served as a warning. They introduced ice hockey tactics of forearm smashes off the ball, plus gouging of the eyes and other such friendly interactions. However, the referee was just as tough. He sent off Pick Axe Pete for a tackle on Steve 'Harry' Harrison that would have made an American footballer wince. Football Tony, watching from the touchline, had the bad sense to comment, 'And about time too!' It was heard by Pick Axe Pete, who went to his car and pulled out a baseball bat from the boot. It was classic Benny Hill as he chased Tony around the field, all the while being chased by several of his own players who were intent on trying to disarm him and so avoid losing their star centre-half on a murder charge.

After the match, Pick Axe had calmed down and even said goodbye to Harry Harrison as if nothing had happened. But all the excitement had been too much to bear for poor Harry. Still fearing retribution, he bottled out of the return fixture, out in the Partington Ponderosa. But he needn't have worried, Pete didn't turn up for that game. Apparently he had been arrested the night before for battering two police officers during a pub brawl.

Lee Athletic didn't fare well that season, finishing fourth from bottom, and the team was on the slide despite the inclusion of Howard Kemp, one of the best players ever to don the Lee shirt. As a consolation, we did win an FA Fair Play Mitre Multiplex ball and the whole team went on a three-day bender to celebrate.

It was clear that we needed new faces to get things moving, and the 1986/87 season witnessed radical change. The diminutive Alex Murray arrived from Wythenshawe League side the Pear Tree. He brought a number of players who we christened the Pear Tree Mob, all of whom liked a spliff before, during and after the match. In fact, there was often so much weed around in the dressing room, that I was moved to design a new badge for the club. This consisted of a marijuana leaf and the Latin inscription which read 'Quidam Amicus Cum Initulis Herba Eqidam Amicus Sane' which was supposedly Latin for, 'A friend with weed is a friend indeed.' It was later shortened to a snappier, 'Quidam Amicus Cum Herba,' and I told everyone this meant 'A friend with weed'. The club went on to embrace its marijuana theme and, in later years, we had the great idea of having a club mascot called Spliffy. This we envisaged as a sub dressed in a big joint suit who would stagger up and down the touchline mumbling words of stoned enlightenment to the players.

Alex wasn't the only new arrival at Lee Athletic in 1986/87. Neil 'Bugsy' Burrows also signed from Bibby's team Mancor. Neil wasn't acquired for his playing talents; he was signed simply because he looked good in the kit and we wanted to glam up our image. In fact Bugsy's career lasted for one game before his dodgy knee suffered a nervous breakdown.

Despite the acquisition of these players, the quest for success proved elusive once more. This lack of glory wasn't down to the inclusion of a further player who I've yet to mention, but his total lack of idea of how to play football didn't help. Dave Blinkhorn was the friendliest bloke you could wish to meet, but on a football field he made me look like Pelé. In one game Dave missed so many chances that Gilly commented, 'If he was a parachutist, he'd be the first one to miss the earth!' But he did have a unique and pragmatic outlook. He was substituted for facing the wrong way while in a wall for a free-kick on the edge of our box. He argued that he saw no sense in getting a gratuitous whack in the knackers for a game of football. Postman 'Blinky' made 12 appearances, which was a measure of how short we were for players (reinforced by the fact that I was an ever-present). Every Sunday evening, it was a custom of many of the local teams to go to the Brooklands Tap for alcoholic discussions about the games played earlier that day. When we were joined by a Stella-fuelled 'Blinky' you'd have thought he'd won each game single-handed.

Our final position in the 1986/87 'Do it Yourself Home Bidet Installation Mega Superstore Altrincham and District Sunday League Division Two' was sixth out of twelve teams. We had recorded a couple of notable victories: 8–0 and 7–1. Such margins were unheard of during the following season. In fact, any margin of victory was almost unheard of, as we only managed to win one game! Once more our fair play won us an FA match ball, signalling another week off work on the sick to recover from the extravagant celebrations.

We lost some of our better players before the start of the 1987/88 schedule, who departed in search of silverware. I, however, was made of sterner stuff. Besides, I was lucky to get a game at Lee and the odds of any other club wanting me were minimal. If I'd had an agent, he'd have been covered in bed sores.

Our first and only victory came in the second game of the season at The Fortress against the Bull's Head. We then had to endure a run of fifteen defeats and two draws before being drawn away in the League Cup to face Premier League King William. Cruel fate had brought about a David and Goliath pairing for this first-round cup tie. At the time, they were top of the Premier League and we were rock bottom of the Second Division – the two clubs couldn't have been further apart. Pete Moore had by now taken over as manager and he was optimistic about our prospects. The game was played on a cold February day. As we took to the field in our short-sleeved shirts without a glove in sight (except for our goalie Phil) the crowd waited in anticipation of lowly Lee being swept away in a blizzard of attacking football. But, due to careful tactical planning and resolute defending and a skip-load of luck, the first half ended goalless. Although the back four received a bigger run-around than a taxi driver on New Year's Eve, manager Moore had seen enough to give him some totally misguided optimism. It was during the half-time break that he uttered the now-infamous words, 'They're not that good this lot, let's have a go at them in the second half.' His plan went tits up, big style.

King Billy finally took the lead on the hour. But the ref should have disallowed it as the ball went out of play earlier in the move. Then it was a case of 'open the floodgates' with another 12 goals in the next half-hour as goalkeeper Knowles was taken to hospital with a severe case of shell shock. This has to be the absolute low point of my amateur career. If you've been in a 'defence' that has conceded 13 goals in 30 minutes you can imagine the despair felt by the players. It was made worse by the howls of laughter from the Eskimos on the touchline.

This was a defeat that signalled the shape of things to come. I tried to become a jack-of-all-trades, but unfortunately, I was a master of none. I actually played in goal, both full-back positions, centre-half, centre mid, and on right and left wings. I even had a bit of a stint up-front during the first game of the season and I was so effective that I was back to full-back the following week.

One thing that I could do well, however, was take a penalty – as explained earlier. I was so reliable, it was suggested that I should be used as an American football-type kicker, coming on to the field of play only when a conversion is required. I had a proud record of scoring 13 out of 14 for Lee and the one I missed was on a mud-bath which was so deep, I could only see the top of the ball let alone hit it properly. Even then the goalkeeper was forced to make a great save.

Despite our solitary victory that season, there was a team even worse than us: Ladybarn didn't manage one win!

The following season it all changed. We'd brought in Bibby as manager once Mancor FC folded and we got to the position where we needed to win the last game of the season to gain promotion. However, that Sunday morning coincided with Stewart Freeman's wedding at which I was best man, as I was one of the few in the team who were expendable. Part of my duties was to keep the groom cool and calm, but the roles were reversed as I was so concerned about whether we would go up. Shortly after the ceremony, the lads arrived from the match with the news of a 3–1 victory. We were promoted – success at last!

A few weeks later the team received their runners-up trophies from City winger David White. It was the first piece of silver-paint-coated-plasticware I'd won in football. I coveted my new trophy so much, I dropped it in the car park while negotiating the short stagger back to the minibus. It didn't look too bad once the Evostick had done its duty. The main thing was that we were on our way up, but it didn't stay that way for long once I took over the reins as manager a few years later. . . .

26

The Art of Football Management

anaging a Sunday League team should be universally recognised as one of the most thankless tasks one could wish to embark upon. I should know, I was manager of Lee Athletic for over twelve seasons and was rarely thanked for my considerable efforts, fruitless or otherwise. Why on earth did I bother? This was a question I asked myself on a regular basis during my lengthy tenure in charge.

My introduction to the higher echelons of Lee Athletic management began with the position of assistant manager to Phil Knowles back in 1988 and Mark 'Bibby' Bowden two years later. I did continue with my playing career, but I also witnessed the varying approaches to management, ranging from the sublime to the ridiculous. Phil taught me how to bawl at players from the touchline until I was red in the face. If the team was performing badly (as was usually the case), the 'Big Man' used to adopt an obstreperous hairdryer approach and regularly read the Riot Act to the players at half time. But not unsurprisingly, the reciting of a piece of long-winded eighteenth-century government legislation had no discernable positive effect on performances in the second half of the game. Phil's early approach was one of total discouragement. It once surfaced when he told one of our strikers, 'just because we haven't got a substitute doesn't mean I won't take you off if you carry on playing like a great big nancy!'

Alternatively, Bibby took a more laid-back option while retaining a red-faced look. He and I spent most of our first season in drunken stupors on the touchline, the mornings after the nights before. As the team staggered from one poor performance to another, Bibby and I staggered from one foot to the other while we watched our beleaguered team. It was an all-too-brief partnership as Bibby was regularly overwhelmed by the usual Sunday morning syndrome: warm pit verses cold field. More often than not he chose the former, leaving me to run the show.

My appointment arrived after I'd served my managerial apprenticeship with 'Bibby the great dictator' and it wasn't long before I was well versed in his ruthless team selection policies. These consisted of picking the team on the basis of the first eleven players to turn up. We had three 'keepers, all of whom suffered from varying degrees of ability absence. They regularly arrived in the dressing room at the same time, and deciding which one to pick caused Bibby's brain to overload! This wasn't too difficult as it was usually pickled in alcohol, but it became apparent that such selection methods weren't always the best policy to follow. This was illustrated when Pete Moore arrived early for one match and was inadvertently selected as a centre-forward. Although commendably willing, a sixty-odd-year-old, short, tubby bloke wasn't perhaps the best option. However, with some of the clueless strikers we had in our forward line, Pete wouldn't have looked that much out of place.

Bibby was also a protagonist of the 'superstar selection technique'. This was the method where he would choose the better players even if they hadn't turned up for weeks. Their regular absences were explained by the usual schoolboy excuses, 'The baby ate my shin-pads,' or 'The dog buried my boots,' or, 'The baby ate the dog then buried it in my boots and shin-pads after it had won a highly competitive kickabout with the cat next door, 4–3 on penalties.' A slightly suspicious excuse, but acceptable in the eyes of gullible Bibby.

Such players also had a regular array of questionable injuries which mysteriously materialised on Sunday mornings after late Saturday nights on the town. These ranged from pulled hamstrings to strained groins, and from slipped compact discs to dislocated willies. Even a, 'damaged knee *cartridge*', once put paid to a player's attendance. Such injuries were dubious enough for lowly tuned amateur players, but when one lad explained his absence due to the severe pain of a blocked fallopian tube, even Bibby raised a Roger Moore-like eyebrow.

Indeed, feigned injuries were a serious problem in selection and they arrived in abundance on those cold, dark, rainy days that we 'enjoy' in Manchester. It was always my experience that, '*when the going gets tough, the tough get injured.*' During one bleak winter, we had so many of our better players missing through calf injuries, you'd have thought we were a rural team rather than a suburban one. When these star players did put in an appearance, Bibby would shove them straight into the side at the expense of loyal but limited players such as me. Such favouritism usually led to bitterness and conflict, but it would all be forgotten the following week when I'd be back in the team because he would be short of players once more.

There were the rare occasions (usually during the warmer late summer months at the start of the season) when we were overloaded with players. In such circumstances, Bibby couldn't make his mind up whether or not to be indecisive in picking his team! Consequently, we had too many hopefuls scrambling for limited kit in the dressing room, and so he introduced the 'pink-eyed eliminator technique.' This was a sort of reduction process for the lads who had been suspected of overdoing it the night before. With naturally pink eyes due to his albino features, this did not enhance Jim Grant's selection prospects. He was regularly and cruelly left out of the starting XI even though he'd been commendably on 'the wagon' the night before.

Following lessons in team selection techniques, there was the art of the pre-match team-talk and Bibby was an excellent role model. By the end of his tenure as manager, we could all rattle it off. He taught me the value of the Churchillian speech. As 'Land of Hope and Glory' defiantly and patriotically blared out in the background, Bibby would recite heart-stirring rhetoric such as, 'never before in the field of amateur football have so many played so shite in front of so few.' This wasn't his only Winston Churchill paraphrase. There was also the classic, 'we'll fight them in the air, we'll fight them on the ground, we'll fight them at Beech Avenue' (Beech Avenue being our former fortress before we moved on to Walton Park), and not forgetting my all-time favourite, 'give me the tools and I'll do the job.' There was never a shortage of tools at Lee Athletic and, overall, Bibby did a good job, particularly the season we gained our first promotion when we were runners-up in Division Two.

I didn't have any serious designs on taking over the reins, but in becoming the manager of a modest little Sunday League team, I had ascended to the height of my footballing potential. Once my appointment was rubber-stamped, following Bibby's self-imposed abstinence, in true Bill Shankly speak, I set about, 'building myself a dynasty,' rather than building a decent football team. This was my first mistake. There was a lot to learn, but as Bibby's aspiring apprentice, I had gained invaluable tuition on how to do it while in a contented state of inebriation.

One thing Bibby hadn't taught me was the use of tactics and they were now up to me to decide. There were, of course, the traditional tactical manoeuvres on which to rely. For instance, when playing against opposition from a superior division in the cup, or indeed being 1–0 up with 10 minutes to go, the trusted 10-0-0 defensive formation was adopted. Conversely, against inferior opposition or being 1–0 down with 5 minutes to go, the trusty 0-0-10 attacking formation would be used. Like every other manager, I had brief dalliances with the 4-5-1, the 4-3-3, the 5-4-1 and even the innovative but ineffective 4-1-1-1-1-1-1 upside-down umbrella formation. I tried every combination going, but, as we know, the English footballer is a simple beast and 4-4-2 usually prevailed so as not to complicate things. However, a further combination I employed to good effect on a couple of occasions was the 4-4-3 formation! Although starting a game with twelve or bringing on a sub without taking a player off was illegal, I got away with it on at least two occasions without anyone noticing, including me. Jim Grant pointed out these numerical imbalances after the match. However, both players and manager alike were well aware that we needed all the help we could get!

I also quickly realised that some players would react well to a bollocking while others needed a paternal arm and a few encouraging words. However, I was soon to discover that other methods of inducement were necessary for some mercenary individuals. Within weeks, I offered a free three-course Indian to anyone who could score 20 goals in the season. Jim got dangerously close on 15, but a couple of own goals meant I chalked two off his tally! I also tried the hard man approach. After one particularly poor performance, I threatened to wash the kit without fabric conditioner if they played like that again. Unfortunately, the fear of an uncomfortable kit minus a spring fresh fragrance wasn't enough to galvanise them into concerted improvement.

Things started to go wrong by Christmas. I had some 'limited' players, but those with a modicum of talent were often the most challenging to coax a performance from. Take Lee Jenkins. He had skill, pace, a shot like a missile, he was good in the air and he could score goals for fun. He was even good looking. But for some reason, I couldn't get him to play to his potential for two consecutive halves let alone two weeks on the trot. What was the problem? It was his inconsistent attitude and my inability to change it. When I got Jenky on a good day, there was no-one better at our level. But Jenky's good days were dependant on his mood. His perfunctory performances drove all around him to distraction. He also knew he could play well when he wanted to and he had the confidence to be greedy on the ball; nothing wrong with that if there is a tangible end-product. Sometimes there was, but usually there wasn't. In fact he could be so indulgent in possession that most of the lads used to comment that if he was ever on *Mastermind* he'd get disqualified for refusing to pass.

One of his many nicknames was 'off-licence eyes', because they never opened until 12 noon on Sundays (we kicked off at 11). Realising Jenky could stir the team to success if I could stir him into consistency, I embarked upon anything and everything possible. I tried praising, screaming, forward psychology, reverse psychology and bribery. I even thought of kidnapping his wife and demanding that he played to his potential at least three times on the trot before releasing her. It probably wouldn't have worked. Their marriage didn't last long and it's likely he wouldn't have been that bothered.

Just as all appeared lost, I stumbled on the answer. Suddenly and without warning, Jenky hit a rich vein of form, which – inexplicably to me – lasted a month and I couldn't understand why. As far as I was aware I hadn't done anything unusual as there was nothing left to try. But his form had clearly improved and was sustained – so much so that he banged in ten goals in the space of four glorious games and I didn't question why. 'If it aint broke don't fix it' is one of my many mottos.

For a while I thought I was a genius of a manager. I was Steve Worthington, the man who somehow finally got the enigmatic Lee Jenkins to discard his cloak of apathy and show the world (well at least fifteen or so people who bothered to watch us), what he could do every Sunday. Then I found the real reason had nothing to do with me. One of those fifteen stood on the touchline turned out to be his long-lost father who'd returned from the merchant navy. He'd taken the opportunity to watch his lad play football and in front of his 'old man' Lee was a different player. Jenky Senior went back to sea and Jenky Junior went back to his old self. Had Mr Jenkins been employed in a regular job on land, Lee Athletic would have been far more successful and I'd have been the greatest Sunday League manager in the South Manchester area.

This lack of tangible motivation was the major flaw in being a Sunday League manager. Unlike our professional counterparts, the amateur boss has little in the way of positive or negative persuasion to offer. All I could do by way of punishment for bad performances was to wield the axe and that was dependant on having twelve players available. But having taken this extreme measure, the player in question would get the hump and march off into the distance. Even if discarded players did show some character and tough it out on the touchline, most would sulk while slagging me off behind (and often in front of) my back. Even my stalwart mate and Lee Athletic captain Stew Freeman went into a strop when I substituted him. The next week just to lighten up his mood, I duped him into putting on the number 8 shirt before the match. A mere 5 minutes into the game, I attracted the referee's attention by holding up a number 8 board made out of a cornflake packet earlier that morning. Even the referee had a laugh. But the moaning and the criticism is something which is part and parcel of the job. There was nobody worse than me at verbally abusing managers during my playing career whenever I was left out, so at least I had an appreciation of the disappointment of being consigned to the bench.

Another huge problem was 'signing' new players, especially someone who had banged in a hat-trick against you the week before. Then the tapping-up process would begin. You would find out where his local was, go there, strike up an innocent conversation about football and then praise him on his brilliant performance the previous week while plying him with free ale. You would tell him how crap his existing team was and deliver tales of how your club was going places with all the local superstars you had in the pipeline. Towards the end of the night, you would thrust a transfer form and a pen in front of him and before he knew it, he'd signed! After a few games he would realise he'd been duped. The other star players hadn't materialised and he'd put in for a transfer. But you'd tell him some tall story about why he couldn't have one because of some made-up league rule technicality. He would soon fall into submission and stay way longer than he anticipated.

I once offered £200 and Dave Blinkhorn in part-ex as a bribe to an opposition manager for a particular player. But he drove a hard bargain and we eventually settled on a straight fee of £100. It was unfortunate that we resorted to such skulduggery because as an independent club, we had little to offer the better players. Some pubs paid some players to turn out – such was the kudos in hosting a top-flight team from local hostelries. The only money we could muster was getting subs *from* the players, which was usually a nightmare. Mysteriously, most of our players could always afford to spend loads of cash in the pub after the game, but couldn't afford the £2 weekly subs! Luckily, our club treasurer was relentless in his pursuit of the weekly charge. Players commented that they'd rather owe the Mafia £50,000 than owe Stew Freeman their subs.

During my first full season in the Lee Athletic cold seat, I was joint-manager with my flatmate Flynny. Being a joint manager seemed the logical move because managing a joint had never been a problem in the past. Flynny had been brought in to help spread the responsibility and we had a great working relationship: I said one thing and he did another. An example of our forward planning came the weekend the clocks went forward. We thought they'd gone back and so left the flat to arrive in good time. It was almost three hours before the kick-off when we got to the ground before sloping off back home and going back to bed. It sort of summed it all up and was a case of the hopeless leading the clueless and, not unsurprisingly, we were relegated taking 8 points from a possible 56 with a meagre three league victories from twenty-six matches. The only highlights we had that season were the ones some of the players had put in their girlie hairstyles. It was a baptism of fire, but mysteriously the 'Worthy Out' campaign failed to materialise.

Such demise could have been seen as a testimony to my managerial ability. What with supporting City and my various indignities as a player, it appeared as if I was beginning to turn football failure into an art form. However, I remained convinced that I could be a better manager than I was a player. I was back for more the following year and proved I could manage. We won a record amount of games for one season in the club's history and accumulated the most points. The latter statistic was principally due to the introduction of 3 points for a win (rather than 2).

Despite the considerable improvement in season two, my third season began with a 4–0 home defeat and completely destroyed my complex, cunning and well thought-out masterplan for the campaign ahead. I gave up on that and decided to listen to Flynny instead. But his wisdom was no greater than mine. Once more we went into a slump and Flynny left me to it, following his usual philosophy of, 'if at first you don't succeed . . . sack it.'

One of my philosophies was that if we couldn't win on the field, at least we could look good in the kit. We acquired a new strip that made us look like Newcastle United in more ways than one, as we were often just as bad as they were on the pitch. We were more the 'Goon Army' than the Geordie version.

Unfortunately, it wasn't sartorial splendour that was the key to successful management. While I knew *my* limitations as a player, my players often blamed *their* limitations on me, particularly when they were left out of the team. In fact, decisions on team selection often led to rows before games, during games, after games, in the pub and at training on Tuesday. It got to the point where long-standing friendships were threatened. Our dodgy start to the 1993/94 season had inflamed a blame culture and I was becoming the focal point. But I soon put a stop to my scapegoat status after our defence blamed me for putting on weight after I'd told them to, 'spread out a bit more on the pitch.'

Despite my early failure, I still had faith in my own thoughtful and studious approach, even though whatever I said never seemed to make the slightest difference. I'd suspected that my team weren't as transfixed by my football counselling sessions as I'd have preferred. To further illustrate my plight, I once spent the whole of my team-talk telling the players that they were in trouble of their own making and if they'd stop giving the ball away with poor passing, they wouldn't suffer half as much in the second half. I even paraphrased Alf Ramsey's famous 'precious gold bar' reference that he used before England took on Brazil in the 1970 World Cup in Mexico.

'Right lads, in the second half think of the ball as a "precious block of weed". Don't give it away.' Stirred by my words, they got up and took to the field shouting, 'Come on lads, don't give the ball away.' The match restarted and the ball went to Stewart Freeman's cultured feet. He controlled it and knocked a lovely 15-yard pass straight to their centre-forward, who ran through to bang in goal number five a mere 10 seconds into the half.

The following week I used the word 'pivotal' in the pre-match address to which Terry Hyland advised, 'Steve, you should stick to words of no more than one syllable if you don't want to confuse them any more than necessary.' I amended my style and offered some strange pieces of advice which would have been perplexing to the most intelligent of players, 'Keep your eye on the wind in the second half,' 'Look for the shout!', 'You're stood walking,' and, 'Fill the plug,' instead of plug the gap!

To my comment, 'I don't want you all going gung-ho in the second half,' the riposte was, 'But if you do, get me two portions of egg fried rice and chicken and green peppers in a black bean sauce while you're there.'

My favourite came when the players looked even more lethargic than normal as I called them into a huddle for a team-talk.

'That's right lads, just amble in,' I said.

'Wasn't she once the Queen of England?' asked John Gillespie. It was a shame we weren't as sharp on the pitch.

1995/96 saw the return of Phil Knowles to the management line-up, this time as my assistant, but even more disappointment was on its way.

Somehow we managed to make it to my first cup semi-final only to lose to eventual winners Hale Barns United.

The following season, 1996/97, was barren once more and by the time 1997/98 arrived, the tables had turned full circle. Bibby had taken over from Phil as my assistant, but that didn't last long. Continual attacks of gout, brought on by regular cider binges meant that the spirit was willing, but the flesh stayed in bed. Finally it was Phil to the rescue once more and he helped see out my days as Lee Athletic manager, which lasted well into the next millennium. But this had turned out to be yet another average term.

In 1998/99 we didn't fare much better as a mid-table finish and early cup exits brought little cheer.

27

Desperation all around

If amateur league football proved challenging, then City failed to set the world on fire in the 1980s. The Blues had started the new decade reasonably enough, but once Trevor Francis had departed for 'pastas' new – he'd been sold to Sampdoria – City's form took an alarming dip and with players in the side like Peter Bodak, Terry Park and Chris Jones the Blues did not appear formidable. 'Chris' and 'Jones' are household names in England, but not when put together in a footballing sense. City's Chris Jones wasn't even unique. Lee Athletic had their own Chris Jones who, despite his weight and limited ability, was marginally more talented than the professional version.

That season was to witness my only 'willing' participation in football violence. I'd gone down to West Ham in the back of a white Ford Escort van with ex-Button Laner Andy Seddon, his mate Jim Yates and another big bruiser called Baz. It was a van load of three handy lads and me. After the match, which City lost 4–1, we were *all* put to the test. On the return to the van – a route march which went in the opposite direction from the police escort – I'd found myself walking back alone.

Within a few minutes, and having no obvious access to fruit or vegetables as the customary failsafe camouflage, I was aware that I'd been sussed out by a West Ham skinhead who started to follow me. As I approached the van he disappeared into a launderette full of shadowy figures. I jumped in and shouted to our driver to, 'Get the hell out of here, pronto!' Andy kicked into *Sweeney* mode and burned rubber up the road, which was just as well as we were soon being chased by a mob of eight West Ham boot-boys. It looked like we'd escaped, but the traffic lights changed at the junction and the car in front braked. With the gang of ten closing in, Andy instructed us to grab whatever we could out of his toolbox in the back: a couple of hammers and a large crowbar. All that was left for me was a set of jump-leads and a sawn-off pencil. As the Cockney crew of fifteen approached menacingly, we burst out of the back of the van screaming, 'COME ON THEN!' We fearlessly ran at them in an 'attack being the best form of defence' manoeuvre. Much to my surprise, they thought better of it and all twenty turned tail and ran off up the high street with me swinging my jump-leads above my head in hot pursuit. It's a good job I was a slow runner or I might have actually caught up with the fleeing mob of twenty-five, and then what would I have done? Offered them a jump-start?

Meanwhile, passing shoppers were aghast and agog and just for one brief, deluded moment, I felt like a real bad boy. Within seconds all four of us were rounded up by the police and I was shoved back into the van with my ticker thumping at the rate of twenty to the dozen. What a result! We'd ran West Ham on their own 'manor' – well, at least fifty-eight of them (without any exaggeration) and I'd saved face, after leading them to us in the first place, and I had lived to tell the tale – which I did once or twice when I got home safely. The 4–1 defeat had paled into insignificance.

◆　◆　◆

With such a lack of talented players in the team, the Blues rapidly plummeted to a position where relegation was a reality. But the prospect of sinking back into the Second Division for the first time since 1966 was unimaginable. John Bond had left the club under a cloud, after the team had been embarrassingly thumped 4–0 at Brighton in the FA Cup. His assistant, John Benson (AKA Ben Johnson), had taken over. The penultimate match of the season was another away game at Brighton & Hove Albion's Goldstone Ground. It was a game City simply had to win and luckily we did, thanks to a solitary strike from Kevin Reeves.

Seven days later I was queueing outside the Kippax, ready for the decisive game against Luton, with my dad and commented, 'Just think, we could go down today,' to which he replied, 'Well, it wouldn't be the first time I've seen it happen.' A cold wave of doom washed over my soul. Every dog has its day and this particular pack of Bedfordshire canines were about to cock their legs in our direction.

There were about 10 minutes to go when Raddy Antić scored Luton's winner: these were the only 10 minutes in the season that City had slipped into the relegation zone. But 10 minutes was enough to seal our fate. The Blues went down in front of 42,843 distraught fans and Luton manager David Pleat ran onto the pitch in a preposterous beige suit, skipping and jumping for joy as the final whistle meant his team had stayed up and mine had gone down. It was a moment the BBC showed more times than that God-damn Ricky Villa goal, and that's saying something. Not that I'm bitter, I always look out for Luton's results and hope they lose! I was glad that they didn't go bust in 2008, because it allowed them to carry on and drop out of the League altogether. Somehow I managed to resist crying on that day of doom, but had I known what dross and struggles that were to follow I surely would have done. Not only did Luton relegate City, but I once lost my Saver Seven bus pass while in Luton for a League Cup tie, and I will never forgive them for either occurrence.

Peter Swales had inherited a successful and wealthy club when he took over the chairmanship from the wily and dignified Mr Albert Alexander in 1971. Twelve years later, the club was debt-ridden and back in the Second Division. The wise old man of City would have not have been best pleased with the profligacy of his successors had he lived to see his fine work unravel in such an irresponsible manner. Perhaps it was then that Swales should have been ousted, but I don't recall any clamouring for his head, and he stayed at the helm for many years to come.

◆   ◆   ◆

The following season was a complete culture shock. Graham Moore's girlfriend was pregnant and the use of his car to away trips was forcibly withdrawn. By now I was firm friends with Bibby and we started going on the Denton Supporters' Club minibus which was run by a massive City fan called Alan Potter. At 40 stone, Alan really was big. He moved about like a waterbed on legs. But Big Al can't have eaten all the pies, because if he had three with his chips, I had at least two! I could never really understand how he could be 28 stone heavier me.

Perhaps a clue to his critical mass was through something other than food? Alan gave new meaning to drink driving. While behind the wheel he drank two litre bottles of Strongbow cider en route to any away ground. But in Alan's huge grip, a two-litre container look tiny. He always appeared to be in complete control and totally impervious to the effects of the 5 per cent proof alcoholic apple juice. He got away with it until a journey home one dark and dreary night when he slowly and inexplicably began to veer from the inside lane all the way to the outside lane on the motorway. Our driver was fast asleep, bless him. Quick to notice I slapped Big Al on the back of the head as hard as I could while screaming, 'WAKE UP!' Despite the sudden jolt, Alan stirred in an instant and thankfully controlled the bus, steering it away from the crash barrier that was threatening to coax us all into a permanent sleep. I was already in Alan's bad books. I had been put in charge of selling 50p cans to the lads on the bus coming home from Sunderland, but had decided to give them all a free drink. Alan couldn't understand why most people were completely bladdered by the time we got back, until he realised I'd given away all 48 cans of lager. He banned me for a couple of away games, but I was reinstated once he struggled to fill the bus and he knew Bibby, John Eaton and I went everywhere together. We travelled the length and breadth of the country year in and year out, never knowing which years were in and which years were out. If City were playing we'd be there. We even went to Glasgow for a six-a-side tournament in which the Blues were knocked out after 10 minutes!

Football was indeed an obsession and it wasn't just City and England that I watched that year. Football Tony took Eaton and I to see his former love, Scunthorpe United, at the Old Showground to play Wigan Athletic in October 1983. We'd been drinking most of the day and on seeing the stadium, Eaton exclaimed, 'There's no way I'm paying to get into a dump like this.' We began to look for an alternative means of entry without handing over the cash. Despite us both being attired in jeans, trainers and trendy Fila tracksuit tops, I went over to the commissioner and told him that we were scouts from Manchester City who'd come to check on Scunthorpe's right-back. No problem. We were escorted straight into the directors' lounge, where we were treated to free drinks and a buffet before being taken into the directors' box! Terry Venables was sitting a few seats behind us on a genuine scouting mission, as he was QPR's manager at the time. The right full-back we claimed to be checking on was in his mid-thirties and had seen better days.

Following City around the country was a way of life. I did have a couple of chances to get away from the never-ending cycle of City's disappointments. Late in 1983 Kevin Cooke, a mate from Button Lane School, turned up on my front doorstep and invited me to go for a pint in the local pub. He'd departed for America a couple of years earlier to seek fame and fortune and had gone some way to achieving it, having climbed his way to the lofty position of manager of a luxury hotel in Miami. He wanted me to go back with him and learn 'the ropes' of the hotel business.

Kev painted a great picture of sand, sea and American totty who couldn't resist the English accent. I had two weeks to think about it, and I did. It was a similar situation to the one my dad had found himself in the 1950s while working as a printer on the Hotspur Press. He had completed a special rush-job order and had impressed an American businessman who was well connected with the *New York Times*. He offered my dad a job on the paper over in the 'Big Apple', which he accepted. Unfortunately, just as he was about to go on his big adventure, his mother was taken ill and he was unable to fulfil his dream. He stayed behind to care for his mum who was on her own by this time.

My choice wasn't clouded by such issues. It was sun, sea and swimming pools or the damp grey skies of Manchester. If only it were that simple. To leave would have meant saying goodbye to my true love, Manchester City. Even though they always let me down and caused me great despair, occasionally they gave me great happiness and joy. Much as I often wanted to walk out on them like a tempestuous lover, I knew in my heart of hearts that I never could. Besides, there was nothing wrong with the girls from Manchester and I liked living through the seasons every year (football and cricket). Regrets, I've had a few, but this wasn't one of them.

I also knew that if I stayed, I had a pretty good chance of ending up with a degree, as my college work had progressed from BEC General to BEC National. Once more I had embarked on the course with my usual economy of effort. But I had got myself in trouble by failing to turn up a couple of times, and one afternoon I returned from the pub 'slightly' worse for wear. College had sent a letter of complaint into work and I was in the soup. So much so that my boss, Dave Howarth, warned me that if I didn't pass the course first time, he wouldn't finance another attempt. However, I still managed to avoid a disciplinary hearing thanks to a crass amateur psychological evaluation from my accusing lecturer. College had also asserted that the reason for my erratic behaviour was due to my sibling rivalry with my more successful *brother*, who had an obvious negative effect on my self-worth and this had driven me to drink. Not having a brother gave me the opportunity to discredit the letter and plead my innocence. It was a close call and after that I determined that I would keep my nose clean. At last I finally recognised that if I could go on to attain the higher qualifications, I might have a chance of promotion to the higher echelons of local government. What I needed was a good woman to help me along my way, although a bad woman might have been much more fun.

28

What is this thing called, love?

Towards the end of 1983, I met my first love in the female sense: Janet Watson. She worked in the Planning Department at the Town Hall and most of the lads in our office were mesmerised by her good looks and seductive wiggle. I wasn't the best 'chatter-upper' when it came to the opposite sex and I was always stuck in the classic catch-22 situation when I went out with my mates. Having never got past first base at school with *any* girl whom I might have liked, I lacked confidence and I could never really relax and talk to women whom I fancied. This was inexplicable to me as I was always dressed in the trendiest clothing. In addition, I was usually plastered with copious amounts of nose-tingling Kouros or pungent Givenchy aftershave and equally large helpings of Dutch courage in the form of alcohol. But in those days being inebriated wasn't seen by girls as an advantage and any seductive powers of my provocative cologne were suffocated within an intrusive cloak of toxic mist as the chain-smoking masses polluted the pubs.

My main objective was to get drunk rather than to 'trap' – mainly because I couldn't be potentially saddled with the demands of an over-possessive female. There were just too many away games to attend. Besides, I was more than happy to go back to Terry Hyland's house and play drunken chess until the early hours while drinking his mother's Courvoisier brandy, which we cannily replenished with water.

I'd been out with a few girls, but they never lasted long, usually due to my pertinacious obsession with City. However, one relationship ended rather abruptly, when an irate father caught his daughter and I in a clinch in his living room. He'd ventured downstairs in the early hours of Sunday morning to unplug the fridge for the night in order to save electricity!

I took a simplistic male viewpoint. The way I saw it, girls knew little about football, so they had little hope of understanding me. Besides, in my limited experience of females, they were an overly expensive commodity for the benefits they provided. Most of those I'd dated never seemed to get their hands in their purses due to some outdated custom that the bloke always pays. This might have been okay up until the mid-1970s when the man was usually the sole breadwinner, but this was the 1980s and I was only too happy to preach the gospel of equality. My limited funds were mostly allocated to City, clothes, music and beer – and not necessarily in that order. Despite my sincere and chivalrous motives to protect my date from the mercy of the elements, they usually had me sussed. They were always clever enough to recognise the old, 'I'll meet you inside,' ruse, thus avoiding having to pay their admittance to the nightclub or cinema. Going out with a lass was always an expensive venture, usually with little reward.

Being a lad's lad, in the strictly non-gay sense, I could take it or leave it. Mostly I left it. I much preferred my mates, drinking beer, talking rubbish, playing the odd game of Space Invaders and then scoffing pie and chips on the way home with nothing on my arm but the odd beer stain or a blob of gravy. But all this was soon to change.

As happens with all groups of lads, my beer buddies bit the dust as they started getting hitched and 'loved-up'. It became a case of if you don't move with the times, you'll end up sad, alone and nookieless. I knew the days were rapidly approaching when I'd have to find myself a girlfriend. The saucy girl from the Planning Department fitted the bill, but would I fit hers? Janet was an outgoing lass with a great sense of humour and the more we spoke, the more we hit it off. As I got to know her, I started to make any old excuse to go to the photocopier in the hope of a brief, flirtatious liaison, so much so that, after great deliberation with the lads in the office as to my chances (of which it was unanimously agreed ranged from f-all to nil), I finally asked her out for a lunchtime drink. To my delight and horror, she accepted. I must have been 'bricking it' because I remember taking along a photograph of Terry and I standing outside Stan Laurel's house in Ulverston. I naïvely thought it would give us something to talk about if the conversation dipped. But she later told me that she thought it was slightly weird and gave her a few second thoughts about my character. Not only that, but there were the numerous stories I told her about my love of City, which should have rung a few alarm bells for her.

I'd just turned twenty-two when I started going out with Janet seriously, although not so serious that I would give up watching the Blues at home and away. Not that she asked me to. Janet always seemed okay with my footballing exploits, even when I took her to Paris for a romantic week on the Champs-Elysées, despite the fact that I had the ulterior motive of seeing Hearts play Paris St Germain at the Parc des Princes in the UEFA Cup (which they lost 4–0).

Miss Watson wasn't really into football, but insisted that I take her to Maine Road to see what all the fuss was about. Most lads didn't want their other half anywhere near the match. Taking a 'bird' to the game made you look like a bit of a wimp. It was always best to make their experience as repugnant as possible. I waited until one dark, damp November Saturday and plonked her in the standing area between the Kippax Stand and the North Stand, known as 'Windy Corner' (later known as the Gene Kelly Stand as in *Singin' in the Rain*). This was well away from my usual cosy spot under the Kippax roof with my mates. My plan was to ensure her hair would get wet, windblown and messed up, and it wouldn't be an experience she'd want to repeat. This was the 1980s: the age of hairspray junkies.

My dastardly ploy did the trick. By the time she left the ground, her make-up had run and she looked like the lead guitarist out of Kiss with a soggy cow-pat on her head. It was more than enough to deter any fanciful thoughts of a City season ticket with the loving boyfriend.

Janet and I went out for over two-and-a-half years, and I didn't miss a game at home or away. But it put a strain on our relationship. After a couple of years of my absenteeism, she took a part-time job as a backing vocalist with former *Coronation Street* star Chris Quentin, but I still didn't foresee a problem. I thought she was happy to go off singing on Saturday nights while I came home from all corners of the country having watched City lose. We'd never discussed marriage and there was no way I wanted to settle down at such an early age. I was more than happy to plod along, living at home with money in my pocket (after paying my mum a weekly pittance for my keep) and enjoying life with a great-looking blonde on my arm. That was until, without warning, she binned me.

♦   ♦   ♦

Getting the sack was a real shock and it took time to recover. I thought we were both happy doing our own thing on Saturdays and being together on Sunday afternoons after I'd played football and had enjoyed a drink with the lads. There was no Sky football on Sunday afternoons, so it was a lot easier to fit her in. Come to think of it, I didn't see her much on Friday nights either as that was lads' night out in Manchester. Still, I could see her in the week, during and after work. I thought this would be more than enough. I was wrong.

Janet didn't tell me why she gave me the grand order of the boot, although I had my suspicions. In hindsight I suppose my unrelenting love for MCFC didn't help. I always got the impression that her mum was advising her to get a secure future with a more devoted bloke. To be fair, she may have had a point. But I never doubted my honourable intentions and, had she stuck around, we probably would have tied the knot. But I never saw myself getting married before I reached twenty-seven. I had a game plan and wanted to live before starting the 'whoopee cycle'. Perhaps I should have told her this when it mattered, but I didn't.

When I got the push, I spent many maudlin days and nights up in my box room playing lugubrious Smiths records and wallowing in self-pity. Not only had I lost my girlfriend, but the rejection had taken a devastating – if ultimately temporary – effect on my self-esteem. Being a loyal type of bloke (somewhat ironically proved beyond doubt with my devotion to my football team) it was all too much to comprehend. How could she give me the boot? Me, the best guy in the entire world (well certainly in my world at least). The realisation that I wasn't the best guy in her world shook me to the core.

This deep sadness couldn't have come at a worse time, as I was about to sit my first year exams for the degree at Manchester Polytechnic. This was not a great time to study – not that there was ever a great time to study. My head was 'in bits' and about a week before the first year exams I was out drowning my sorrows with Terry in the Hare & Hounds in Timperley. While staggering back to his girlfriend's house, I got caught short and went for a pee behind the back of the shops on Shaftesbury Avenue, where it was pitch black. Consequently, I hadn't noticed the steps down to the cellar of the back of one of the shops. I fell into the eight-foot chasm landing on a pile of bricks trapping my hand between the bricks and my right knee. I broke a couple of fingers and once more injured my right leg. It was a painful blow, although with cock-in-hand it could have been a lot worse. I didn't know it at the time, but it was *the* best thing that could have happened.

I was patched up in the familiar surroundings of Wythenshawe Hospital Casualty Department and I was physically as well as mentally unable to take the exams. I explained my plight to the tutor. Luckily he saw me hobbling towards him and was shocked at my physical state. Immediately he said, 'There's no way you can take the exams like that. You'll have to take the re-sits in September.' By the time the re-sits arrived, I was fit and ready and passed without difficulty.

♦　♦　♦

By the time December 1986 arrived I was on the lookout for a 'Christmas chick' – and she was duly hatched in the most unlikely of places. There are not many married couples can say they met in the modest and diminutive lounge of the Jolly Angler. The 'JA' is a traditional end-terraced Victorian pub set behind Piccadilly station.

Neil 'Bugsy' Burrows decided to hold an all-day birthday bash in these unlikely surroundings at which both his girlfriend Judith Croasdale and her best friend Jane O'Dwyer were present. Judith worked with Bibby in the car parks office and Jude and I had become good friends. I'd seen Jane with her a few times and she always had an unattainable air about her, confirmed by the fact that a number of Bibby's mates had tried unsuccessfully for a date. Given my total fear of rejection, I hadn't considered, 'puttin' in a bid', as Bibby's mate Grybo called it before he had asked her out and failed.

Bugsy's birthday bash lacked nothing in booze. As usual I noticed the stylish, alluring and apparently single woman but hadn't taken the opportunity to do anything about it. After a few hours of heavy drinking with my mate Stew Freeman, an impromptu mixed doubles pool competition began. I was paired-up with the classy-looking brunette, but failed to recognise the opportunity. However, that changed as Judith and Bugsy provided the opposition. Bugsy and I were highly competitive. I was trying to concentrate on my game, but Judith's friend proved to be a welcome attraction but also a distraction through my beer-goggles. It turned out that my new partner could hold her own playing pool and when she hit the winning shot I gave her a celebratory peck on the lips. To my delight, she responded positively with the most delicate and subtle return kiss. It was indeed a romantic moment and one which would have benefited from the shield of my old plastic briefcase.

Sure enough, after a few more drinks and 'stimulating' conversation in which I totally avoided anything to do with MCFC, I asked her out and I'm pleased to say that I didn't go the way of my other 'failed' mates.

Nursing a hangover the next morning and watching my dad frying an 'egg banjo', I decided to inform him and the world of my impending date.

'Dad, I think I might have copped off with a rich millionairess last night.' Suddenly his attention perked up from the frying pan and he replied, inadvertently nicking a line from *Arthur*, one of my favourite comedy films, 'You have my permission to marry her.'

As it turned out, it was Dawn, another of Judith's friends, who was the potentially rich one. But as I was to discover, Jane was wealthy in other ways, namely love and loyalty – the two main ingredients for a long and happy relationship.

Our first date came the following day at Belle Vue Bowling in my then recently acquired first car: a beige Ford Fiesta that came complete with go-slower rust spots. Jane turned up in a dress that had red and black parallel stripes that, I later commented, made her look like Desperate Dan, to which she instantly replied, 'More like Desperate Jane to be going out with you.' She was sharp and gorgeous with it – a fine combination.

Over twenty years later, the brunette I fancied as my Christmas chick is still by my side. If Janet was my first love, then Jane is my true love. After six years of dating, we were married in 1992.

29

Trials and Tribulations

ity's relegation in 1983 was a severe blow and so began a yo-yo period in the club's history that brought a cycle of promotions and relegations. This season saw the beginning of a new and now time honoured tradition where the club shop would commence its end of season sale at the beginning of February.

Before the 1983/84 season started, John Eaton and I went on our pre-season travels, but this time it wasn't for footy. On Sunday 3 July 1983, a couple of months after I'd turned twenty-one, we both ventured down to Milton Keynes outdoor bowl to see an extravagantly bleached blonde David Bowie in his Serious Moonlight tour on a glorious summer's day. As neither of us had enough money to afford an overpriced ticket on the official coach from Piccadilly Records, we 'thumbed' it. John produced the smallest cardboard sign possible in an effort to persuade motorists to give us a lift. The sign simply stated 'Bowie' and John had shown artistic flair by putting an elongated 'Z' underneath the word, presumably in tribute to *Aladdin Sane.* I made scurrilous remarks about the sign commenting that the uninitiated would think 'Bowie' was a small town near Hornchurch. My abuse proceeded for 5 minutes before the first car that came towards us screeched to a halt at John's sign! The driver turned out to be the freaky DJ in the Bowie Room located within the Pips night club in Manchester. I'd regularly clocked him on Friday nights dressed up in Ziggy Stardust regalia as he entertained the crowd with his brilliant dance and mime. There were three Bowie disciples from Burnley and were more than happy for us to join them with the comment, 'We weren't going to stop for anyone, but when we saw the sign that just said "Bowie" we thought, "quality", we've got to give those boys a lift.' Within minutes I'd wiped the egg off my face and replaced it with a serene and contented look with which first-class weed will bring.

We got there and back for a song (or two), got stoned, watched Bowie and got back home all in one piece.

♦   ♦   ♦

Down to earth again with football. City's first game in the old Second Division was at Crystal Palace. It was a trip where Bibby and I decided to try to finally settle our long-standing argument of who could drink the most beer at an away game. By the end of the day the score (including cans) was Worthy 23 – Bibby 23. But crucially, the big fella nodded off and I took the opportunity and drank the last and deciding can in extra time to take the all important trophy 24–23. I played for Lee Athletic the next day!

City started the comeback campaign well enough winning at Palace 2–0, but it was the same old story a couple of days later losing 2–1 at Cardiff. During the season, City were drawn at Torquay United in the League Cup. Bibby and his mates Rosie and Paul 'Gilly' Gilsenan went by car as I followed behind in Potter's mini-bus. It was a hot, sunny day but the clear blue skies were slightly blotted by the silhouette of the police helicopter circling overhead as our van approached Taunton. Little did we know it, but the 'chopper' was tracking Bibby's car a few miles ahead.

Apparently, Bibby, Gilly and the others had earlier staggered into a service station with a beer can in each hand. Concerned locals had informed the police that there was a drunk driver with a load of hooligans on the loose. As Bibby & Co were pulled pulled-over by two patrol cars with lights and sirens blazing. The police were happy to find the driver hadn't touched a drop and so on they went.

I met up with Bibby in the ground, and Rosie and I almost came to blows as I shouted my usual abuse at Paul Power and his usual struggle with lack of ability, as far as I was concerned. Rosie – who was *the* most irritating person I knew – was wearing a plaster-cast pot on his leg so I decided not to shove him down the concrete steps from the top of the stand.

After the match, Bibby and his car load headed straight back to Manchester. However, 'Potter's Tours' stayed on behind and the remaining eight 'likely lads' (minus Big Al) walked from the ground towards the bright lights of downtown Torquay in search of entertainment – as if a 0–0 draw on the south coast against a Fourth Division team wasn't enough for one night?

On Potter's bus that day was Neil 'Blinny' Blinston, a long-haired hippy looking lad who never took his City shirt off, even in the Town Hall where he worked in the collar-and-tie planning department. Blinny was a live caricature of the laid-back hippy Neil from *The Young Ones* except that he wasn't as soft. Neil's mate who accompanied him on 'Potter's Tours' was 'Simmo'. He was a thick-set lad sporting a severe and distinctive Mohican hairstyle with heavily gelled-up spikes. It made him look an intimidating prospect although he really was quite a cool bloke.

On our way into Torquay town centre, Simmo decided he needed a pee. He used the facilities of a huge front garden and relieved himself on the 'For Sale' sign stuck in the middle of a large lawn on which you could have landed a passenger plane. The local constabulary rounded us all up into the meat wagon. We were then unceremoniously whisked off to the cop shop and into a communal cell.

As we sat there awaiting our fate, Blinny realised that he was carrying a ready-rolled joint. It was decided that the best way of getting rid of it was to smoke it, and we did. You've never seen a spliff passed around so quickly. It was like playing pass the parcel with a hand grenade. Eventually, Simmo was the only person to be charged and had to revisit Torquay, a 420-mile round trip, on a trumped-up rap of 'Peeing on Posh Bloke's "For Sale" sign Without Due Care and Attention'. The case came two weeks later. Simmo took a consolatory block of weed he'd brought with him in preparation for the anticipated and inevitable train journey home. He decided to play it safe in case he was searched on his way into court (as it turned out he wasn't). He ducked into the gents at the station and placed his chunk out of sight high on the window ledge of a cubicle.

After picking up a hefty fine at the dock while dressed in a suit and tie sporting his outrageous Mohican haircut, he returned to the station bogs. To his horror, he found that workmen had decorated the gents from top to bottom, finding and removing his treasured block of black in the process. That pee cost him a day's pay, a £30-odd train fare, a £50 fine and a big block of Moroccan Black. At least City won the second leg 6–0 at Maine Road.

♦   ♦   ♦

At the start of that season, all Blues hoped that City would bounce back at the first attempt, but it soon became apparent that this was not to be. Ignominious defeat in the FA Cup on 7 January 1984 at Fourth Division Blackpool showed that we weren't ready to return to the big-time of the First Division. It was also a game which signalled our first fancy dress effort and one to which my dad terrified Eaton, Bibby and I with his woeful driving ability as he gave a graphic illustration of why it took him seven attempts to pass his test. Bibby suffered the most, screaming, 'Derek, roundabout, Derek, roundabout, DEREK ROUNDABOUT!!!' Finally my dad hit the brakes at the last moment having failed to see the incoming circular junction from at least half-a-mile away.

Despite failure to get promoted, City's new Caledonian manager Billy McNeill (or Neil McBelly as Bibby and I called him) did sign a number of promising players who were all Scottish. These included names such as Duncan Davidson, Gordon Dalziel, Jim Tolmie, Dominic Sullivan, Neil McNab and Gordon Smith – the latter missed a late sitter which would have been the winner for the seagulls of Brighton against United in the 1983 Cup final. Smith is now the Chief Executive of the Scottish FA. To be fair, Gordon Smith was a popular player for City and added some much needed extra class to our largely Caledonian team. His cup final miss was a pity in more than one way. . . .

The Friday night before that particular cup final, Bibby and I had stayed behind in work putting our cunning plan into action. We'd spent hours cutting out and pinning up huge cardboard seagulls all over the front of Manchester Town Hall's giant windows which fronted Albert Square in hopeful anticipation of a United defeat. It was to be our personal welcome home! Unfortunately, Piccadilly Radio DJ Suzie Mathis spotted our cardboard flock just before the United team arrived on the Sunday morning for their subdued homecoming having drawn the final. They were quickly removed, a pity really because the seagulls looked absolutely massive and brilliant. It would have been a great mickey-take but for the combined efforts from Gordon Smith and Suzie Mathis!

That 1983/84 season also witnessed John Eaton and I at our most prolific at getting into away games for half price. We'd head for the juniors then complain 'innocently' to the stewards or coppers about being in the wrong end. We were usually led out to safety and into the City end. We carried out this sketch at Grimsby that year. But once in the ground – contrary to usual practice – the police told us that it was our own fault and that we'd have to stay put in the home end. Not long into the game, Derek Parlane – a former Scotland striker who was a bit one-paced, but knew where the net was – banged in a belter at their end and ran off towards Eaton and me to celebrate. We both jumped onto the perimeter fence as we leapt in celebration knocking Grimsby fans all over the place. Within seconds, we were gripped by the police and led around the pitch over to the City end.

Several weeks later, John and I were sat in the dressing rooms at Lee Athletic when club manager Pete Moore came shuffling in. He'd just returned from a trip to Australia where he visited a one-boomerang town in the middle of the Australian outback. As he was sat in a bar, the English football from the previous day came on the box. City's game at Grimsby had been on *Match of the Day* and sure enough, when Parlane scored, Pete could see in crystal clear view Eaton and I celebrating the goal. All Peter could say was, 'All the way to the Australian outback and I still couldn't get rid of the flippin' pair of you.'

It was often comical watching City off-and-on the pitch – and sometimes both at the same time. On 17 March 1984 on a bright and breezy sunny spring afternoon, City played at Fulham who were way below us in the Second Division. This was also the day of the Oxbridge boat race and it wasn't just the Oxford boat that sank that day, City were thumped 5–1! Future City 'legend' Gordon Davies knocked in a hat-trick for the Cottagers. By the time the fifth went in, City's mass travelling army had long since lost interest. Instead they found better entertainment by hanging over the top of the back of the ground to watch a schoolboy game. Those young boys displayed a level of skill that was way in excess of anything City had shown that afternoon. The City supporters really got into the action cheering the team in blue. So much so that when a decision went against them from the referee (who was presumably a teacher), a chant of 'We all hate Sir' went up. Minutes later there was an invasion of the park pitch as some City fans ran off with the ball. It wasn't the nicest thing to do, but at the time it was absolutely hilarious. Following that for comedy was going to be difficult, but somehow City's Neil McNab managed to come close. At 5–0 down, 'Nabber' actually put one away for City to make it 5–1 and he ran off celebrating as if he'd just scored a late extra-time winner in the World Cup final. Although it was his first goal for the Blues, none of the City fans present could raise a smile never mind a round of applause and McNab's triumphant gestures to the crowd were met with total apathy.

City ended the season just out of the promotion places in fourth. The penultimate game was at Hillsborough where Sheffield Wednesday were neck-and-neck with Chelsea for the Second Division title. We arrived late on Potter's mini bus and we were all 'worse for wear' as we queued to get into the Leppings Lane End just before kick-off. We were squeezed into a cramped tunnel by the weight of those pushing behind us, forcing me straight into a tightly-packed pen at the front of the stand. Four years later the Blues were away at Blackburn and as

City were getting thumped 4–0, news came through that there were serious crowd problems at the FA Cup semi-final between Liverpool and Nottingham Forest. I commented to Bibby, 'I'll bet it's at that end where we got crushed against Sheffield Wednesday.' Unfortunately it was the same spot.

◆   ◆   ◆

Season 1984/85 was a big bag of laughs and began with a 2–2 draw at Wimbledon's modest Plough Lane ground. By the time we played at Brighton in November, City were in a decent position. For some reason it was decided that we'd go to Brighton away in fancy dress. I was dressed as 'The Invisible Jock' in my older sister's kilt, a knackered old pair of Doc Marten boots, a shirt and tie, a pair of odd socks and a stack of bandages. I also wore a pair of sunglasses and a bowler hat!

There were only about twelve of us on the trip, with half having the courage to dress up as daft as possible (a task not too difficult for those in regular clothing). I attempted to enter the ground via the junior turnstile in my 'Invisible Jock' outfit. Not only could the turnstile operator see me, but he spotted the beer stains around my bandaged mouth. I ended up paying full price in the visitors end and City managed a 1–1 draw.

After the success of the first fancy dress trip, Bibby went into full swing sorting out next season's excursion to Brighton. He hired a fifty-eight-seater coach which arrived at the Cornishman Pub Disco at midnight on the Friday. At this time we were all suitably mellow while 'Travolta-ing' it in the in full fancy dress. There were all sorts of characters such as 'the Black Adder', 'the Pink Panther' and 'Casey Jones'. There were knights in shining armour, two American footballers and even a 'Deputy Dawg'. My former Chorlton and college mate Steve Graham went in a Kenny Everett type suit which was totally cut away at the back revealing women's lingerie. His girlfriend went in a nurse's outfit also in stockings and suspenders. Believe me, she looked far more attractive as a woman than John Eaton who'd turned up in his mam's slippers, nightie and dressing gown with a brown wig and a couple of days' stubble on is face. My favourite was little Billy Kenny, who went as a boxer, complete with silk dressing gown which had the words 'Paper Weight' stitched on the back. Bibby and I were dressed as Laurel and Hardy, complete with green dungarees shirt and tie/dicky bow, masks and bowler hats; mine being authentic, unlike the plastic moulded version sported by Bibby. The bus left for Brighton in the dead of night with everyone in buoyant mood having boarded straight from the Cornishman. But minutes before we'd reached motorway, John Eaton grabbed the bowler hat from off my head and threw up in it.

The trip lives in the memory for many reasons. I was forced to wake up Terry Hyland, an American footballer who'd fallen asleep on the bog during a touchdown. After a long and challenging drinking session, the bus took us to the ground where the coppers didn't always see the funny side of fifty-four drunken Mancunians in fancy dress. We were requested to leave boxing gloves, crash helmets, cardboard swords, polystyrene clubs, toy pistols and plastic machine guns behind some bushes near to the bus, for fear we might attack the Brighton fans. Half of us could hardly stand up let alone cause trouble. The bus was parked near a recreation area close to the ground, which was frequented by a waggle of 'winos'. It was hilarious watching them rubbing their eyes and dropping their bottles in disbelief as various cartoon characters disembarked from the coach and walked nonchalantly towards the ground.

As usual, City let us down on the pitch, mustering an uninspiring 0–0 draw. Our coach load caused more amusement than the match and I only managed to get an idea of how fantastic we looked once the game had ended. When we came out of the ground the bus had been moved and we had to walk down the main road. I'd gone on ahead and was in the queue in a chip shop as 'Shag' walked past. He was dressed as Deputy Dawg, but he had his body on back to front thus making his tail look like his todger as he marched down the middle of the road proudly swinging it as if it were his own. He was followed by a gorilla, a viking and a Mickey Vernon who was riding an emu singing 'We are City, super City from Maine Road' despite him being a Manchester United fan.

On the way home, after Mike Greenwood had tried to set fire to several costumes while their wearers were asleep, we stopped off at Coventry for a few beers. This was coincidently the same city to which Millsy had moved the previous week to set up residence for his forthcoming degree course at Coventry University. As he was unfamiliar with his new surroundings, he made the decision to come with us and return to Coventry the next day fearing that he wouldn't be able to find his new digs. When he arrived all the way back from Manchester the following day, he was horrified to see that the pub he'd been in the night before was in fact his local and he could have been at his new flat within a 2-minute walk.

♦   ♦   ♦

Four days before the Brighton trip, City had been away in the League Cup against First Division West Ham. Upton Park was always a dodgy place to go as I'd learnt from past experiences with the jump leads sketch, but it didn't stop Bibby and I going in the Hammers' end in order to get in at half-price. I'd regularly come across West Ham's ICF (Inter City Firm) on my travels with England, and knew we needed to keep our mouths shut. The problem was we didn't get a transfer from the West Ham end and, after about 10 minutes City got a throw-in taken by Paul Power down by the corner flag. He looked up, recognised Bibby and I and waved to us! Everyone looked at us in an accusing way, but we looked at the nearest person to blame, and nobody pinned us down. We'll never really know whether or not Paul Power was waving at *us*, but he could have inadvertently exacted revenge on me for all the rubbish I had shouted at him throughout the years. City won the game 2–1 with goals from Steve Kinsey and Tony Cunningham and we were in the next round, again in London, at Chelsea.

In those days Stamford Bridge was vastly different in shape and atmosphere than the multi-tiered view-obscured stadium it is today. The ground had an eerie graveyard-like atmosphere which added to my overall sense of foreboding of the place. It also had a fearsome reputation for violence. However, that didn't deter John Eaton, who insisted on trying the half-price junior ploy in the Chelsea end. It was the last time he would try it. After my near miss with Bibby at Upton Park I had second thoughts. Even so, I might have taken a chance with John but I was twenty-two and looking decidedly older than fifteen, the West Ham experience having aged me somewhat. But John was a couple of years younger and he thought he could still get away with the junior admittance fee.

Getting caught wasn't the primary concern. My main worry was that the Chelsea end was the infamous 'Shed' and home of every nutter in West London, or so I thought. I was soon to realise there were plenty of other nutters located in the east side of the ground. Once the game kicked off, John quietly let it be known to the police that he was a City fan who'd somehow come in the wrong end. But he was quickly sussed by some Chelsea fans and was quickly ejected from the Shed accompanied by two coppers with a mob of irate locals interested in tearing him apart, limb from limb. We could see John's look of terror even from our far-away vantage point at the top of the large, open away end. He was as white as a sheet. It was hilarious to see the visibly shaken John Eaton walk pastey-faced into the City section to a hero's welcome that he didn't deserve.

But that was the only relief we had. City were 4–0 down at half time, although it could have been worse, Chelsea had also missed a penalty. John, Bibby and I called it a day at half time deciding to nip into the pub only to find it packed with like-minded City fans.

Despite the League Cup exit, and the FA Cup exit at a freezing cold Coventry, by the time the end of the season approached City were well placed for promotion. Our main rivals were Portsmouth, who we played at Fratton Park with only four games to go. We travelled on a double-decker bus hired by Dominic Cosseron at the height of the popper-sniffing craze. We literally fell off the bus at Pompey. It was only a few minutes before we managed to lose Bibby only to find him being marched around the side of the ground. He revealed that he hadn't gone in there on the usual half-price act; he just didn't know where he was, being wasted on other people's fumes from the bus. The cops weren't going to let him out until he put his hands in the air and shouted 'Come on City' at the top of his voice.

After the match we all got lost in search of the bus. Eaton, Bibby, Millsy and I were wandering around Fratton Park only to be stopped by some kind-hearted coppers. They knew there was a heavy mob just around the corner waiting for away stragglers. The cops put us in the back of their van and drove us around the ground to the visitors' car park. Millsy was that drunk he thought he was in a taxi and insisted we had a whip round for the driver. The police constable was not amused. He was even less happy moments later when Millsy got out said 'Cheers mate' to the driver and immediately relieved himself on the side of the police van in the middle of the High Street.

City's 1–0 win set up promotion, but we then stuttered to a 0–0 draw at home to Oldham. However, all was not lost. The following Easter weekend presented City with another opportunity to gain promotion at Notts County, who had already been relegated. But in typical City fashion, the Blues lost 3–2, in a game that saw a pitch invasion when Justin 'He's black, he's sound, he's worth a million pound' Fashanu scored County's third. The next day Eaton and Mills had their pictures all over the Sunday papers as they'd somehow wandered into the City dressing room during the 'riot' and were shown coming out looking totally bemused. After all, they had been inhaling 'Big D' gas and Zoff Floor Cleaner all the way to Nottingham on the mini bus.* Apparently they'd sought refuge in City's changing room from a giant meat pie with arms and legs which had chased them across the pitch while wielding one of the corner flags. Both ended up with First Class Honours degrees a few years later. Daft but not thick.

The following game produced the best success at City I had experienced, the date being 11 May 1985, the day we were finally promoted after two years in the wilderness of League Division Two. City faced Charlton Athletic at Maine Road and 2 points would foil Portsmouth's aspirations for second spot. It would also give City revenge for the 1926/27 season when Pompey 'pipped' City to promotion by six two-millionths of a goal, (or something like that). John, Bibby and I set off for the match laden with cheap fizz, in readiness to celebrate. We gathered in our usual spot at the top of the Kippax near 'windy corner' and witnessed the Blues' triumphant return to the First Division with an emphatic 5–1 victory. City were 'Back in the Big Time' and the nightmare of Division Two was over for good, or so I thought.

♦   ♦   ♦

The following Monday, I was in the snooker club on Oxford Road (now The Cornerhouse Cinema), during my lunch break when I bumped into City player Jim Tolmie at the bar. Despite my better judgement I let on and, still euphoric from the promotion, I enquired, 'Hey Jim, did you enjoy it on Saturday, it was brilliant wasn't it?' Mr Tolmie – who hadn't played through injury – looked at me with his Marty Feldman-like nomadic eyes and said, 'Aye, I suppose it was alright.' I knew I should have known better than to let on to a footballer and encourage almost certain disappointment in his response. Jim Tolmie never played for City again. After such an unenthusiastic answer, I can't say that I was too bothered, despite the fact that he was a very good player.

....

* This was about the time when the infamous 'Glue Tune' was composed by those great lyricists 'Nasher' and Marky Morgan to the tune of 'Singing the Blues'. It went:

Oh I never felt more like sniffin' the glue,

With a Lewis's bag, and a tube of UHU,

Oh City, you got me sniffin' the glue!

30

Courting Success

By the time Jane and I started dating, my short-term outlook on City began to change. I'd realised that I couldn't carry on watching the Blues both home and away with total abandon for the rest of my life without having to make sacrifices. I had plenty of 'mates' but I needed a literal one from the opposite sex, as is a young man's wont.

Football means different things to different people and Jane had a limited concept of football and its importance to a fanatic like me. It was difficult to explain my compulsion of travelling 'all over the show' to watch City being beaten at most of the dilapidated and archaic First and Second Division grounds of the day. Understandably, she couldn't see the attraction of my spending all my spare cash on a dodgy football team that had little or no prospects of improvement. Despite this irrational behaviour, she still allowed to me get on with it and this was one of her many endearing features. It wasn't that Jane asked me to put the brakes on my travels. In that regard, she couldn't have been more accommodating. Putting a stop to going to *every* game City played was a decision I made for myself.

Jane's LBW (Life Before Worthy) had a virtual omission of the 'beautiful game' and her naïvety in all things football was almost legendary, despite her dad being a Blue. At one point in the 1950s, before severe hostilities broke out between the two sets of fans, Steve O'Dwyer went to City one week and United the next. He was not alone and it was a common practice in its day (although not a concept to which my dad ever subscribed).

Despite her apparent football naïvety Jane always knew better than to assert that football is 'only a game'. To her eternal credit, since our meeting, she always sticks up for City in an argument, despite not knowing much about the Blues. But she does know that City last won the FA Cup in 1969 and that City's best ever player was Francis Bell – or was it Colin Lee? Jane has been to a match at Maine Road, just the once (due to my tried and trusted hair-and-eye-make-up-wrecking tactic) and she even witnessed a Scotland v England game at Hampden Park on 27 May 1989. I don't know why she made the journey; perhaps I needed her petrol money? She wasn't overly impressed with England's 2–0 victory, despite Steve Bull's rare goal in a lilywhite shirt. In fact, she was more entertained by the emergence of the Scottish pipe band during the interval.

It's not just football she doesn't care about. Cricket is a complete mystery. In addition, she doesn't drink to excess and would never contemplate eating a vindaloo or indeed a more sedate 'pie on barm'. Furthermore, Jane can't abide my love of Indie music. For her, it's more a choice of crooners such as Frank Sinatra, Tom Jones or Michael Bublé (AKA Mickey Bubbles).

When Jane and I officially became 'an item' I realised that she was the girl for me. There were indeed plenty of fish in the sea, but there weren't too many that swam in my direction – particularly on Fridays, when I was usually floating in ale. Having found a good catch, I didn't want it to slip through the net or put another promising relationship in jeopardy. It might have been more difficult for me to give up my unbroken six-season attendance streak, but previous experience told me that I shouldn't miss out on a 'top bird' for a second time due to my misguided loyalty to the beautiful game.

A negative experience of a different sort at Ipswich Town on 12 April 1986 helped me decide a way forward. By this time, John Eaton had all but given up on away games. This left me with Bibby and new boy Stew Freeman, to enjoy the not-so-glamorous away-game circuit without John's amusing but often dubious charms. For some reason Bibby didn't go to Portman Road. It turned out to be a blessing in disguise.

Stew and I had decided to make a variation on the fancy dress sketch and spent most of the day with our clothes on back-to-front. We imaginatively called it 'back-to-front day'. It was an innovative concept, but it didn't really work. Unless your clothes are ten sizes too big, it's really difficult to do up the buttons and make them fit properly when wearing them the wrong way round. On arrival in the away end car park, I was relieving myself against a fence (as you do), when I was hit by a volley of punches from behind. I quickly turned round and instinctively returned with a couple of useful digs of my own before being forcibly separated from my attacker, Ron Pryor.

Ron was a few years older and had been a notorious football hooligan during the 1960s, or so he told us. But after years of minibus ridicule his hard-man reputation had somewhat diminished. He'd become quite the figure of fun between me Bib, Shay, Dave Parr and Roy Nutter (I'm not big on tattoos but Roy Nutter had the most impressive decorative scar I've ever seen; he tattooed 'City' on the inside of his own bottom lip with India ink and a pin. It was incredibly neat seeing as though he'd done it upside down and back-to-front using his bathroom mirror).

During a post-match beer stop on the way back from a 0–0 draw, I confronted my assailant and it transpired that Pryor had only attacked me in the absence of Bibby, his number-one target. Apparently, his pent-up anger had taken him to the malevolent decision, as he put it, that, 'I was going to have a go at Bibby because I was sick of all the stick I was getting on the minibus.' Although most of the jokes at his expense were good-natured, we did have a propensity to go over-the-top, particularly under the influence. His annoyance was somewhat understandable to a degree. But then again, it wasn't our fault that, 'Ron Pryor, Ron Pryor', rhymes with, 'His arse is up for hire'. His threats and actions hadn't intimidated me to the point of being scared, but they did contribute to my eventual decision to sack Potter's minibus. I needed a push to stop my away-game obsession and, although the flurry of windmill punches left no physical scars (as most of them missed), they did have a contributory effect. I was deflated by the incident and didn't bother going to the next away game at Newcastle.

After this unfortunate episode, my away days in the 1980s were never the same again. My dismal record at Southampton's old ground, The Dell, summed up how I felt. I'd been down to that dump no less than eight times and City had lost on each occasion. It was getting to the stage where I was starting to wonder how many times I needed to visit such places before I'd finally get some satisfaction.

♦ ♦ ♦

Not going to *every* away game also allowed an opportunity to concentrate on other things. As consolation for not going to the World Cup in Mexico 1986, I ventured on my first non-football lads' foreign holiday that summer. For £100 Bibby secured me a fortnight in Ibiza on a Club 18–30s sketch with Bugsy and a dozen others.

Every night I was tormented by our Cockney brethren to the point of total distraction. You could easily tell who was from the South and who was from the North. The Southerners drank halves and chatted up the women while the Northerners sank pints and chatted up the pavements. One night my patience was wearing thin and I'd warned Bibby that, 'If I hear another story from a Southerner about how many women he's shagged on this holiday, I think I'll flip my lid.' Right on cue, we were joined at the bar by a couple of Cockneys who were quick to strike up a friendly conversation with us. Sure enough within a few minutes they were onto the subject of women, telling us both about their numerous conquests during their brief vacation. Finally they changed the subject to politics. I hadn't uttered a word so far, but they sociably tried to bring me in.

'Well mate, what do ya fink of the old North/South divide then?' he enquired. I replied, 'It's not 'kin wide enough mate. Now please "go forth" and shag some imaginary women.' In hindsight I was more than rude and was lucky not to get a smack in the chops. But sometimes, enough is enough. Besides, there were fifteen lads in our party and not one of them had got as far as undoing a bra strap. After all, they are quite tricky to negotiate, whether you've had a few or not.

♦　♦　♦

1986 was also the year when I saw arguably Manchester's greatest band, The Smiths. Their gig at Salford University on 20 July was described as: 'seminal' (a word often overused by the music press, but its adoption was totally accurate on this occasion). Four of us went to this gig armed with one original and three 'hooky' tickets that I'd photocopied onto pink paper and perforated with a scalpel. This was the tried and trusted method of getting into many a set at the Manchester Apollo during the mid-1980s, until they adopted computerised photocopy-resistant versions.

However, we saw buckshee performances from some of the great bands of the day, including U2 on their 'Unforgettable Fire' tour of 1984. On the second night of that sell-out weekend, we even had the cheek to flog a couple of photocopies to the touts at an over-inflated price. Meanwhile, at the impressive Smiths' gig, Stew Freeman managed to slide past the doormen on his dodgy pink copy, but Flynny was caught (our only ever knock-back during the whole ticket reproduction era). We always had the plan if we were ever caught to plead, 'I've just paid a fortune for this ticket off a tout,' so passing the blame in the event of possible recriminations. After the gig we found Stewart's car had been broken into and our coats stolen . . . except for Flynny's! Three of us were gutted at our loss, but we had a laugh at Flynny's expense, because they hadn't bothered taking his leather jacket, presumably because it was so shabby. By the time we got home, Flynny was indignant his coat hadn't been nicked!

The 1980s was an excellent decade for freebie gigs. Having gained promotion at work to the post of Trainee Committee Administrator, my job was to write minutes and sort out committee agendas. One of the committees to which I was assigned was the Maine Road Consultative. This body had been set up jointly by MCFC and the City Council to provide a vehicle for local residents to raise issues of concern and generally have a moan about the fact that the ground attracted large crowds thus causing them inconvenience. My main contact with City was with director Chris Muir – a jolly Scottish chap. It wasn't difficult to like this amiable fella; not only did he have an easy-going manner, but he also had an obvious love of City, and told me that he was also a Hearts fan before he moved down south – a fine combination if ever there was one.

During this time, the club had started promoting lucrative outdoor concerts at Maine Road and – on Mr Muir's insistence – I was provided with tickets for all the gigs because, as he put it, 'How will ye know what the residents are talking about at meetings if ye have nae seen it for yeself?' Sound logic, but the other three tickets he gave me every time were presumably in case I missed something and my mates could point it out later. Watching a gig from most vantage points within a football stadium is not the best and probably wouldn't have been my choice but for Mr Muir's generosity. From the stand, bands look as big as ants so you inevitably end up watching the set on the big screen. If I want to watch a band on telly, I can stay at home and watch a video. But because of this nice little outlet, on separate occasions, I got to see David Bowie, the Rolling Stones and the Stranglers. I could have seen Pink Floyd and the artist formerly known as Prince, but I didn't want to lose my street cred. I couldn't even give the Prince tickets away! One band I reluctantly went to watch was Fleetwood Mac. Our Julie used to play their *Rumours* album incessantly. Familiarity had bred a grudging tolerance towards it and I took Jane that night thinking that we might have some common musical ground for enjoyment. We sat impassively on the cold, dusty, haemorrhoid-inducing concrete Kippax terrace.

Towards the end of the gig, lead singer Stevie Nicks asserted, 'This has been the best night of my life,' to which Jane dryly replied, 'She must have had some pretty grim nights then,' which summed up exactly how we felt about the show.

Later that year I also saw The Smiths at the Free Trade Hall for the second and last time. Once again they provided the sombre background music to even more personal trauma; City were relegated back to Division Two. It took another couple of seasons before we returned from the Second Division, which meant a few more new grounds to visit, not least Millwall at The Den in December 1987. This was my first visit to Cold Blow Lane: a place that proved to be about as warm and friendly as a North Korean border patrol. On our way into Bermondsey, an ordinary-looking bloke, standing at a bus stop with his young son, picked up a dustbin from outside an adjacent wine bar and hurled it at our stationary coach. As the bin crashed against the glass window, his son continued munching impassively on a bag of chips as if this was normal behaviour from his dad.

The hospitable 'Welcome to Millwall' dustbin message proved to be the start of an eventful day. Rosie had made his own way up in the car with 'Laughing Les' Hare, owner of the legendary King Bee record shop in Chorlton. Unfortunately, Rosie didn't see the game. He was knocked out cold while walking around the ground, without even opening his mouth or displaying any colours. When he came back to the land of the living, Rosie found himself in an apartment in an adjacent block of flats to which he'd been carried by a couple of local Samaritans. He later described it as starring in his own mini episode of the soap opera *EastEnders*. Once he'd been bandaged up and had enjoyed a plate of jellied eels, followed by pie 'n' mash and a good ol' sing-song on the old Joanna, he was out of the door and back in Manchester with a sore head and an equally sore stomach later in the day.

The injured Rosie was pals with City striker Paul Simpson who later told him that the police had warned the City players not to celebrate a goal as they could be in mortal danger. The dirty Den was undoubtedly the most intimidating place I'd visited to date and what arguably made matters worse was that City had the audacity to win 1–0, thanks to a solitary Tony Adcock goal just before the break. At the end of the match the Millwall fans – located on the terraced bank at the side of the ground – didn't budge an inch. Their dark, shadowy silhouettes remained rooted while defiantly chanting, 'WAR, WAR, WAR'. This came as the majority of the away fans stood there nervously twitching in a well-protected and fenced-off pen. I remember with a smile our defiant riposte of, 'We're gonna get our 'kin heads kicked in!' It has been my experience over the years that City fans can usually find good humour even in the darkest of situations.

Eventually, the Millwall mob was forcibly moved by the police, but the ordeal still wasn't over. The cops led us behind the back of the main stand to where the coaches had moved, just to keep the Millwall mob guessing. It was a covert operation, which proved successful, and so we got home in one piece, as did the coach.

♦   ♦   ♦

In 1987/88 City were out of the promotion places. I was back going to most of the away games in the car. One that sticks in the mind was the first trip of the new season to Oldham Athletic. It was a bright, sunny August day. But we could see from a distance, *the* darkest clouds imaginable rolling towards us. It was as if they were announcing the arrival of doomsday the shading was so sinister. Meanwhile the 16,008 fans were enjoying the 1–1 draw in sunglasses and short-sleeved shirts. The Caribbean weather was swiftly pushed aside by an Indian monsoon. Within less than a minute I couldn't have been any wetter had I dived into a swimming pool fully clothed.

After the game there was nothing for it but to strip off down to our underpants for the journey back to the Jolly Angler in Manchester. Bibby, John Eaton, Millsy, Stew and I piled out looking like highly-toned lifeguards. Our chiselled muscular torsos must have impressed Joe Public, well apart from the image of Millsy and Eaton playing pool in their damp Y-fronts. Not a pretty sight.

♦   ♦   ♦

The following year City made it back into Division One. By then the music scene in Manchester had changed. The Stone Roses were on their way to being top dogs following the acrimonious split of The Smiths. My attention had first focussed on The Stone Roses as their names had been daubed all over town by graffiti 'artists' – not least on the Town Hall extension where I now worked. Our office junior at the time was a lad called Tony Jefferson (later to become Anthony Jefferson and then Anthony H. Jefferson). He was a young Northern Moor music protégé who was clued up on all the latest bands. Tony had acquired a demo cassette tape of The Roses, which must have been copied to the limit. When we first saw them at Legends in Warrington in November 1988 they hadn't yet released their eponymous debut album, but the lucky 200 present knew all the words by heart.

There are a few things about that *seminal* night (as no doubt the music press would have said had any of them been there). Before we went into the gig's glamorous venue – which was, in reality, a room in Warrington Rugby League Club's Social Club – we visited a nearby pub. This was full of trendy-looking teenage Mancs who made me feel really old, even though I was only just on the wrong side of my mid-twenties. It was perhaps my first awareness that I was no longer a carefree spotty youth. I took the opportunity to get them back for this inadvertent offence by going around the pub asking most of them in an overly deep Lancashire accent that was probably well wide of the native dialect, 'Anyone know 'ow bloody Wires went on t'nite?' None of them knew what on earth I was on about. Milking disdainful looks from haughty individuals has become a bit of a hobby of mine over the years.

It was soon evident that I was in the presence of greatness. Before the end of the first track, we'd managed to shove our way right to the front and within touching distance of the band that was inadequately elevated on the shallow stage. By the time lead guitarist John Squire edged a half-smoked spliff towards Ian Brown during 'I Wanna Be Adored', I'd intercepted it, took a drag and passed it on to the now-grinning frontman. It was a great rock 'n' roll moment for me. Years later this was arguably topped when I signed an autograph at the request of a young rock chic, having been mistaken for a member of the mighty Manchester outfit Puressence. I was collared as I re-emerged from their dressing room having sneaked backstage with Eaton for a chat. I obligingly signed, 'All the best, Worthy'.

The night after Warrington, I took Jane to see The Stone Roses at The International on Plymouth Grove, and even she was moved to comment, 'They weren't too bad. At least a bit better than your usual rubbish.' It was high praise from one who would rather listen to a mixed tape of road works and nail-scratching on a blackboard than be subjected to my personal harmonic bliss. The next gig we attended as a couple was at the Manchester Academy 2 where headliners the Happy Mondays did a pathetically short set where they messed about on stage for a mere 40 minutes. Smiths' bassist Andy Rourke shook his head as we all filed out of the hall, feeling thoroughly cheated and dejected.

I saw The Stone Roses three more times before their premature demise, choosing not to go to the now-legendary open-air gig at Spike Island, near Widnes. I swerved it because they now had a massive following and I preferred to see 'my' bands at small venues with small crowds.

◆   ◆   ◆

City's promotion at the back end of the 1980s was accompanied by a craze that was to temporarily sweep the country, inflatable toys on the terraces. A few bananas had appeared during the previous term and this wasn't just among the playing staff. By the time of the first away game of the new term, on a sunny day at Hull City's Boothferry Park, the craze had blown out of all proportion. It was a bizarre spectacle to see masses of inflatable toys of every type size and shape appearing at City games, including the odd paddling pool. These unique exhibits gave a light-hearted side to what was a serious season for the Blues. In fact, it became so light-hearted that plans were afoot to make the Boxing Day game at Stoke in 1988 something rather special.

There were 24,056 at the old Victoria Ground, of which it appeared half were Blues, with the vast majority in fancy dress. Never one to miss an opportunity to dress up, I went to that game in full tuxedo, dicky bow and cummerbund. I'd previously bought this 'get-up' for the polytechnic celebrations at the Last Drop Village, which had been held for those who'd passed their Batchelor of Arts qualifications. After all my trials and tribulations at school, I'd come through with a creditable educational qualification: a decent honours degree. It was only a 2:2 'gentlemen's degree' in the highly coveted subject of Public Administration, and acquired with the minimal effort. I could have attained a 2:1 had my thesis not been inexplicably downgraded from 65 per cent to 59 per cent by the external examiner. How could I complain? I'd got there in the end and, consequently and perhaps more importantly, I had a ready-made bonus fancy dress outfit to wear at the match!

I went to Stoke as a 'Hooray Henry' complete with slicked-back hair, pencil moustache and an oversized inflatable bottle of champers. The police also caught the act. They displayed inflatable bananas on the dashboards of their vans in acknowledgement. The number of Blues in fancy dress was staggering and, perhaps, the most surreal moment arrived when I was having a pee in the pungent Victorian bog just before half time. As usual, City were losing and some bloke commented rhetorically in the obligatory slurred voice that, 'This game is rubbish. They always let you down, don't they?' Finally I looked up to see the Pink Panther nonchalantly staggering out as if we were both dressed in normal attire.

However, City didn't ultimately let us down. Promotion was achieved in the final match at Bradford City after we'd almost thrown it away the week before. Such was the unbearable tension at Valley Parade that I almost fainted at 1–0 down when we needed at least a draw to go up. The week before City had been 3–0 up at home to Bournemouth, when a victory would have assured promotion. But one of their players (a certain Ian Bishop), orchestrated a Cherries' comeback of Lazarus-like proportions as the game ended 3–3. Bishop was so impressive that the Blues signed him during the close-season. City managed a point at Bradford thanks to Trevor Morley and we returned home on the M62 cock-a-hoop.

♦   ♦   ♦

With Ian Bishop on board for the next effort to stay in Division One in 1989/90, things were on the up. Indeed Bish was on hand to pull the strings for perhaps City's most famous victory in the 1980s: the 5–1 demolition of United at Maine Road on 23 September 1989. However, it wasn't the best performance of the decade. The 10–1 home thrashing of Huddersfield Town – together with the resulting teary, high-pitched, post-match voice of Town's manager Malcolm 'Supermac' MacDonald – arguably gave the most satisfaction.

It also occurs to me that to state that your best win is against United is to over-inflate their importance and, besides, we couldn't hang on to the lofty bragging rights for as long as I'd have liked. My best memory of 'The Maine Road Massacre' was Andy Hinchcliffe's, 'chance at the far post,' which he converted to make it five. After the game, Jane picked me up outside Maine Road. We were driving towards home when I spotted Lee Athletic's Pear Tree Mob, with heads bowed, forlornly trudging along the tree-shrouded pathway that hugs the side of Wythenshawe Park. They were all Reds who'd left early to avoid further humiliation and embarrassment. I got Jane to stop about 30 yards ahead and gave them some suitably creative verbal abuse with accompanying hand gestures from a distance at which they couldn't hope to catch up with me, even though they tried. It was tremendous. Once they got close enough I jumped into the car and got Jane to stop another 30 yards on and the whole process repeated itself until they finally gave up.

The next day they'd all calmed down and I met them prior to the Lee Athletic home game. Big Red Andy Smith was apoplectic as he impatiently waited to get some serious grief from my direction. But I purposefully said nothing before, during or after the game in the dressing room. By the time we got to the Brooklands Tap for a traditional post-match beer, he was almost at bursting point and shouted, 'For God's sake Worthy, will you get it over and done with and let me have *it*!?' I realised he'd suffered enough of my provocative silence and so I gave *it* him big style.

The following Monday came the *pièce de résistance*. I was walking through the city centre during my lunch break when I noticed a chauffeur-driven black limo pulling up at the traffic lights just in front of me. Sitting in the back was United manager, Alan Ferguson (name changed to protect anonymity). I caught his eye by smiling and putting the thumbs up, to which he returned in similar fashion. I smiled once more while subtly changing my hand gesture to a wide-open-palm-full-digit-salute. As I did this I exaggeratingly mouthed 'five' in the same manner as Hinchcliffe had during the game to Reds in the Kippax. His car pulled off as the lights changed and, to be fair, he smiled and jokingly put his roadmap-face in his hands. It was the final satisfaction of the ultimate weekend. Like all true City fans I'm magnanimous in defeat, but a supreme mickey-taker in victory.

31

My Flat Mate

Towards the end of the 1980s living at home was becoming tedious and claustrophobic. Mum and I weren't seeing eye-to-eye on most things and by now I'd outgrown my far from spacious box-room; I was looking to fly from the family nest. Besides, my mother was beginning to suss out that the pungent aroma emanating from underneath my locked door wasn't that of my stale socks (as I had so vehemently protested on a regular basis). Several years later our next-door neighbour, Mrs Steele, asked, 'How's it going Steve? Are you still smoking that marry Joanna stuff?'

'No,' I replied. 'How did you know I used to?'

'Because you would blow the smoke out of your bedroom window, and the wind would take it straight into our bedroom. It always gave me and our Bob a laugh.'

'I'll bet it did,' I replied.

When I'd weighed up moving out in the past, the pros always outweighed the cons. These boiled down to the fact that living at home was cheap. As early as 1984 I went as far as considering the purchase of an end terrace in Didsbury. This was located right next to the Albert pub, in front of the old Heald's Dairy from whence an armada of milk floats ponderously invaded South Manchester every morning amid a clinking cacophony of glass bottles. My main motive was not for an early investment in what would be an increasingly valuable asset, but instead was to be near to Fobs Wine Bar. This was my regular Friday night haunt where Rosie was the DJ and he played the Mancunian gear I enjoyed. Indeed, every weekend was a Smiths, James and New Order fest. The price of the property I fancied was around 33,000 beer tokens. This might not sound a lot. But it would have meant virtually all my money going into the place with little manoeuvre for anything else, so I sacked the idea. Who needs that sort of weight and responsibility at the tender age of twenty-two?

By the time the new decade arrived I was twenty-eight and somewhere along the line I had matured into a fully-grown adult, not that my mum had noticed. In all probability her angst was mostly because I was still underfoot and had outstayed my welcome. I started looking at local authority luxury apartments within the Northern Moor area (AKA Council flats in Wivvy).

I'd just been promoted to a post in Cheshire County Council and I had more money in my pocket; theoretically, at least, as most of it went on increased petrol costs on the daily 70-mile round trip to Chester. I was allocated a top floor 'penthouse' flat at 45 Hazelhurst Walk. The rent was cheap and it was only a couple of minutes away from my mum's. As a boy I had delivered Sunday morning papers to this humble abode and now I was to reside here. I had come a long way in life.

My individual dwelling was located within a chip-stone grey, water-stained two-storey block of six. Although the lobby and stairwells usually reeked of the acrid combination of cat wee and stale refuse, once through the door, the apartments were deceptively spacious. They had real potential for a palatial life . . . well, in comparison to the cramped confines of my box-room at Greenham Road.

Jane's mum, Joan, and her sister 'Aunty Eileen' – both in their mid-sixties – decorated the place with a job lot of Next wallpaper that had fallen off the back of a lorry! Consequently, the rolls were ruffled around the edges and a bit grubby as it had been raining that day, but they looked nice enough once hung. One of the main pieces in the jigsaw came when the sky blue lounge carpet was fitted on the Friday before the weekend I was to move in.

At that time the suite and the furniture hadn't been acquired. On the way home from the pub while walking in far from straight lines, Terry Hyland and I decided to go to my new flat for a chat. Terry couldn't resist a fag despite the new decorating and I allowed it, but I was soon to adopt a no-smoking policy once I officially moved in. I ended up crashing in the flat that night as Terry went home. The next day I woke up face down on the floor, dribbling onto my new lounge carpet. Consequently, I admired my beautiful new shag-pile at very close quarters, only to spot from a wider view, Terry's fag butt sitting in a plastic beaker on the floor within reach. Unfortunately, I soon discovered that *his* dimp had burnt straight through the beaker and down through the carpet. It left a brown crater which resembled the top of a large, burnt-out volcano amid a Nylon sea of MCFC blue, as viewed from an elevated helicopter vantage point. Still not completely sober from the night before, I marched round to Terry's house, knocking him up to demand that he make it right, while exclaiming like a big girl, 'My beautiful new carpet's ruined and I haven't even moved in yet!' Terry replied in his usual casual manner, 'I don't know what you're moanin' about. At least I didn't burn down the whole block!'

Terry being Terry – coolness personified – he soon calmed me down with his simple and mercurial plan to make good. Once the suite arrived, we would place it where the hole could be covered. However, before it arrived, we realised that there was no way that the couch could be placed over the hole without having to sit two feet from the gas fire. Terry's next bright idea was to collect the loose bits of wool from the edges of the carpet and glue them into the hole. He reckoned the final repair job looked great but, in reality, a blind man would have spotted it. If not, he would have tripped over the mound. Once the glue had dried, the patch swelled up to leave a small blue hill which I later christened 'Wool Mountain'.

Before you could say, 'I'm off to Habitat to pick up some dodgy furniture off my mate who works there,' I had a tidy bachelor pad all to myself . . . well, technically at least. Jane and I had been going steady for almost four years and we were engaged to be married but we decided against living together. This was out of the question even if we'd wanted to. Her mum and dad had old-fashioned morals and I was more than happy to respect these. Besides, Jane stayed over most weekends, allowing me space during the week to chill . . . and then warm up again when I had enough money to turn on the central heating.

I have to say, it was a happy existence living on my 'Jack Jones'. If I made a mess I had to tidy it up; it was nobody else's fault or responsibility but my own. I could cook whatever I wanted, when I wanted (mostly thanks to my prospective mother-in-law Joan, who kept the larder and freezer well stocked with tins and home-made pies). I could also listen to music whenever I wanted to and at a decent volume. The Stone Roses, the Mock Turtles, Echobelly, the Psychedelic Furs, the Charlatans, Ride and particularly Public Image just weren't done justice by spinning their respective vinyl discs quietly. I could also drink whenever I wanted to and leave the bog seat up all the time without my younger sister moaning. In short, my new existence was 'slobberific' male bliss.

Virtually every Friday night Terry would come back to the flat after we'd fallen out of the pub which, in those days, was usually the Carters Arms in Sale Moor. We could chat, drink and, in his case, smoke until the early hours, as I'd usually lift the smoking curfew when drinking. Besides, I'd learnt my lesson and bought several new ashtrays. I was living the carefree life that was my utopia – until Jane was due round and I had to commence the weekly tidy-up.

Living on my own provided few difficulties. I could cook, clean and iron – no problem. Sometimes I did all three at once: cleaning the cooking, then ironing it just for good measure. As for the washing, I'd banned my mum some years before I left home after she'd stuck four expensive Jaeger and Pringle lambswool sweaters into the washer. After a tumble on a hot programme, they come out small enough to fit the Action Man 'Perry Boy' – a popular doll in the early 1980s. Consequently, I'd successfully taken over this chore.

Of course, there were the new responsibilities of paying the bills, but once the various standing orders were in place, it was a doddle. Consequently I could never understand why people always moaned about, 'not going out tonight because I've got loads of bills to pay.' Why didn't they all just get standing orders sorted?

♦   ♦   ♦

After a year or so of solitary bliss, things were about to change. Paul 'Flynny' Flynn (a good pal and occasional Lee Athletic player) had told me about the breakdown of his marriage. He'd moved back in with his parents, and they were giving him constant grief about his failed matrimonial alliance. Flynny hadn't want to get married in the first place, but parental pressure had pushed him into the ceremony at a church located not far from the 'Prestwich Loony Bin' (as the local mental hospital was irreverently known to its neighbours). The way things were going at his mum and dad's place, Flynny was on the verge of taking up permanent residence there.

Flynny was a career postman and a traditional Northern lad who wanted to live the traditional Northern male life. Domestically he was hopeless. He couldn't cook, clean or iron and when it came to handiwork in the house, like me, he took the sensible DDIY option, as in *Don't* Do it Yourself.

Flynny was quite a few catnaps in front of me in the laziness stakes. He couldn't even be bothered to plug in the vacuum cleaner and take it for a little walk around the lounge every now and then. Or was it that he just didn't know how to power the thing up? That job, among all others, was left to the slave that was his missus. She was a young lass who he'd been dating for the best part of four years prior to wedlock. Debbie was the 'Little Lady' at home upon whom Flynny would traditionally expect to sort out all the domestic chores. As far as Mr Flynn was concerned he brought home his share of the housekeeping, put his feet up, sat back with a can in his hand and with his dinner in the oven, prepared by a loving wife. It was the good life to which he was entitled . . . or so he thought.

At first, all was well in his two-up two-down, terraced love-nest in Bury. That was until, perchance out of boredom, after almost a year of 'married bliss', he actually read one of the many regular letters that had been arriving from the building society. They had been trying for months to inform him that the mortgage was not being paid. Not unnaturally, Flynny had left this along with everything else to the Little Lady. Following her subsequent interrogation it was revealed that she hadn't been paying the mortgage. Instead, she'd been spending the money on cocaine with one of the numerous fellas with whom she'd been having affairs. This was after it had also come to light that she'd been shagging their 'best' man on the side and that she'd also been pilfering money from her employer in order to maintain her expensive Class A drug habit. Had she set up a simple standing order for the mortgage in the first place, surely all this could have been avoided?

When the police finally caught up with the Little Lady, she ended up in jail. This left Flynny home alone, a forlorn man buried beneath the wreckage of a broken marriage and the debris of the used chip wrappers and beer cans he'd failed to clean up in his lounge once she'd been carted off at Her Majesty's pleasure. At least Debbie did manage to keep the house tidy which was well beyond Flynny, without help. There was nothing for it but to move back to his mum and dad's place in Ashton-on-Mersey.

Unfortunately, his parents blamed Flynny for the breakdown, despite the fact that his newly betrothed had turned out to be squarely at fault. They weren't as astute as Jane and I had been. We had quickly suspected Flynny's new wife wasn't all sweetness and light, an early clue coming when we arrived at their wedding reception. The bloodshot-eyed bride bounded over in her white wedding dress with a cigarette dangling out of her mouth as she yanked the large wedding present from my grasp and asked, 'Is that for me?' before bounding off in search of the next ribbon-tied box; a quality bird who was neither little nor a lady.

A few months after the wedding, I saw Flynny's wife with a fella on her arm who was definitely not Flynny. For a start, he wasn't wearing a postman's outfit. She walked past, clearly having recognised me, but showing no concern whatsoever. I literally couldn't believe my eyes and presumed Flynny's wife had a twin sister. That was until it all came to light once the scandal had hit the local papers. Flynny explained the whole sorry tale during a Stella session in the Carters Arms. Following several hours of increasingly slurred debate there was nothing else for it, Mr Flynn would have to come and live with Dr Worthy. I had a ready-made chaise longue in the form of a second-hand couch in my lounge which awaited my disturbed pal's truculent patter. However, once I sobered up the next day, I had some reservations, but I needn't have worried. Flynny and I had a 'right laugh' over the next eighteen months.

It took Flynny a few weeks to finally cut his mother's apron-strings once more and move out. But when he arrived, in true odd couple style, we quickly agreed a few ground rules. These were limited to no smoking in the lounge, except when we were both drinking and other domestic pleasures mainly to do with ablutions and smells. They didn't call our block 'Trump Towers' for nothing. I should have added a rule of no punching my brand new freezer, which he did one night after he'd had a few too many having endured a provocative telephone conversation with his soon-to-be ex-missus. But he bought a new door the following day and there was no need to amend standing orders. Besides, my effective psychotherapy over many late night sessions soon had a positive calming effect.

Flynny occupied the back bedroom, which I'd spent many a long hour decorating on my own much against my better judgement. It would have been far quicker had I had the slightest idea about what I was doing. I should have got in a proper painter and decorator, such as Jane's mum or aunty. Had I done so, the task would have been completed in hours rather than weeks and with far less rolls of wallpaper.

After a few weeks of settling in, I soon realised that Flynny's anecdotes of his own domestic ineptitude were not exaggerated. If anything, they were understated. As he didn't have a clue on most things practical, I set about providing him with a crash course on domestic science. Flynny's tuition began not on how to wire a plug, but how to put one in the socket and turn on whatever appliance he was seeking to use, thus confirming my earlier suspicions about his ineptitude rather than total laziness. We moved on to the complicated process of how to vacuum-clean a carpet with the use of a stand-up Hoover. He soon became proficient at this, and we quickly progressed onto more advanced techniques such as how to iron a shirt and how to peel a potato. Had these been attempted simultaneously he could have been excused for his dismal failures but to my initial surprise and delight, he didn't try to peel the shirt and iron the potato. However, it soon became apparent that ironing was way beyond his capabilities and, consequently, I was quickly running out of white shirts for him to practice upon. Although large brown triangles had quite a fashionable look back in the early 1990s, I was also running out of burn cream and bandages and so his ironing lessons were abandoned. Unfortunately he fared no better at the peeling of spuds. By the time he'd finished removing the skin from a Maris Piper the size of his head, there was barely enough potato left for a solitary chip. It was agreed that I'd do the cooking, the ironing and the washing and he'd do the vacuuming and nothing else. It was the *safest* and most economical arrangement.

I tried to give Flynny a few cooking tips, but I realised I was flogging a dead postman when inquiring as to what he'd had for his dinner? Flynny replied, 'Weird soup!' He explained, 'I opened up the tin as you showed me, poured it into a pan and gave it a stir. It heated up okay, but it was just like steaming red sludge, so I threw it away.' I suspected what he'd done wrong.

'You're supposed to fill the tin with water and add it to the pan. It's no wonder it looked like molten lava. It's condensed soup, you clown!'

'You never told me that,' he replied incredulously. 'How can it be my fault?'

It wasn't long before I started to realise why his wife had soon become hooked on cocaine after only a few months' marriage with good old Flynny-boy. There were several memorable sketches to follow, like the time I'd asked him to put a low light under two pans of vindaloo curry when he got home from work in mid-afternoon. I always cooked in bulk, intending to freeze the batch for future use. But to the contrary, Flynny put a high light underneath both pans and promptly fell asleep. By the time I'd got home, the curry was welded to the pans and I had to throw both curry and pans in the bin. Although he offered to buy sixteen portions of vindaloo from the local take-away, I was starting to dine out on Flynny stories with friends and acquaintances alike.

His best effort arrived one afternoon when I was at work at Cheshire County Council. We didn't have a phone in the flat so, to make a call, we had to traipse a few hundred yards to a dilapidated, red public phone box. At about 2.30 p.m. the phone rang on my desk and, to my surprise, it was Postman Paul back from his round.

'What's up mate?' I enquired, fearing the worst.

'Have you been paying the rent?'

'What do you mean, have I been paying the rent?'

'Just that. I can't get in the flat. There's a big metal grille on the front door with a big padlocked iron bar!'

'Of course I've paid the rent, and even if I hadn't there's no way the council would board it up without a truckload of warning letters first,' I replied. But this wasn't good enough for the irate postie.

'I'm stuck out here and I can't get in!' I ended the conversation with an assurance that I'd leave work early. When I arrived at the flat a couple of hours later, I wasn't at all surprised that – contrary to Flynny's assertion – there was no bar or grille on the front door, and no evidence that one had been there in the first place. As I entered the flat my interrogation began.

'Flynny, what's going on mate?'

'You wouldn't believe it, Worthy. When I returned from the phone box, all the metal stuff had been removed!'

'Why don't you nip out to the block of flats at Vawdrey Drive next door, go up to number 45 and tell me if that's boarded up?' I suggested. He nipped over to the adjacent block of flats to our right, only to return with a cadaverous look on his face. He had indeed tried to get into the boarded-up flat at no. 45 Vawdrey! How he'd made a living as a postman for all those years was beyond my comprehension.

'I'm never ever gonna hear the end of this am I?' he asked. You've just read the answer to that one.

♦   ♦   ♦

To be fair, I was capable of a few gaffes of my own, such as my plan to remove the squirrels that had taken up residence in the roof space in the loft. I'd been lying awake at night listening to their irritating scratching noise and I'd written to the council to ask them to remove the itinerant rodents. However, as they weren't prepared to do anything for a few weeks, I took matters into my own hands. I'd seen the Carling Black Label advert showing the agility and intelligence of squirrels when confronted by a complicated garden assault course accompanied by the theme tune to *Mission Impossible*. They always ended up with a pile of acorns having completed the difficult tasks ahead. I followed suit and opened the ceiling hatch that led to the loft space and left a trail of assorted chick peas, peanuts and raisins from the top of the hatch. The trail of food went down the step ladders and out of the front door and into the lobby, now perfumed with the comparatively pleasant pong of disinfectant. Not surprisingly, my cunning plan failed miserably, much to Flynny's delight. The squirrels failed to take the bait as Flynny had predicted. In fact there was no sign whatsoever of the little pests. To this day I still think it was a good idea. How was I to know that squirrels aren't partial to extra hot Bombay mix?

My most infamous flat sketch also involved sleep disturbance. This came in the form of a couple of somewhat larger rodents in the bulbous shape of two well-seasoned ladies of the night who had moved into one of the flats below. One had all the allure of an East German shotputter in a Freddy Krueger mask, while the other looked like she'd styled her hair out of chip pan fat and had been sleeping rough in a bin-bag under a canal bridge for the last three years. Why anyone would pay for sex with either of these two odious 'glamour girls' was beyond me. But there were plenty of customers, both male and female alike.

Neither of our new neighbours had even scant regard for the karma of the rest of the block. Until their arrival it had been a relatively peaceful existence. I'd been known to play my music overly loud on occasions, but I always told my fellow residents that if it was too loud to let me know and I'd reduce the volume. Nobody ever did. Our relatively quiet life lasted until 'the neighbours from hell' moved in. Not only were they on the game, but both were also selling heavy drugs. This meant that all sorts of unscrupulous characters arrived in the early hours of the morning for their daily fix of one thing or another. I had no problem with this – for me it was live and let live – if only they'd have kept it quiet.

Unfortunately, the front door security system buzzer was permanently on the blink and anyone and everyone could enter the block unchallenged at any time. Whenever their shifty clients came in and then shuffled off into the night, the main door would crash shut. Its piercing thud reverberated all around the block, making it shake like an earthquake. They also had a huge Alsatian dog, which barked and howled incessantly whenever they left it alone, which was frequently. We couldn't get any peace.

Nobody else in the block appeared upset by the constant shenanigans in the early hours. If they were upset, they'd probably been intimidated into silence. Perhaps their apathy was born from the fact that only

Flynny and I were in work and had to get up in the mornings. But Flynny was normally up at 5.00 a.m. to do his glorified paper round and I was up an hour or so later in order to get my usual early start in the rat race to Chester for my glorified secretarial work. This meant that, in the main, we both had to get to bed before midnight to get any worthwhile sleep. It wasn't as bad for Flynny, as he was the type of person that could have slept through an air raid on a clothes line during a thunderstorm. But I'm usually such a light sleeper that a gnat's burp would stir me from my slumber. Their noise was intolerable – I was kept awake most nights and my patience was severely tested; so much so that I'd been down several times and naïvely asked them to keep the noise down, but I'd forgotten the basic rule that you can't be rational with irrational people. Besides, my reasonable requests for quiet were totally lost on a couple of scum-bags whose livelihood was mostly gained through banging as often as possible. The late night/ early morning partying was now a regular feature and it seemed there was little I could do, well legally at least.

By the time I had the sleep-deprived facial features of a cartoon character, complete with red veins which had invaded the whites of my eyes, I was nearly at the end of my tether. This arrived one Friday night on the way in from the Carters Arms when I had a gallon or so of Stella slopping around my system. As I sauntered up the steps to the first-floor level and past the council brothel, I noticed that the infernal racket had already begun. This time I didn't bother asking them to turn down the disco, stop the dog barking and generally shut the f*** up. Instead I gave the front door a belligerent boot that would have sent a medicine ball 35 yards into the top corner of the net. It felt so good. I did it again and again and again while shouting at the top of my voice, 'Come on everyone, let's have a boogie on the landing!' This unsurprisingly sent all three dogs within – and their dubious 'guests' – barking mad. I'd lost the plot and raged at them as they raged back from behind their battered door, with a torrent of abuse and a pan of boiling water in hand. The commotion had stirred Flynny, who was in his room with his girlfriend. He came down and ushered me back up to our flat just before the cops arrived.

When the inquiry began, I didn't really have a leg to stand on; a skin full of Stella had seen to that. I was carted off to the awaiting 'Black Maria' protesting, 'You can't arrest me. I'm not a scum-bag. I've got a degree, you know!' It was freezing cold sitting in the van in just a tee-shirt and beige lightweight pants. However, the ever-caring

Flynny came down and gave me his multi-coloured shellsuit top, which had all the subtle patterns of the old TV test card. But at least it kept me warm as I articulated my protests to the police with a slurred but determined tone. Flynny also told me later that I was exclaiming to the arresting officers how big a catch I was, that I was both Jimmy Boyle and Ronnie Biggs rolled into one and that they were both sure to get promoted once I'd gone down for the heinous crime of kicking a door.

Remarkably my protestations earned me one last chance from the cops. They could see I didn't like doors, but meant no real harm to the dogs, although I had put my point over with greater enthusiasm than necessary. The police clearly didn't want to take me in (paperwork and all that) and said if that if I apologised to the so-called girls and their male 'friends', they'd let me go. The officers knocked on their battered door and explained that I would apologise.

'Well go on then,' said the Communist shotputter, to which I replied in a suitably slurred slowed-up voice, 'You can both eff off, you pair of noisy slags. You wouldn't get an apology from me even if it means me going to jail.' Unfortunately it did. I was immediately carted off with my arm up my back with Flynny laughing his head off as both coppers shook their heads in frustration.

Early the next morning I woke up in a cell in Hall Lane cop shop. It was the best night's sleep I'd had in weeks, although bit of a shock to the system waking up in an austere, iron-barred concrete cell. Once I'd got my bearings and taken in the magnitude of my ill-advised actions, I sat there patiently waiting in vain for the succulent bowl of porridge that I thought was sure to arrive. Instead, the desk sergeant entered the cell and offered me a deal. If I would admit to the attack on the door, then he'd see about me getting a caution. If not I'd be charged with criminal damage or even the more serious offence of, 'Booting the crap out of a wooden door with malicious intent to throttle its owners'. He'd checked the police records and my name wasn't on the list. But by complete contrast, the inhabitants of the flat below had a schedule of offences that read like a Christmas list for a shopaholic.

Having admitted my crime, true to the sergeant's word, I received a slap on the wrists and I was set loose, but not before I graciously thanked them for their hospitality as I walked out of the front door. At last the 'Northern Moor One' was free . . . free to walk the mile-and-a-half journey in the 'persisting' rain through Wythenshawe Park at 5.30 in the morning. To make matters worse, when I arrived back at the flat some 40 or so minutes later, Flynny had set off to see Altrincham away against some fifth-rate non-league outfit way down south. I was locked out!

Embarrassingly, I had to knock at my mum and dad's with a made-up story that I'd been to an all-night party and had lost my keys. Later that day City were at home and I scrounged a lift from my dad to Maine Road without a penny in my kitty, and I didn't have my season ticket either as it was still in the flat. Luckily, Bibby was on hand in the Beehive to lend me some money from the ever-open 'Bank of Bibby' and the City ticket office gave me a duplicate once I'd given them an amended story of leaving the season ticket in the flat by mistake.

Predictably, City lost at home, but that wasn't by any means the worst part of the weekend. It wasn't the night in the cell, nor the row with the hookers, the soaking in the park or the lies to my parents. The worst part of the weekend was being forced to wear Flynny's awful multi-coloured shellsuit to the game and suffering the merciless stick in the Beehive. But was it all worth it? Despite arresting me, a few days later the police paid a visit to our 'friends' in the flat below. I don't know what was said or done, but they soon moved out, never to be seen again. Perhaps it was all worth it. After all, nobody had thought to take a picture of me in that hideous shellsuit top. I'd pretty much got away with it.

♦ ♦ ♦

Looking back, my days in the flat both on my own and with Flynny bring a smile to my face. We both put on about a stone during that time. At first my 'Gordon Blur' speciality of egg, chips and succulent Cumberland sausage from the butchers in Chester was our Thursday treat. Later we were putting away this delicacy at least three times a week, and it was with some relief to my waistline that I left the flat in March 1992 for pastures new – a couple of months before Jane and I got married. Flynny retained the flat for a while with his new girlfriend Sue and, eighteen years later, they're still together and now blessed with their beautiful daughter, Chloe. Eighteen months of eventful therapy with Dr Worthy had got him back on track.

32

A Fistful of Travellers' Cheques

Moving away from Flynny and the flat in 1992 was the stark confirmation that my bachelor days were well and truly over (but long live the 'single married man' as Pete, my trusty but overly expensive window cleaner, often puts it). My imminent departure to Timperley, after thirty years on the north side of Wythenshawe, signalled the beginning of a new life with my patient and understanding girlfriend of six years.

Two years earlier and, having duly secured the appropriate permission from her devoted dad Steve, I'd made the not so difficult decision to pop the classic and all-important question, 'Which early '70s City Continental-style away strip did you prefer: the white one with the red and blue sash or the blue one with the red and white sash . . . and will you marry me?' In order to 'woo' her into a positive state of mind, I'd whisked her off to the salubrious surroundings of a refined, swanky French restaurant in Sale. It was a no expenses spared meal and I was suitably armed with the necessary persuasive inducements. These consisted of a bunch of blue roses (difficult to acquire without the use of a tin of spray paint) and a diamond-encrusted ring which had been provided by my mate 'Jim the Jeweller'. Judging by the miniscule size of the stones, he'd seemingly won this potential engagement insignia in a 'lucky bag' the previous Thursday. What did I want for 20 quid?

After a few slurps of the inexpensive yet surprisingly subtle and full-bodied red wine, the mood was right and the ambience perfect. As the pianist tinkled exquisite tunes, I took a deep breath and ventured down on to my left knee (as the right was way too dodgy from playing too much five-a-side). I took a deep breath as I optimistically sought Jane's slender and slightly trembling hand in marriage. After I'd shoved, rather than swept, her off her feet and with no better offers in the pipeline, she thought for an overly protracted minute, and then finally said, 'Oh, go on then.'

Before I could flit the flat in pursuit of domestic bliss within an idyllic suburban setting, I knew that we would have to buy a house. Rather than dreamily romantic and fun – which it perhaps should have been – I found the process of buying a home a tedious and often provocative affair. This was particularly exacerbated, as Jane and I initially had different ideas of what sort of property we should buy. Neither of us fancied a new 'semi'. My preference was for a large, multi-storied Victorian terrace with an attic and cellar. Such a dwelling could cater for my deluded visions of setting up an illicit underground cottage industry of home-brewed beer or moonshine whisky with a solar powered 'weed' farm in the attic. But my meagre contribution to our joint deposit was more in the class of a wigwam on the disused land near the old Wythenshawe brush factory. In contrast, Jane courted aspirations of a 1930s type of property with a garage and a garden. Not for the first time, her choice prevailed and it proved to be a wise retreat on my behalf, as Jane's preference was far more suitable than mine.

We finally donned the khaki suits and elephant gun and began house-hunting. However, having waded through the boring and tedious blurb of the estate agents' brochures, I switched off on the idea. We spent many a fruitless evening trudging around the 1930s 'Royal' estate viewing semi-detached properties located within the regal surroundings of Timperley. After a hard day at work, perhaps the last thing I should have been doing was walking around other people's houses. At the best of times I found it difficult to feign enthusiasm for the pride and joy of artexed ceilings and rounded alcoves in the home of some DIY clown who was only too quick to tell me, 'I did that myself you know?' I wanted to reply, 'I can see that. It's absolute rubbish mate!' Perhaps I'm not the most patient individual or the nicest bloke on the planet when I'm knackered and after a short while the house-buying process started to get right on my nerves.

As soon as the front door was opened Jane and I could tell immediately that the prospective purchase wasn't for us, but still we had to go through the motions. It was on such occasions when my lack of patience and innate sarcasm would get the better of me. One house had a lingering stench of smoke. The lady smiled as she let us in, to reveal a set of molars yellowed by both time and cigarettes.

'This is the hallway,' she said with a glowing pride that belied its dreary décor, to which I replied, 'Never!' She maintained her false smile and confirmed, 'And this is the kitchen,' to which I replied, 'Really? And what goes on in here then, cooking and stuff?' This prompted a swift dig in the ribs from Jane. My mum says, 'Sarcasm is the lowest form of wit.' True, but it's helped to preserve my severely tested sanity throughout the years.

◆　◆　◆

The house we settled on was bought from an old lady and needed a new roof and every room decorating. There would be a delay before we had the money to hire the required specialists, as my DDIY policy also met with approval from my better half. The romantic image of a young couple hanging up rolls of wallpaper before spontaneously splattering each other in paste as foreplay to a roll-around love scene on a tarpaulin dotted with Jackson Pollock patterns wasn't enticing enough for either of us to don the dungarees or erect a pasting table. However, we did manage to get the house into some sort of decent shape before I moved in prior to our wedding. When I say 'we' I really mean Jane and her mum. It had been many a spring since the house had received the 'Mrs Muscle' treatment, and there's nothing like a mucky habitat to make a woman roll up her sleeves and get some serious scrubbing sorted.

◆　◆　◆

Once all the Ts had been dotted and the Is crossed prior to Jane's decantation from her mum and dad's into our new humble abode, there was the small matter of a wedding to sort out. But before that, there was the large matter of a stag weekend. Predictably enough, this involved sixteen lads crammed into a minibus pointed in the direction of Auld Reekie (or Edinburgh to the locals). With all my beer buddies on board, it was off to 'Bonnie' Scotland for a final Highland fling. It started with a visit to the Edinburgh Beer Festival at the Caledonian Brewery. My insistent whinings of, 'It's my stag do and I want to go to the beer festival,' became a bit of a catchphrase throughout the weekend and in the following years. The real ale and jazz fest was followed by a few beers at Haymarket and the traditional pub crawl of Rose Street taverns. This was where I was treated to the traditional spirit sweep, with a pint made up from all the optics on show, topped up with a small bottle of barley wine. It wasn't really surprising that I threw up all over my trendy Pierre Cardin blazer and then had to be carried from pub to pub from then on. Oh, what fun!

The party was based at the Trust House Forte Hotel, which provided a unique jungle noise alarm clock due to its close proximity to the city's zoo. Another thing out of the ordinary was that the hotel was to become the venue for the great Subbuteo mystery of 1992. Even though I'd stopped playing the game well before the turn of the 1980s, for some reason Paul Conlan decided to bring his Subbuteo set. When he and his room-mate, Noel Bayley, came back from the Friday night festivities, they had a game, no doubt emulating the players by swerving all over the room as they played. The next morning they left both teams and the pitch in a mess and departed for another day on the ale. When they returned late that evening, they found the pitch straightened out, the nets upright and both teams lined up on the touchline in position for the national anthems and ready for their next match! Was something really weird going on or was it just a case of cleaners with a great sense of humour?

That Saturday night brought more copious drinking and I managed to navigate the watering holes of Edinburgh without the assistance of a couple of male crutches. The following Sunday morning we set off back to Manchester, worse for wear but significantly better after the 'hair of the dog'. On the journey back, we stopped off for some cans in an obscure Scottish village, when Bibby and Gilly tried to persuade me and best man Terry Hyland to go for a soothing paddle in a nearby stream. But, fortunately, we were sharp enough to realise that they were trying to leave us both up in Scotland, penniless and without shoes and socks. I knew that I was in danger of some prank or other as I'd been one of the main instigators of John Eaton's stag episode.

◆   ◆   ◆

The week before John's marriage we took him on a pub crawl in Manchester, but not before a lead ball and chain was clasped securely around his right ankle. Towards the end of the night, after a lock-in at the Green Man in Ancoats, we nipped into an Indian restaurant for a late curry, but John was missing. We'd locked him and his ball and chain into the attendant's cabin in the Piccadilly station car park, courtesy of

Bibby's contacts in the council's car parks' department. John was freed from the hut before the end of the night, but on the way home in the black cab, I showed him the key to his ball and chain. Before he could grab it from my grasp, I promptly dropped it out of the window as we chugged past Southern Cemetery. The next morning I went round to John's with the real key to let him loose, but he thought I had thrown away his only means of escape. When I arrived, his ball and chain was gone. He'd already had the fire brigade around to saw the shackles from his blood-red ankle.

◆   ◆   ◆

Once we'd crossed back over the border into England, I naïvely thought I'd ridden out the 'let's do something daft to the groom' threat. By the time we arrived at Charnock Richard service station near Bolton, I'd completely dropped my guard. As I casually strolled out of the gents toilet, I could see the minibus disappearing into the distance with my mates' delighted faces hanging out of the window. I was half-cut and stuck 20-odd miles from home and wearing a beer-stained, tacky-looking MCFC shellsuit. My first thought was to ring Jane and ask her to retrieve me, but with only 2p in my pocket I was compelled to make a reverse charge call to her house from a payphone in the car park. Her mum Joan informed me that Jane had gone on her 'hen do' in Southport and wasn't due back until later that evening. Next, I tried asking motorists for a lift, but nobody was going back to Manchester.

As I was standing in the middle of the car park, I noticed a coach emblazoned with the words 'Lambs Coaches – Stockport, England' and that gave me an idea. Once all the occupants had slowly disembarked, I meekly scuttled onto the bus and had a word with the driver. As Stockport wasn't too far from the flat in Wythenshawe I begged him for a lift. But he told me that he was on the way back from the Lake District with the Liverpool Pensioners' Ballroom Dancing Society and he had to drop them off before he could return. However, the driver was happy to give me a lift via 'the Pool' if I could square it with the group leader. She turned out to be a 'dolled-up' battle-axe of a woman who would take some persuading, particularly from a semi-sloshed, slobby-looking, unshaven bloke in a beer-stained shellsuit. Luckily I managed to turn on the charm, and the promise of not causing, 'any trouble nor distraction in any way,' swung the deal. I took up a vacant seat near the back of the bus. There was further humiliation to follow. The lady deemed it necessary to pick up the microphone and explain my plight to all the passengers. She relayed the story of how my so-called mates had left me stranded on my stag do. It brought much needed laughter on what I suspect had been a fairly strait-laced trip.

It was all working out perfectly, until a few miles from Liverpool when I started to feel the ominous need for a 'comfort break'. Unfortunately there was no toilet on the bus and so I had to sit there in ever-deepening discomfort. I realised I was in trouble when the driver stopped on the outskirts of the city and stated, 'Right ladies and gentlemen, here's the first stop.' I was compelled to just sit there as my teeth began to float. It was a total nightmare.

By the time we'd taken the complete tour of Liverpool and had reached the final drop off at Aigburth, my bladder was the size of a beach ball. Finally, and just as I was about to burst, it was all clear to get off. But the agony was still prolonged as the last protracted well wishes for my big day came from a delightful old biddy who had unknowingly added a couple of extra years on to my life in the space of 3 minutes. Once she finally disappeared into the distance, I staggered off the coach and I enjoyed the longest leak ever. The definition of the word 'relief' should have been changed in the *Oxford English Dictionary* to read, 'Worthy's slash on an oak tree at Aigburth on 5 June 1992.'

Despite the main collaborators in my abandonment being Bibby, Gilly, Steve Maher and driver Phil Knowles, it was poor old Flynny who incurred Jane's wrath the following day. She'd found out about my plight shortly after I'd phoned her mum and she spent the rest of her hen trip in a frenzied state of panic. By contrast, I wasn't overly concerned as I knew that, one way or another, I'd make it safely back.

♦ ♦ ♦

A couple of weeks later it was time for the wedding, which was held at St Matthew's church in Crumpsall. This was an away fixture for me as the bride had home advantage. Besides, the church was far more architecturally ornate that my home ground of St Michael's and hers was also located nearer to the reception, to be held at the Britannia Hotel in Manchester.

Jane and I made sure we both had a great time on our wedding day; after all it had cost a small fortune and with any luck, we'd each only do it the once. Just for one day, all the best people in our world were there. As neither Jane nor I had many living relatives, the rest of the guests were mostly made up with friends whom we both love. The highlight of the day was the speeches and Jane's dad delivered his with great gusto. He was followed by best man Terry who gave me the traditional slating: concentrating particularly on my lack of footballing prowess, both in playing and in managing Lee Athletic. He even had the temerity to assert that all of City's woes weren't down to Peter Swales, but instead were my fault. I was a football jinx and he backed his theory up with the similar downward plight of Lee, who'd also never won anything since I had become involved.

Unfortunately, as with everything I enjoy, it was over in the blink of an eye (well perhaps not *everything* I hasten to add). One minute I was in the Cleveland in Crumpsall having a 'pre-match' beer with all the lads, the next it was three in the morning and I was having a 'post-match' sing-song with all the lads. Somewhere in between, Jane and I had got hitched and I couldn't have been happier, except for the obvious: an away win at Old Trafford and a couple of silver cups in both City and Lee's trophy cabinets. But now we really are within the realms of fairytale weddings.

My late-night session crooning with Bibby, Gilly, Steve Maher and Bugsy made it a short wedding night, particularly as Jane and I had to catch an early morning flight to Orlando. We had a mini-panic as we grabbed all our things and lobbed them into a taxi. In the departure lounge there was another catastrophe when I realised that I'd left all the travellers' cheques back home. I rushed back out through the check-in barrier to phone my younger sister, Joanne. She shot around to the airport to get a set of keys in order to scour our house. As I hadn't a clue where I'd left them, Joanne recruited my older sister, Julie, and they turned our new gaff upside down in pursuit of Thomas Cook's valuable pleasure vouchers.

I waited and waited – and waited – outside the airport until the very last minute, but there was no sign of our Joanne. I decided I'd have to get on the flight or Jane and I would miss the whole holiday. The plane was due to leave at 11.00 a.m. and at 10.50 a.m. I legged it back through the check-in as fast as I could and boarded the jet red-faced and out of breath. But there was one more 'slight' problem as there was no sight of my new wife. The stewardess told me that Jane had gone back to get me and that I must have run back past her without noticing. The airport had been frantically 'bing-bonging' me, but now they were bing-bonging Jane as 'Mrs Worthington', which she failed to recognise. The whole thing was like a farce. As the plane's departure was imminent I had a decision to make. Should I get on board and wait at Orlando airport for

Jane, who would surely have found the travellers' cheques and boarded another flight? Or should I get off? Just as I was pondering what to do, the hallowed vision of my younger sister and my new wife appeared across the apron with Jane clutching a fistful of travellers' cheques.

We were both red-faced in more ways than one as we finally boarded the plane to an embarrassing round of applause from the rest of the passengers, who'd already been informed by the cabin crew of the reason for the delay. Having turned the house upside-down, my frantic sisters, Joanne and Julie, had finally located the travellers' cheques wedged in my work briefcase behind the latest copy of *Big Jugs Monthly*. My glorified butty box/conker bag had hidden the secret of the missing travellers' cheques for more than a week. I'd had a few beers on my last day at work and had forgotten all about the stack of travellers' cheques that I'd collected from the travel agents.

33

Paul Gilsenan 1963–96

I first met Paul 'Gilly' Gilsenan in the early 1980s. He arrived on the Kippax as 'partner in crime' with Bibby, who once described Gilly as, 'the greatest man I have ever met'. Although I don't know everyone who Bibby has ever met, I wouldn't argue with his assertion that Gilly was indeed the greatest of men. Bibby and Gilly's friendship went back to early childhood. Apparently, the Bowden and the Gilsenan families were formally acquainted even before the outbreak of the Second World War and Bib's parents, Ernie and Bella Bowden, went to Matt and Margaret Gilsenan's wedding, and vice-versa.

Both families left the bomb-battered Hulme area of Manchester in the early 1960s. Along with other working-class people from all over the Manchester and Salford areas, they migrated to Woodhouse Park – one of the many new neighbourhoods in the vast new Wythenshawe council estate. This flagship area of South Manchester was a planner's dream; a promised land of greenery and inside toilets for all. It was a Garden of Eden located within an idyllic urban setting, purpose-built for the new and prosperous postwar future so coveted by the downtrodden masses.

Bibby and Gilly went to the same junior school (St Anthony's RC Primary) and then on to their respective grammar schools of St Augustine's in Sharston and St Gregory's in Ardwick. By no stretch of the imagination are my mates thick (especially not these two) and they were certainly streetwise. Despite eventually aspiring to an elite school, Gilly often used to 'wag' primary school and would get nine-year-old Bibby to write excuse notes to the teacher. They always got away with this due to Bib's extraordinarily neat handwriting, for one of such a tender age. Gilly and Bibby also had a cunning (if unoriginal) method of skipping church and not getting found out at the Monday morning teacher's inquisition. They would nip into St Anthony's on a Saturday night, check on the vestment colours and which priest was saying Mass and then nip back to Bib's for a game of cards, all while both sets of parents were at the pub.

Gilly had an early and unjust reputation for being of questionable character (or a bit of a 'rum un'), so much so that he once got hauled off a school bus by the police, being mistakenly identified as the culprit who'd pushed a child off the bus and to his death the previous day. Investigations proved beyond any doubt that he was innocent. In fact, Paul had been locked in a classroom with a teacher at the time, in detention.

In later life, Gilly would be up against the police once more, when he was inadvertently rounded up with a gang of lads who'd been running amok in a Manchester pub. Gilly was innocent of any crime and only guilty of being 'slightly' inebriated but he was roped in by the cops and falsely charged with 'suspicion of theft of a pint pot'. In court, all the other lads pleaded guilty, as did Gilly. The lead magistrate asked if anyone had anything to say. Gilly commented that he hadn't nicked a pint pot and he hadn't been with these lads who were causing havoc. He'd just been in the wrong place at the wrong time. The magistrate asked the other defendants if this was true and they all admitted that they hadn't the faintest idea who this Gilly lad was! The incredulous magistrate asked Gilly, 'Why on earth were you arrested? Did you do anything to antagonise the police, and if you weren't with them why did you plead guilty?' Gilly replied, 'My legal brief didn't show much of an interest so I thought it would be quicker if I admitted it. As for the police, all I said was, "Cuckoo hiya," and they nicked me.' Apparently, the gang of lads fell about laughing and Gilly received a £20 fine.

♦ ♦ ♦

Paul Gilsenan was from good Irish Catholic stock and all his brothers and sisters were fervent United supporters, as was Gilly up until the age of seven. This changed after a serious family row about the sterilised milk he was forced to have on his cornflakes. In protest against the force-feeding, Gilly vowed to 'get his own back on his family' and gave them a serious body-blow by deciding that he would support City. Being the awkward, stubborn little kid that he was, Bibby and his mates were all delighted that he stuck to his guns and remained a Blue for the rest of his life.

My first impression of Paul Gilsenan was that he was a bit of a nutter because of his sturdy physique, his home-made 'Lity' tattoo and gruff voice. But I soon realised that my initial opinion was totally wrong. This ebullient, likely lad from deepest, darkest Wythenshawe was as Pete – his father-in-law-to-be – later put it, 'a little rough diamond with a cheeky smile, who will be all right once I knock a few corners off him.'

Gilly always had good manners, courtesy and a great consideration for others. To his eternal credit he also had a great respect and special warmth for pensioners. He said to me, 'It's important to respect older people. They have been through all of life's ups and downs and have come out on the other end.' As a single lad, Paul would often stay at his nanna's house on Saturday nights just to offer her a little extra protection and security when she was of an octogenarian disposition. She made a rule that he had to be in the house by 11 o'clock, and he'd always make the deadline – although on one occasion he arrived there a few minutes late to find that his nanna had turned the lights off and gone to bed. But he regularly stayed over even at the age of twenty-four, such was his devotion.

Gilly had a deep passion for life and for football. He was an excellent player and regretted that he never pursued a career as a professional, although he'd never have made it as a striker. I played against him in friendlies between Lee Athletic and Mancor. Gilly would often beat two or three players and then go back and beat them all again, always neglecting to shoot when he had had a clear opportunity to score; he just enjoyed taking the mickey too much.

Unlike Bibby and I, Paul wasn't an ever-present at City's fixtures. He played both Saturday and Sunday League football and trained hard in between. He astutely realised at an early age that 'there is only a short window of time to play football; there is plenty of time to watch it in later life when your legs have gone.' However, Gilly was in our little corner of the Kippax often enough to brighten up the usually dour proceedings with his razor-sharp one-liners.

Because of his regular absences from Maine Road, Gilly decided not to invest in a season ticket for one particular season. When it came to the home derby, he'd forgotten to join the membership scheme and hadn't acquired a ticket. On the day of the game, he went down to Maine Road and, concerned that he'd miss the match, elected to pay a tout £35 for his ticket.

'I told you I'd get one,' he proudly announced, waving his ticket to us all in the Beehive. However, his happiness was soon cut short when it was pointed out to him that for just a tenner more, he could have bought a season ticket that would have got him another twenty-one home games that year!

In those days Gilly wore a trademark knee-length zip-up parka coat. It had a built-in hood which folded flat across the shoulders and when zipped, created a tubular effect with fur around the edges. The front of this unfashionable monstrosity was splattered in paint and curry stains. It was a fine example of Wythenshavian sartorial splendour and resembled the wizened old relic found on Scott of the Antarctic when it had finally thawed out. He wore this knackered coat everywhere he went; he even wore it on his first date with what turned out to be his future wife, Joanne Kenny, before finally having it surgically removed a few years later.

As a tender sixteen-year-old, Joanne first saw Gilly on her first day at British Gas. She was in the tearoom and thought to herself, 'He's all right; a bit fat, but all right.' Gilly told her his name was 'Sid' from the stores. In fact, Sid was the store manager – responsible for ordering all manner of essentials for British Gas. He once ordered 500 pairs of workmen's overalls, and was delighted with himself for negotiating such a great price with the seller . . . until they turned up. Unfortunately, 500 pairs of pink overalls wasn't the colour the macho British Gas burly fitters required! And then there was another time when he was asked to order 10,000 crayons for the company magazine as a gift to employees' children as part of a drawing competition. Luckily Gilly found out that the crayons were toxic just before they were all sent out.

A year or so after first meeting, 'Sid' and Joanne went on a works trip to Blackpool at which Gilly later insisted Joanne, 'threw herself at him', when they came home on the coach together. They had certainly 'clicked' and for their subsequent first date, Gilly arranged to meet his 'posh bird' and her friends for a cosy little foursome in a quaint Timperley pub. But he turned up an hour late in his paint-stained snorkel coat with his cousin Baz, just in case the date went sour. Joanne later commented, 'Paul came over to our table in that minging coat that was zipped up so high that all you could see was a circle showing two eyes and a nose. The other couple thought he'd come over to rob us.' Joanne drove Paul home back to Wivvy, and when they arrived at a large brick building, Gilly said, 'This'll do. I live here.' Joanne didn't think it was too bad for a house in Wythenshawe, before later realising that this was in fact his local, the Cornishman.

Their next date was in the 'Corny', where Joanne was given a clear and serious briefing before being introduced to his 'rough diamond' mates.

'Don't call me Sid, don't touch my hand and don't kiss me,' implored Gilly, not wishing to blow his street cred. But Joanne soon forgot the rules. A few weeks later at Jimmy Kelly's wedding, Joanne managed to persuade Paul into a slow dance to a Phil Collins love song. They were both subsequently pelted with pork pies by some of his 'less desirable mates' – as Joanne put it.

It wasn't long before the couple were an item and could have had a 'Gilly 'n' Joanne' sun visor on Paul's new car . . . except for the fact that, despite having taken out a car loan for £2,500, the new motor never materialised. Having virtually taught him how to drive, Joanne had nagged Paul into getting a car, but the pressure of having so much money proved too much. He and his enthusiastic mates effectively 'drank' his car over a six-month period – a time that Gilly not surprisingly described as, 'one of the best of my life'.

It was another eight years before Gilly finally started driving, previously preferring a rusty old crank of a bike. His bike would often be seen discarded on Friday nights in the middle of the Moss car park behind Altrincham's football ground. He abandoned it, knowing full well that nobody would ever nick such a rusty heap of junk! After a few pints he would pedal all the way home and never fell off.

Despite the car setback, Joanne and Gilly were on solid ground, so much so that in a bid to get his feet under the table, he was introduced to Joanne's family, the Kennys of Timperley. Joanne's dad Pete had two attractive daughters of whom he was fiercely protective. The first night he stayed over at Joanne's Gilly was put in solitary confinement in the spare room. Pete had given a briefing of his own before the night was out. This was to deter any amorous aspirations Gilly might have had in tip-toeing into Joanne's room for a clandestine liaison.

'If I hear the slightest noise on the landing, metal doors will come crashing down. Bells, whistles and alarms will start ringing and lights will start flashing. Do you get the picture?' The next morning the Kenny family were sat around the breakfast table as the unshaven and bog-eyed Gilly came ambling into the room. Before Joanne's dad could greet him, Gilly announced with his cheeky grin, 'Mornin' Pete. How's it going? By the way, your alarm doesn't work!'

Gilly and Joanne were engaged on 7 November 1987 – the day when City beat Huddersfield 10–1 at Maine Road. This was no coincidence.

Gilly once promised her that they'd get engaged on the day that City scored ten, not that he ever thought it might happen! They went to a Chinese for their first ever restaurant meal at which Gilly ordered fish, chips and peas followed by jelly and ice cream before going down on one knee and proposing. Nobody could argue that the lad didn't have style.

They were married on 25 July 1992 and moved into their new home in Timperley village. Their marital nest was only about a mile down the road from where Jane and I had moved after our wedding in the same year. It was a real bonus to have Gilly living nearby, as Jane and I regularly joined the other happy couple for nights out in the local. One Christmas we all went out to the Hare & Hounds for a celebratory drink. Midway through the evening Gilly nipped into the gents. I followed him a minute or so later and he was standing next to a stranger, who was unaware we knew each other. Both Gilly and the stranger were minding their own business in silence as I took my place leaving the stranger between us. The tune of 'White Christmas' was suddenly piped over the speakers. Gilly promptly added in the City lyrics, 'I'm dreamin' of a Blue Wembley,' and I nonchalantly joined in, 'Just like the ones I used to know.' Neither Paul nor I knew whether or not the stranger was a Blue or a Red, but we quickly found out when he casually added, 'There'll be blue flags flying . . . to see City win the cup.' The three of us fell about laughing. I suppose it's one of those moments that you have to be there to enjoy, but the memory still brings a wry smile.

Gilly's sense of humour was, perhaps, his most endearing trait. I've met some riotously funny guys, with razor-sharp wit and brilliant comedy timing (Tony 'Friz' Freeman for one), but Gilly was the grand custodian of my metaphorical tickling-stick. I always looked forward to nights out with him, because I knew I was always going to have a 'right laugh', as we say in these parts.

In 1987 I persuaded Gilly to sign for Lee Athletic from Bibby's team, Mancor, who were on the verge of folding. When he first arrived, Gilly spent most of his time asking his new team-mates how many fish they thought they could catch in our goal nets. It was a perplexing question for most players in our team, intelligent or otherwise. However, Gilly was one of our most competitive players and, beneath it all, he always wanted to win. This showed occasionally when he was over-enthusiastic in the tackle, so much so that he became the self-proclaimed 'Gilly the Hard'. He even used the terminology to his wife after he'd been extra cheeky. Joanne told him off once, to which he replied, 'You can't speak to me like that; I'm Gilly the Hard.' Joanne instantly replied, 'If you carry on like that, you'll be Gilly the box room!' That happened when he returned home minus his wedding ring after playing in a match at Hough End. He'd lost it during the game and he and Joanne drove all the way back, combing the churned up pitch for hours in the ever-decreasing light of a cold, damp evening in vain pursuit of the elusive gold band.

Gilly wasn't a dirty player, but he often fell out with referees as he had his own interpretation of the laws of the game. The funny thing was that most of the refs in the league knew his name through previous experience – Paul was the kind of bloke that you never forgot. One particular game at Beech Avenue sticks in the memory. We were losing and looking for a late equaliser when the ball went straight into the brook after a deliberate clearance from one of their defenders. Anxious that we were running out of time, Gilly shouted to the referee, 'Never mind the ball ref, just get on with the game!'

Gilly played for Lee for five years and always protested that he didn't play as well as he could have done because he never took it seriously. There were just too many opportunities to mess about, which he did before, during and after the match. He'd be at it in the dressing room before the game, particularly if we were sharing with the opposition. He'd soon let it be known to all present that he was on 'cock-watch' as he put it, in a deep, overly gruff voice, resembling that of an American movie preview announcer. At this point he'd wander around the dressing room unsettling the opposition as he commented on the size of their 'todgers'.

Out on the pitch, he'd never miss an opportunity to feign a throw back to our goalkeeper which would send an opposition player sprinting towards our penalty area, before quickly turning around and throwing it the other way while laughing. He also liked nothing better than to 'nutmeg' a player (putting the ball through an opponent's legs and retaining possession) while saying, 'Cuckoo!' He even had the audacity to chip an opposing goalie when scoring a penalty for British Gas. Apparently the 'keeper was so incensed he had to be restrained by his team-mates as Gilly jogged back to the centre-circle with a broad grin on his face, unaware of the chaos he'd caused.

After the match the fun would continue in the pub and on the way home. There was nothing Paul liked better than winding down his car window and asking one of the local girls standing at the bus stop, 'Excuse me love. Can you tell me the way to the beach?' Once he started dating Joanne properly, Gilly used to take great pleasure in going up to total strangers and telling them, 'I've got a bird.' One of his other favourites was to walk around Altrincham during his lunchbreak and inform passers by of 'Haircuts, 5p.' Nobody had a clue what he meant. Nor did we know what, 'Chocolate on the radiator,' was all about, but he used to shout it at the top of his voice when playing for Lee Athletic.

He left to play for Timperley Labour Club so that he could, 'take my football more seriously and stop messing about.' This was a laugh in itself. And yet, despite leaving, Paul never stopped supporting Lee Athletic and we heard him shouting, 'Come on Lee Athletic!' while he was playing for his new club over on the adjacent pitch at Beech Avenue. So much for taking it seriously!

In the early 1990s I suffered hard times at Cheshire County Council. I found the place devoid of fun and humour and at first I struggled with the work. But my days were often brightened up by a phone call from Gilly. Sometimes he would come through on someone else's line if mine was engaged. I could always tell it was him because there would suddenly be an outburst of laughter in the open-plan office. He would say to the lucky recipient, 'I'll just have to put you on hold for a minute.' Instead of the customary piped music, Gilly would sing, 'If I was a blackbird I'd whistle and sing' (from his favourite episode of *Boys from the Black Stuff*). It was that or, 'When the red, red robin goes bob, bob bobbin' along' in the 'club style' way before Reeves and Mortimer came up with the idea.

There was always fun to be had when Gilly was involved. For instance, closing a round of golf at Altrincham Municipal Course I was about to tee off when I heard a raucous voice shouting, 'Worthy you . . . (rhymes with 'tanker')!' He'd stopped playing in the middle of his five-a-side game on the pitch behind the course just to hurl abuse at me. Needless to say, I duffed the shot 10 yards into a gully that was hidden under a bush.

One of Paul's work colleagues, Chris Hullah, once told a story of how he was out with Paul on Christmas Eve. Following their annual festive session in the Moss, they embarked on their usual drunken argument about football. By the time they reached Altrincham bus station, Gilly was losing the argument and kept telling Chris to, 'shut up.' As matters progressed, Gilly became more and more cheesed off with his pal's persistence in trying to win the debate. He suddenly stopped in his tracks, took his trousers off, folded them up neatly and crammed them into his parka coat pocket. He walked through the station, and got on a bus and disappeared off into the night, minus his pants. It was Gilly's unique but passive way of ending an argument.

In fact, Altrincham bus station is not without further significance in the life of Paul Gilsenan. When he worked in the Gas Stores, there was the usual heavy stash of girlie mags that did the rounds among the lads. One Monday morning after a weekend of salacious 'studying' Gilly was in the process of returning the stack of literature back to the store library. It didn't reach its destination. The bundle of 'dirt' wrapped up in brown paper remained on his seat on the bus. It was in the days of IRA bomb threats and when he arrived at work, Gilly was told the exciting news by a colleague. The town centre was at a total standstill as the bus station had been evacuated due to a suspicious-looking package found left on a bus! Gilly realised his big mistake and was absolutely mortified. His deep concern wasn't so much for the chaos he'd caused, or indeed the repercussions for the loss of the porn, but he also realised he'd left his sandwiches behind! It was a good job they didn't bother to carry out a controlled explosion that morning or there'd have been tits, fanny and cheese butties flying all over the town centre, courtesy of Paul Gilsenan.

Gilly's humour prevailed at every opportunity. Lee Athletic had a Swiss player called Benno Stauffer, who worked in the Swiss Consulate in Manchester. Benno was a clever, friendly bloke and he spoke at least five languages. But every now and then, he made the odd comment in his pidgin English that was tailor-made for Gilly. Benno and Gilly became involved in a discussion about the political constitutions of both Switzerland and England. Benno commented, 'In Switzerland we don't have a prime minister, we have a syndicate of senior ministers who dictate policy; the decision process is very slow.' Gilly replied, 'So I've heard. In fact, I believe that Switzerland is still deciding whether or not to enter the Second World War!'

On another occasion, Benno invited us and our respective partners to sample a traditional Swiss fondue at his luxurious home in Hale (an exclusively affluent area to the south of Manchester where most of the rich pro-footballers reside). Gilly wasn't too sure about the ingredients of fondue, so Benno assured him, 'It consists of every type of cheese imaginable.'

'What, including bell end?' Gilly asked as Benno sat there looking totally bemused. After that fondue evening, Jane described us both as a couple of naughty boys after sitting at Benno's table giggling away all night. Unfortunately, the fondue and its complex and sophisticated combination of cheese and bread didn't agree with Jane. Straight after we'd finished, she just about made it to the downstairs loo to be ill. The other five of us remained sitting at the table in an embarrassing silence as we could clearly hear my darling wife in distress. Gilly saved the day when he commented, 'Don't worry Benno. Being violently sick after a meal is the English way of showing your appreciation to the chef.'

Gilly also featured in an episode with a Saudi Arabian player at Lee Athletic named Mansoor. He turned up in an all-in-one dazzling white sheety outfit, complete with cranial tea towel. The attire remained spotless until Gilly started having a kickabout with him just before the game started. Gilly continually and purposefully knocked the ball at Mansoor at such a height that he had to chest it down every time. The poor lad was covered in mud within minutes. Not that he minded; over the next few months Mansoor became a great admirer of Gilly, both for his genuine encouragement and football ability. Indeed, Mansoor was once moved to comment at five-a-side that, 'Man with two bald patches on head has great skill.' It wasn't long after that Gilly acquired the irreverent and temporary second nickname of 'Baboon Arse Head'.

♦   ♦   ♦

It was after one of these training sessions when we started to realise that all was not well with Gilly. His family suspected that he had a serious problem on holiday in Tenerife. Paul complained that he was finding it hard to swallow. He'd been to the doctors several times, where he'd been assured that it was nothing worse than a temporary condition caused by stress.

Paul started to lose weight, and things came to a head at the 1995 B&H Lord's final between Lancashire and Kent. As usual we stopped off for our traditional pre-match fry-up at a 'greasy spoon' café in St John's Wood. All he could muster was a plate of scrambled eggs, which he hardly touched; given that Paul enjoyed his food, scrambled eggs was completely out of character. I had a go at him for such a feeble attempt at breakfast, but he calmly explained that he was really struggling to swallow anything, including liquids.

We were all aware that Gilly wasn't well, something that wasn't lost on his astute father-in-law, Pete. He'd had enough of the GP's ambivalence and led Gilly back to the surgery on the Monday following the Lord's final and insisted that Paul be sent to the specialists. The following day I took a phone call from Gilly, who was at Withington Hospital with Joanne and her dad. Paul asked, 'Can you get over here mate? They've told me they think I've got cancer.' When I arrived at his ward, he was sitting up in bed wearing both his England football shirt and his cheeky smile. The timing of this couldn't have been worse, with Joanne five months pregnant. Gilly had been diagnosed with oesophageal cancer, but there was hope. During that summer Paul endured a course of chemotherapy. He'd just had his second blast when Joanne went into labour and produced the best gift Gilly could have wanted, a baby boy they named Sam. Pete and Gilly were at the birth of Sam and cried tears of joy.

Sam was immediately given a bib to wear with a Manchester City badge on it which read, 'Cos my dad says so.' Paul would sit with his new baby repeatedly saying, 'My boy,' and, 'I love you.' As he fed him from a bottle he sang him lullabies while kissing and cuddling him, with both arms wrapped around him and a look of total admiration and pure contentment on his face. All this love and affection was given although Paul's body was being ravaged by chemotherapy and illness. But he didn't complain. He couldn't understand why he'd fallen to this illness, but often confided with Pete that he was glad that it was him and not Joanne who had to suffer.

We kept in touch with Paul as often as his illness would allow, but time was getting short. The last derby match Paul attended came on 14 October 1995 when he and I visited Old Trafford for a league fixture. Work was in progress on a new stand and so United decided not to give City supporters any tickets due to lack of space. Fair enough. I'd have expected the same if the roles had been reversed. It had been years since either Gilly or I had missed the big clash but we had to be there. Like me, he saw it as his duty to be present at the derby. Jill, an old friend of Paul's from British Gas, had managed to secure him a ticket and he persuaded her to find another one for me. It was a measure of people's affection for Paul that, despite the fact that she lived in Canada at the time, Jill was willing to go so far out of her way to make him happy with her United season tickets, even though she was in Manchester for the weekend. Due to the scarcity of tickets, at most there were probably only about 100 City fans at the game. It was to be the last time I spent any personal time 'alone' with Gilly, and even though City lost to a solitary goal, I look back on the event with a lot of happiness.

When the day arrived, Paul's attendance was in doubt. He had been very ill and was sick just before he left the house. However, he still managed to find the strength and determination to get to Old Trafford. Once there, we overheard a Red saying, 'There'll not be many City fans here today.' Gilly replied out loud in a voice full of pride, 'Well there's one here mate,' and I added, 'Make that two.' The bloke turned around and we quickly realised that the Red was England's cricket captain, Michael Atherton.

Gilly somehow mustered up the strength to cheer on the Blues with his usual fervour. We were sitting just behind Mike Summerbee, and the three of us almost had cause to jump up and celebrate Niall Quinn's equaliser. He was put clean through, but shoved it wide and we lost 1–0. It would have been 'A goal for Gilly' had he scored. It was a triumph in itself that Paul managed to attend the game. Joanne drove us to the match and picked us up with Sam gurgling in his baby seat. For once, derby defeat paled into insignificance.

Paul made one last appearance at Maine Road just to say goodbye to the place he loved. He looked so pale and ill that Steve Maher asked, 'Is he going to die, Worthy?' Although I couldn't bring myself to say it, in my heart of hearts reality had finally dawned on me. It was becoming apparent that Gilly would be lost. I, like many others, could not believe that the inevitable would happen, but it did.

Christmas 1995 was the only one that Paul, Joanne and Sam Gilsenan shared together as a family. Paul began x-ray therapy on 3 January for the cancer that had by now developed in his brain, lungs and liver. He succumbed to his illness at home twenty days later. It still came as a deep shock when Joanne phoned me at 5.30 on the morning of 23 January 1996 to deliver the grave news. Paul had died 10 minutes earlier. I then put into motion the plan to ring around his many friends for them to digest and pass on the bad news. It was the hardest thing I've ever had to do.

♦   ♦   ♦

The night before the funeral there was a vigil with the coffin at St John the Baptist Church in Timperley, where all of his large family of friends and relatives were present. Gilly's dad went through the Hail Mary routine, which I'd never heard before. With his broad Irish accent, it sounded to me like horse racing commentary – something which gave me a fleeting smile as I knew it wouldn't have been lost on Paul. But when I got home, the magnitude of the event hit me hard. I finally went to sleep that night crying like a baby.

The next day, the funeral was the toughest and saddest day of my life. I can't imagine how his loving wife Joanne must have felt. She had been a guardian angel, totally devoted to Paul throughout his illness, even when she was pregnant with obvious needs of her own. It was a dimly-lit, perishing, snow-covered day, appropriate to the cold, dark mood that prevailed. When an older person dies, it is nice to celebrate the full life they have led; but Gilly was only thirty-two years of age and with a four-month-old baby boy, who had just lost probably the best dad that could ever have been.

Bibby, Bugsy, Gizzard, Johnny Copper, Steve Maher and I carried the coffin into the church, which was packed to the rafters with distraught mourners and all manner of people – so much so that one of the seasoned undertakers was moved to comment, 'Who was this guy? I've never seen so many people at a funeral before.' Gilly was a soulmate to everyone who liked having fun. During his eulogy, the priest said that Paul had once commented, 'We are on this earth for a short time in preparation for the eternal life that is to follow.' I still can't help but think of him up there with his beloved nanna – who died a month or so before Gilly – looking down on us all with his cheeky smile. It is a fanciful notion perhaps, but also a comforting one.

After the solemn and moving church service – during which his older sister Karen sang like an angel to her solo acoustic guitar – Jane and I drove off a mile or so through the snow and sludge to Altrincham Crematorium for a short cremation service. It was a service we missed. We'd inadvertently got stuck behind the wrong hearse down a country lane en route and by the time we got there, it was all over. We weren't best pleased with ourselves, but Jane and I comforted each other in the fact that had Gilly been looking down from above, he would have been chuckling at us for missing the service in such a daft manner. The following weekend Manchester slowly continued in its snowbound existence. It was, in all probability, a coincidence, but the following Saturday, City's match and all of the Altrincham Sunday League fixtures were postponed. They say that God works in mysterious ways and nothing could have been more fitting than such a mark of respect to my dear friend from his master.

As you get older, you hear people say, 'This person was special,' or, 'That person was special.' Its meaning gets diluted with familiarity, but in the case of Paul Gilsenan, he truly was a special individual and a real measure of his unique qualities came after he was gone. Every year his many mates still get together on the anniversary of his death for 'Gilly Night' where a bottle of his favourite Holsten Pils with ice is always kept on the table and we all toast the memory of the lad who gave us all so much pleasure and warmth. It's now over fourteen years on and the numbers in attendance have not diminished.

Without Gilly's company, life has never really been the same. Whoever Paul came into contact with, their lives were touched by the magic that was only Paul's to give. Joanne told me that it was once written that some people are a gift. They are only destined to be here a short time, but they bring joy and happiness to the people whom they touch. It is a true description of Paul Gilsenan. If there is an afterlife, as Paul truly believed, he'll be up there right now patiently waiting to hold his beloved son once more. Rest in peace mate . . . until then, Sam is in good hands.

34

'The Best Chips in the Land and all the World'

The date 29 January 1997 is one that will remain forever tattooed into my memory. It coincided with one of the biggest disasters to occur in M14 since the Blues lost that infamous relegation home game to Luton Town in 1983. That evening, City's Nationwide First Division game against that most cavalier collection of football impresarios from Yorkshire – namely Sheffield United – was not a classic. But in those days a profound absence of anything resembling even a mediocre exhibition of footballing prowess was nothing new. The eventual 0–0 draw can hardly be described as a catastrophe, but even a 7–0 defeat would have proved insignificant in terms of my own bigger picture, which was to suffer a blow that was tantamount to vandalism.

By the end of the 1996/97 season City had endured no less than five different managers in charge – if you count Asa Hartford and Phil Neal's respective stints as caretakers and we didn't get to the bottom of why Steve Coppell came and left in such a hurry. By the time the Sheffield United home fixture arrived on that fateful winter's night, the legendary Frank Clark had taken over. He was legendary because he was soon to show that he didn't have the first, nor faintest, idea about how to get City back on track which, at the end of the day, was his job. However, under his tutelage, the club was going somewhere all right. By the time Clarke shuffled off into the sunset, we were on our way to the Second Division, the old Division Three.

Even in the face of the regular and severe adversity offered by my team throughout the 1990s, I always found more than adequate consolation at the diminutive but homely Victorian end terraced establishment located at no. 300 Claremont Road. This wasn't the address of a shabeen or, indeed, a house of the red light variety. I had spent this particular Wednesday looking forward, not to the impending goalless war of attrition that prevailed, but instead to the traditional culinary delights available at the greatest fryery on God's planet: the City Chippy. You can't imagine my horror when I arrived at 5 o'clock to find the place unlit and with a home-made sign on the window inconspicuously announcing, 'Due to unforeseen circumstances, the City Chippy has closed.'

Once I'd recovered from the initial trauma, which sent shock waves reverberating around the Beehive, I decided to look on the bright side. After all, closure might have been due to temporary illness or come as a mark of respect for a bereavement. Things turned out to be much worse than I had first imagined when the landlord of our pre-match boozer announced those dreaded words, 'The City Chippy has gone bust!' It takes relegation or to lose in a cup final to make some supporters put their heads in their hands and cry, but for me it was the closure of the City Chippy. Its loss left me as gutted as one of the numerous cod that had been fried there. The City Chippy (formerly Edwards') was a charming little shop and was usually a very friendly place to visit, although there was a big fight in there one night and two blokes beat the crap out of each other (shame on you if you thought I was going to tell you that two fish got battered). Not only did its closure bring to an end one of my sacred match-day rituals, but it also represented yet another nail in the coffin of the traditional English chip shop.

The City Chippy was a welcome throwback to the good old days when fish 'n' chips were a cheap alternative to home cooking. Perhaps this was ultimately the problem. When your dad interminably talks of a time when he got a taxi to the match, sat in the Main Stand, had a skinful afterwards, grabbed a fish supper on the way home and *still* had change out of a shilling, he must have called in at the City Chippy because the prices were always so ridiculously cheap.

Not only was a visit to the City Chippy part of the important pre-match build-up, but it was an important part of the weekend's pre-pub build-up. When I worked at Manchester Town Hall, I would often collect my tea from there on the way home on a Friday. Unfortunately, by the time I had got to Northern Moor 5 miles down the road, 'the sog factor' had set in and those little crispy delights had wilted down to the status of mere mortal pieces of deep fried potato.

In later years I would often tear back from work in Chester to get to the City Chippy before 4.55 p.m. on a match night. This was to avoid the bloke from City's ticket office who got a shipping order in for the rest of his colleagues, delaying my liaison with fried heaven longer than my tolerance would allow. Queueing was never one of my great virtues and I always used to speed up my walk on the way to the City Chippy whenever I noticed a potential customer approaching from an equal distance. An outright sprint to the door would be rude and uncool, but a brisk amateur runner's jog never blew my cover. Once safely inside the door and in the queue with the line of sad-looking locals and City fans alike, I would soon be cheered up by the aroma of spudulicious bliss which was eagerly hoovered up by my nostrils. It was just a matter of time before that fried finery would tantalise my tongue. It was at these times that I was most vulnerable to the dreaded delay. That horrible shout of, 'Does anyone just want fish?' prompted a 10-minute fidget as, 'We're just waiting for chips,' was added to the equation. The worst part of the prolonged agony came whenever the asbestos-fingered owner picked one up to test it, gave it a loving squeeze and declared, 'They're still not ready!'

There was also 'Old Lady Syndrome' which caused irritating delays, but this was somewhat easier to deal with. Whenever some old dear couldn't decide after six seconds what she wanted, I'd quickly but respectfully shove her out of the door until she finally got her act together and sorted out her order. The thing is, when you're in a big chippy queue, what do you think about? All you should be focusing on is that last fish and whether or not the potential spoiler in front of you is going to order it. Then there is the dilemma of whether you should put your chips on your 'barmcake' (bread roll, bap, bun to non-Mancunians), eat the barm separately or, if you're bladdered, whether or not you can get the whole pie, chips, peas and gravy on the barm and scoff the lot without dropping any. There is also the further problem to consider of whether or not you should get a side order of scallops . . . just in case. I can't understand ditherers in chippy queues; after all, they've had all day to think about it. But these are dilemmas that I won't have to face ever again down in Moss Side.

It's no use crying over spilt gravy. The City Chippy and Maine Road are dead. Long live the Golden Fish outside the club's new home: the City of Manchester Stadium.

35

Seasons beyond Reason

C ity had enjoyed better times at Maine Road than those served up in 1997 by the forlorn figure of manager Frank Clark. 'Old Sad Eyes' was a fatherly looking man with little idea of football management. Prior to his arrival, the 1990s had not been City's greatest decade. It started well enough when we finished the 1990/91 season fifth and one place above United. Howard Kendall was at the helm until November 1990 when he left City to rejoin Everton, the club to whom he said he was 'married'.

The popular Peter 'Reidy' Reid then took over as player/manager and steered City to another fifth place spot. But the following year we started to slip down the table with an alarming lack of resistance. It was a descent that coincided with Reidy's retirement as a player, which was really no coincidence. City's reliance on Reid as a midfielder was graphically illustrated when we played United at home that season. At the interval the Blues were leading and we'd all nipped behind the back of the Kippax for a half-time pie and a pint of overpriced ale, when Gilly spotted Johnny Copper. He was in his uniform, patrolling behind the back of the stand on his own. John was big mates with all the lads (he grew up with Bibby's Mancor team and later played for Lee Athletic), but he was also a big Red. Gilly playfully attacked him by surprise and knocked off his helmet as we all piled on for a laugh. On the face of it, a policeman was being duffed up by City fans and, as reinforcements from the local constabulary came rushing to his aid from all directions with their truncheons at the ready, John was heard frantically shouting, 'It's my mates! IT'S MY MATES!' Unfortunately, our friend was to be a laughing policeman that day. With about 10 minutes to go and with City 3–1 to the good, Reidy substituted himself and it all went wrong – United scored two quick goals and almost went on to win.

Fifth place in Reidy's first year – and yet again in 1991/92 – was promising and something upon which to build. But in season 1992/93 we'd slipped to ninth. In hindsight a 'top 10' position should have been more than acceptable. City began the next season badly, however, and Peter Swales started to get a little more than twitchy. In order to do his dirty and unpopular work, the chairman temporarily hired a brave and ruthless hitman named John Maddock to fire his bullets. He soon disposed of Reidy together with his scary-looking sidekick, Sam Ellis. Getting rid of tough-guy Ellis was not a job I would have fancied nor relished – certainly not without the backing of a flame-thrower and a gang of hired Ninjas.

On the morning after a totally nondescript Friday night 1–1 home draw with Coventry City, Brian Horton was appointed in Reid's place. The tabloids greeted this 'swoop' with headlines saying, 'Brian Who?' I had to agree; I didn't know who the heck he was either. But had I studied the Luton relegation tape of 7 May 1983 a little harder, I'd have spotted his bearded head being chased across the pitch by John Eaton, Millsy and the rest of the angry mob in pursuit of our Bedfordshire slayers. The season also saw the start of the demise of both Swales and the old Kippax terrace. The metamorphosis of Maine Road had begun. The last game of the season was the end of the Kippax stand, a place that had been a second home to me and many others. It was a sad loss.

The Kippax was replaced with a building site, which bore witness to some great games, such as a 4–0 hammering of Everton and a 5–2 home demolition of Jürgen Klinsmann and his showbiz Tottenham XI. But such results hadn't been the norm and, later that season, a fine 3–2 away victory to eventual champions Blackburn served to banish any lingering doubts about City's possible relegation. Although City stayed up, sixth from bottom wasn't good enough for new chairman Francis Lee, who had been installed in a wave of emotion under the 'Forward with Franny' campaign that finally saw Swales accept his end. Much to most people's annoyance, the popular Horton was given the grand order of the boot soon after the season's fixtures had been completed. Forward with Franny? Not really.

Then came Lee's masterstroke: he appointed Alan Ball, a man who'd failed at most places he'd managed, but at least he had a few good stories to tell of how he won the 1966 World Cup. In all probability, existing players such as Immel, Mazzarelli, Kavelashvili, Ekelund and Frontzeck wouldn't have known who he was. Ball also signed Martin 'Buster' Phillips from Torquay United, whom he predicted would be 'the first

£10m footballer in this country.' I couldn't tell you who that turned out to be but, needless to say, it certainly wasn't 'Buster' Phillips. In my experience 'potential' is one of life's great hallucinations.

By the time this football genius of a manager had been appointed in his flat cap, I'd been writing regular articles for City fanzine *Electric Blue*. It was a publication that had joined the 'Forward with Franny' campaign to help to oust Swales and insert Lee into the City hot seat. To all of my mates, bar one, Lee's appointment was seen as the dawn of a new era. The one abstention came from Gilly. He prophetically warned us all that, 'Franny Lee is only in it for himself. He doesn't care about City and it will go tits-up once that *portly chap* gets in.' An astute man was Gilly. Things did deteriorate.

Mr Ball's tenure wasn't the best and, unfortunately, I always associate Oasis' classic 'Wonderwall' track with our struggling but honest enough manager as, 'After all, you're my Alan Ball' was adopted as his anthem by many, although not by me. After a season which saw the team rely mostly upon Georgiou Kinkladze's brilliance, 1995/96 saw City face relegation on the last day of the season. The Blues were at home to Liverpool in a game we *had* to win to stay up. If only the management had been aware of that small fact we may well have done so. Despite having some more than capable performers in the team – such as Niall Quinn, Uwe Rosler, Keith Curle, Peter Beagrie, Paul Walsh and the brilliant Kinkladze – City had slipped into a desperate position. Liverpool had nothing on the game except pride. A couple of fluke goals put City 2–0 down at half time. But we managed to pull it back to 2–1 in the 71st then 2–2 in the 78th minute; 12 minutes left to find salvation. But fortune floundered as farce unfolded. Ball took heed of a misinformed rumour relating to the other scores and now thought a point would be enough to save City from the drop. He conveyed this onto the pitch. Instead of going for the necessary win, the players then started time-wasting for a draw (illustrated by Steve Lomas messing about with the ball by the corner flag with only a few minutes to go). It wasn't until the substituted Niall Quinn took matters into his own hands and ran up and down the touchline in a frantic effort to make his team-mates aware of reality. But City played out a draw and went down with 38 points – the same tally as Southampton and Coventry, both of whom also drew but stayed up due to their superior goal difference. Alan Ball was never really held to account for such a basic error, although he only survived a mere three games into his next and final season on the MCFC managerial merry-go-round.

Mr Ball once said confusingly that, 'I'm not a believer in luck, but I do believe you need it.' City did have some bad luck that day, but our overall misfortune was purely and simply down to choices: the wrong choices made by Alan Ball and ultimately by Francis Lee.

Yet another final-day relegation was a crushing blow and after the match I wandered into the Parkside for a consolatory gallon of Stella. None of my mates had yet joined me and as I stood there fighting back the tears, a complete stranger spotted my obvious distress, came over and handed me his half-smoked spliff. Although he didn't know me, he could see that I needed something to stimulate an improved demeanour. Just to help usher my tenebrous mood into plummeting even further, news came through that United had simultaneously won the league at Middlesbrough. I've had better days.

♦   ♦   ♦

We started 1996/97 back in the now-familiar surroundings of the Second Division. During a pre-season visit to Maine Road while showing a group of Euro 96 Germans around our hallowed, if disjointed, stadium, Francis Lee had commented to me somewhat arrogantly that, 'We don't need any new players to get out of this division.' He was obviously so confident that he promptly sold Niall Quinn to Sunderland – a big mistake as he was City's most consistent player of the decade.

In fact, we did need some new players and we needed some new managers as well. Alan Ball was sacked after a couple of shambolic away defeats at Bolton and Stoke. Asa Hartford took over from Ball as caretaker, to be replaced by Steve Coppell and his mysteriously brief tenure of six games. With uncharacteristic charity, I advocated in the fanzine that the former Manchester United winger should be given a fair chance by the supporters, while Bibby's article focused on the view that he was a Red who was bound to let us down sooner rather than later. Unfortunately it turned out to be sooner. By the time the next issue of *Electric Blue* had hit the streets, the former England winger had already departed to leave me looking like a right plonker.

Following another temporary appointment (this time the dignified Phil Neal), Frank Clark took over in December 1996. What a nightmare he turned out to be. We played his former club, Nottingham Forest, at home and their supporters had produced a huge banner which catalogued all the many poor signings he had made while he was in charge at the City ground. I also remember commenting to my dad at the time that, 'I think we might have signed up another duck-egg here,' and I was right. City finished just below mid-table. If that wasn't bad enough, the following year was an absolute disaster.

Clark's reign was thankfully terminated when he was sacked in favour of Joe Royle with a third of the season to go. To describe City as *awful* that year doesn't do justice to the word. Things came to a climax at home to lowly, little Bury on 14 February 1998. Without wishing to sound arrogant or patronising towards the Shakers, there was no way in this world City should have been losing 1–0 to a team of that calibre. The natives were restless and, suddenly, a fan walked onto the pitch from the Kippax and ripped up his season ticket and threw it onto the floor in disgust. Three days later Clark was booted out. As for the disgruntled fan whose sole protest had so poignantly summed up the feelings of the rest of the 28,000 City fans present that day, the ground staff pieced together his season ticket and a replacement was sent to his home. It was apparently accompanied with a message which read, 'If I've got to suffer this, then so do you!' City's desperate plight had become comical to outsiders. But to committed supporters, it was no joke and I'm convinced that the way your team performs can have a profound and significant effect on your overall wellbeing. Indeed, during those dark days, Jane could usually tell if City had won or lost by my demeanour as I walked through the door. Before long I did start to lighten up and accept our role as England's biggest cock-up team, which was just as well as it was having a negative affect on our marriage.

♦ ♦ ♦

'Sir' Joe Royle was a former player who came to City as an overweight and struggling striker discarded by Everton. I saw him playing for City's reserves in the 1970s and Joe enjoyed a number of second string outings in the Central League until he managed to get into a conventional shape. Once he was fit for purpose, 'Genial Joe' was to become a fine acquisition for City. But, years later, he turned down Peter Swales' overtures to becoming City manager while succumbing to the 'Don't Go Joe' pleas of the Oldham supporters. Royle finally arrived as boss at City in 1997 when Swales had departed from City, and indeed, life itself. The demise of Swales was sad. The man was vilified and ridiculed towards the end and he should have quit with dignity. He held on to the chairmanship too long, failing to recognise when his time was up. But in every Annual

General Shareholders' meeting from 1980 onwards, I can remember Swales at his charming best. The man certainly had charisma. Although he had many faults while in control of the club, I have no doubt that his heart was in the right place. It isn't something I could say with great confidence about his successor.

Royle had fifteen games to save the club from an unthinkable drop into the Third Division. It was a similar amount of time that Alan Ball was given by Portsmouth to avoid the same fate. At least we had a shout as they had roughly the same points as us at the time. I'm not having a veiled pop at Joe Royle, but for some reason Georgiou Kinkladze – one of City's most outstanding players of the decade – was treated as some sort of circus act and was out of the team for the majority of the remaining games. Big Joe did a good job, but he had a tangible weakness in handling big-name players. By the time City played at Stoke for a fateful last game at the Britannia Stadium, even a win couldn't keep us up without having to rely on a Portsmouth cock-up, which didn't materialise.

My mate Gary Tipper had organised a chauffeur-driven limo to take us to that game. The vehicle was brand new and only had about 20 miles on the clock when it arrived to whisk us off to the Potteries in search of an unlikely salvation. After the match – which the Blues won 5–2 – there was trouble in the car park behind the City end and a huge rock landed on the roof of the new car. It wasn't the only thing severely dented that day. City and Stoke were relegated and Portsmouth stayed up. The following day was my thirty-sixth birthday and it wasn't the early present I craved!

I soon picked myself up and started thinking of the up-side. At least I'd get to go to grounds like Colchester United, Wycombe Wanderers and Northampton Town. But then I considered the down-side. I'd have to go to new places like Colchester United, Wycombe Wanderers and Northampton Town (at whose Sixfields Stadium I apparently sat next to 'Rogue Trader' Nick Leeson in inebriated oblivion despite his global infamy at the time). The following season 'down among the dead men' was one which all City fans will look back at with mixed emotions. Following the Blues was a true test of character, but the supporters came through it with flying colours. I was worried whether the majority would desert the cause, but they didn't . . . far from it. The opening game of the season was a 32,000 sell-out which became a statement of defiance against our own adversity. City's fabulous support stayed intact all season despite us plummeting still further to the lowest ever position in the club's history, on 19 December 1998.

Bibby, Andrew 'Charlie' Charles and I went to York City in Gary Tipper's Aston Martin. En route to Bootham Crescent (now the Kit Kat Crescent), Gary stopped off at a colleague's home to discuss business. It was located in an idyllic little village. Gary's colleague's hospitality was superb and he took us to a restaurant in the village, then back to his house for drinks and cigars. He'd even secured us VIP seats at the game and we took up position in the main stand of the dilapidated stadium. City were appalling and we departed with the score at 1–1, thinking that the great Craig Russell had saved our considerable blushes with what we thought was the second and last goal of the game. As we got back to the car we heard a roar from the ground and I commented, 'That doesn't sound good.' Indeed it wasn't. We'd conceded a late goal which meant that Manchester City were now in twelfth place in the third tier of English football. It was also a fateful day for the York City bloke who had welcomed us into his home before the match. Gary sacked him on the Monday!

After the York game, the only way proved to be up. Perhaps Joe Royle had spotted a similarity to his former playing style in Shaun Goater when he signed him the season before from Bristol City. With a few games under his belt, 'The Goat' (as he was famously christened) had started to deliver the goals. After an unlikely home win against Stoke at Christmas, the season gained momentum and City battled a way through to the end of season play-offs and a Wembley play-off final against Gillingham. The game was played on the Sunday, but we were living it up on the town so much the night before that a German couple asked Bibby, 'Who won the game?' A few minutes later I managed to clamber up and maroon myself on one of those large lions that guard Nelson's Column in Trafalgar Square. I had crawled out onto the neck of one of the statuesque lions 'for a laugh'. But once I was out on a limb (or its mane in reality) it suddenly started raining and I found that I couldn't get back along the slippery surface without severely testing my 'bouncebackability' to the limit. It would have been a 15ft drop onto unforgiving hard stone had I slipped. Luckily I was helped back to safety.

Another lesson Bibby should have learnt that weekend was never leave a ground before the final whistle. But at 2–0 down, and with a minute to go of normal time, Bib persuaded me, Bugsy, 'Big' Ian Eastaugh and Gary to head back to the warm consolation of the Wembley Conservative Club. At the time it seemed like a sound idea to drown our sorrows after what appeared to be certain defeat. On our way down the steps at the back of the ground I heard a muffled roar. I instantly told the others I thought I might have heard a goal and invited them to join me as I pushed my way back into the ground. This was one of the better decisions I have made because Kevin Horlock had pulled it back to 2–1 in the 90th minute. With 5 minutes of injury time and with only a minute left on the clock, the diminutive Paul Dickov equalised with possibly *the* most dramatic and important goal a player will ever score for City. I ended up face-down on the concrete steps screaming with joy with at least four delirious lads on top of me.

On hearing the news of the equaliser from Tipper's dad on his mobile, Gary, Bibby, Big Ian and Bugsy did a quick about turn in the car park and 'strolled' back for extra-time. Dickov's effort was the sixth goal Bibby had missed out of the last eight that City had scored at Wembley, but at least he was there to see City triumph in the penalty shoot-out.

Sir Joe had taken us up and he did it again in 1999/2000. A memorable if somewhat fortunate last day of the season victory at Blackburn meant that we'd quickly returned from the nightmare of the lower divisions to the financial rewards of the Premier League. Returning from 'Eehbygumwood' Park, my pals and I celebrated our unlikely 4–1 victory and equally unlikely return to the top flight in the Rain Bar in Manchester. Promotion was a marvellous achievement for both manager and club – an achievement which was somewhat spoiled by relegation from the Premiership the following season. Arsenal arrived from another planet that term and took a 3–0 lead at Maine Road after 15 minutes. The subsequent 4–0 hammering provided an all-too-real illustration of City's deficiencies. Big Joe had been found wanting in the top flight, again struggling to accommodate big-name players such as former FIFA World Player of the Year George Weah, who was unbelievably left out of our Anfield line-up at the expense of Paul Dickov. Joe and City endured an acrimonious split at the end of that season as the club entered a rollercoaster era, with Kevin Keegan in charge.

Keegan's arrival stirred things upwards and his first season in 2001/02 was a humdinger. Yet another sentence in the second tier started with a 3–0 home win over Watford. However, a couple of early away defeats left us all guessing as to what to expect when we set off for a night match at Coventry in September 2001. Gary had arranged a corporate hospitality sketch and Bibby, Charlie, Big Ian and I arrived at Highfield Road suited and booted in the 'chauffeur bus' ready for a good time at Gary's expense. Before, during and after the meal we were plied with all the beer we could drink. Just before kick-off we were all invited to take our seats through an adjoining door into the stand, which happened to be in a small section up at the top of the home end. Coventry took the lead, but when the mercurial Ali Benarbia equalised minutes later, all of our somewhat conspicuous party celebrated with the added enthusiasm copious amounts of pre-match alcohol will bring. Our antics didn't go down well with the locals.

Coventry took the lead once more, but this time the home fans overdid their celebrations just to rub it in. They took no time in turning towards our small party with clenched fists, mouthing the usual vitriol as is customary in such situations. By now it was all descending into anarchy and the stewards had positioned themselves around us in order to make sure it didn't kick-off. Just before half time, Kevin Horlock equalised for City and once again our ties were swinging around our necks as we leapt around punching the air. The Coventry fans tried to get at us and we were hastily escorted back into the restaurant area so as to avoid any fist-swinging.

On the insistence of the stewards, we were forced to watch the rest of the game on the 'live' TV feed in the bar and none of us were happy about it. But in consolation, it was a lot warmer inside than out and the free beer continued to flow throughout the second half. Unfortunately, City conceded a late goal near the end to lose the match 4–3 and we weren't best pleased. My lot were the last ones to leave and I staggered over to the minibus to see the rest of the lads in hysterics. Charlie was helpless and in tears as he led me to the back of the minibus, saying, 'Come and have a look at this, Worthy.' He opened the doors to reveal the booty. Somehow they'd managed to nick an enormous 6ft by 5ft wooden Coventry City crest from the restaurant wall. Charlie had unscrewed it with his tie clip.

An incredulous Bibby phoned me at home the next day to tell me that he had found an enormous Coventry City badge in his lounge! He only remembered it when he'd gone downstairs to make a piece of toast to go with his customary chicken Cup-a-Soup hangover cure. Bib kept the badge in his shed for a while and we had a few ideas about taking it to exotic places (such as Rotherham or Walsall) then sending pictures of its location back to Coventry City. But we never got around to it. Eventually Big Ole Fuglestad from City's Scandinavian Branch wrestled it back to Bergen from Manchester via train and ferry. He then passed it on to his pal who happened to be the chairman of the

Coventry City Norwegian supporters' club. It remains in Norway to this day.

Despite the defeat that night, City more than made up for it by eventually winning the league 10 points clear of our nearest rivals and scoring 99 goals into the bargain. Not that winning 'The Championship' is recognised as winning anything. According to United fans we haven't won anything since 1976, so only God knows what that big silvery thing was the team paraded around the pitch.

Fünf – Eins!

upporting City in the 1990s resembled the kind of excruciating and painful endurance test experienced by a contestant in a Japanese game show. It got to the stage where I needed a few footballing vacations away from the Blues just to see some top-class football, but I settled for watching England instead. Following my country had previously provided me with some much-needed respite from City, but it had been a while since England's national footy team and I had been acquainted on foreign soil. Although I had attended a lot of home games at Wembley, these tailed off from the mid-1980s onwards.

In an ideal world I would have loved to have gone to the Italia 90 World Cup, but at the time Jane and I were saving up for the wedding and deposit for the house. With Pavarotti keeping us awake with his rendition of 'Nessun Dorma', England marched all the way to the semis. We would surely have beaten a weakened Argentina in the final had our lads been able to take penalties. This lack of clinical ruthlessness has hindered the nation's aspirations for footballing glory more than once. Had we won this and subsequent penalty shoot-outs, England would have made it through to one World Cup final, a European Championship final, a European Championship semi-final and a World Cup quarter-final. Where was our Joanne when she was needed?

England failed to qualify for USA 94 so when France 98 waved an enticing *tricolore* on the horizon, the country was desperate for the team to make it to the finals following an eight-year gap. The final group game in Italy would determine England's fate. Graham Moore, Bugsy, Noel Bayley and I set off on Wednesday 8 October 1997, for an adventure across Europe to the Eternal City, without even bothering to take a road map with us as we knew that whatever turn we took, all roads would lead to Rome. We spent the first night in a shoe-box hotel in Merlebach, France. The second night was spent with all four of us on the lounge floor of a one-bed apartment in Munich. Given the hours of interminable journeying in Graham's car, this proved to be a more intimate trip than we'd bargained for.

Our host in Bavaria was Noel's German mate, Lothar (or 'Silk Cut' as he became affectionately known: Low Tar). Lothar turned out to be the leader of the local supporters' branch of TSV 1860 Munchen, whose bar treated us to a triumphal playing of the City song 'The Boys in Blue' on the jukebox as we entered the pub. I was instantly converted into an 1860 fan.

The next morning, I peeled open my bleary eyes and discovered that I'd taken an unconscious and somewhat dangerous leak on Lothar's large pride and joy: a cactus plant. It left me with a few splinters to get rid off in a sensitive area which made the hangover suffered on the car journey through the snow-covered Alps into Italy an even more challenging one; it was more than difficult to effectively use tweezers and remove the thorns under such bumpy conditions. Saturday was the only full day we had in Rome and we decided to make the best of it. We took an early morning trip to the Colosseum and recited all the predictable jokes about the place being in ruins. While we were queueing outside for a protracted amount of time, Noel was moved to comment, 'They've had a couple of thousand years to get this right, and it's even worse than the City ticket office!'

We were stopped by an Italian TV crew and asked for an interview. I was on my best behaviour, taking on the diplomatic role for my country as the microphone was thrust into my face as the interviewer asked, 'What will you be doing for the rest of the day?' I replied, 'We are looking forward to enjoying the many cultural and historical delights your beautiful city has to offer.' He then asked, 'So you won't be drinking beer later?'

'No, only mineral water. Otherwise we won't be able to gain a proper appreciation of the majestic splendour of Rome that it deserves.'

Later that morning, we spent a hilarious 20 minutes outside the Vatican watching Noel get a knock-back from entering the Sistine Chapel by the fashion police. This was because he'd been caught wearing shorts and black patterned ankle socks (thus denying him the private audience he'd granted to the Pope just before he left his mam's 'ouse in Wythenshawe).

We then made our way to the Piazza Navona for a few afternoon 'scoopies'. All was well as we sat outside a bar happily watching the world pass, and the oodles of hot Roman totty strolling sexily by, through our cool designer shades in the lazy haze of a hot Azzuri afternoon. Suddenly an Italian bloke clocked us and did an instant double-take. He'd seen us on Italian TV that morning in our distinctive laser blue City shirts. He was delighted to see us.

'Ah, you!' he said pointing to me enthusiastically while sounding lika da Chico Marx, 'I see you ona da TV this morning and you say you don'ta drinka da beer!' He was smiling as he pointed to our table full of half-drunk and empty bottles of Peroni. He then aimed his accusing finger at me once more and continued, 'Before he spoke to you, da interviewer had tolda da audience that he would picka da first Englishman at random. He said you would say you were going to drinka da beer all day and then starta da trouble. Instead you say dat you only drinka da water and enjoya da city. It was a very funny and you make him looka very stupido!' I was well pleased with my result and we all raised our bottles of 'mineral water' in his direction as the impressed Italian walked away with a wry smile. We did have something further to celebrate with the eventual goalless draw. It was enough to send England through to Le Coupe du Monde and France 98.

The following summer, Bibby, Bugsy and I took a brief sojourn over to France for the first-round England v Tunisia game in Marseille. We based ourselves in Nice and, on the day of the match, took a train journey to the drug-importing capital of France in a carriage packed with England fans and a solitary French lass. The heat in the train was stifling and, after a while, the marooned young French girl sitting in the corner tried asking us a question in her native tongue. I was the first to twig what she wanted and I replied in my best seductive French accent, 'Ouvrez la fenêtre?' She replied, 'Oui monsieur,' in an equally gravelled voice. The other lads in the compartment looked suitably impressed as I opened the window, but Bibby quickly set the record straight by saying, 'It's the only bit of French he knows!' The French girl's apparent lack of English soon gave the other lads in the carriage a few ideas and one of them commented like the big, bad wolf, 'My, what nice pert little boobies you have,' to which she replied, 'I do understand some English you clown!'

England won the game 2–0 and there was the usual fisticuffs which accompany many an England match – not at the ground, but at the beach where the big screens had been located. England went out in the second round, losing to Argentina on penalties. They should have won with a late Sol Campbell goal but it was inexplicably disallowed. David Beckham's petulant kick at Diego Simeone led to his sending off and didn't help the cause, but at least it allowed us City fans to blame United for the eventual penalty elimination.

♦   ♦   ♦

Saturday 7 October 2000 marked an historic occasion in English football. This was the end of an era. It was the last game at the seventy-six-year-old dump known as Wembley stadium. The match was a key 2002 World Cup qualifier and it was fitting that the Germans were coming to the 'Home of Football' to provide an appropriate foe for the last match on the hallowed, if rain-sodden, turf. Once in 'The Smoke' we located our usual free parking spot and huddled under Bibby's lone golfing brolly as we set off for the 18-mile hike towards the stadium. I made my ascent up those dreary concrete steps for the last time and entered the prison-like barbed-wire-clad gates leading into the ground itself. Once inside the dark, damp, decrepit old stadium, I had little choice than to wade through a waterlogged forecourt to find my seat, which left me far too close to pitch level to get a decent perspective on the game.

After the formal un-pleasantries it was down to business. Given its billing, and the realisation that there were four overrated United players in the team and Gareth Southgate in midfield, perhaps I should have realised that the day's scriptwriter would not be writing with the finest quill from England's capital. Predictably enough, England's attacking prowess during the whole 90 minutes was expressed through a solitary Tony Adams header and one shot from 'Golden Balls' Beckham which was worthy of note. It was a pretty dire affair from an Englishman's point of view on a day when the Germans won with a goal from future City player 'Didi' Hamann. At the end of the match – defeated and deflated – I stood silently as the teams disappeared down the tunnel for the last time to the traditional cockney cry of, 'Wotta loada rabbish.' It was a local show of appreciation that had alas been heard at Wembley more times than 'Abide With Me'.

Once the dust had settled, Wembley would be no more. From Paul Power to Puskás, from Maradona to Mark Lillis – all the greats had been there. But now they are just ghostly memories flattened by the new super state-of-the-art stadium that stands in its place. For the short-changed supporter, Wembley's yellow lakes of urine had finally filled their last pair of receptive shoes.

England's qualification to Korea & Japan 2002 now looked decidedly dodgy. Having seen England qualify for Spain 82 and France 98 by attending the respective away games in Hungary and Italy, I made it my business to get over to Germany for the rematch in Munich. I flew to Germany with Bugsy and the Boden family on a trip organised by Bugsy's neighbour 'Swiss Tony,' a larger-than-life character. We spent the day in Munich's open beer market sampling the delights of the local Klinkerhoffen brew. I had numerous chats with Germany supporters and warned them of my total confidence, which I retained even when Carsten Jancker scored an early goal for the home team.

I was perched on a strange stanchion-cum-seat thing in the England section as the historic events unfolded. Michael Owen soon equalised and just before the half-time break, Steven Gerrard's fabulous strike from outside the box gave us a 2–1 lead. At half time all of England's fans were in dreamland, which is where we remained during the second half as the score went from 1–2 to 1–3 to 1–4. There were still over 15 minutes left when Emile Heskey banged in England's fifth. As England went 'nap' I had a beer in each hand and was thus unable to rub my eyes at the sight of 'GERMANY 1 ENGLAND 5' on the scoreboard. Heaven.

I'd like to be able to report the great night back in the bar celebrating our victory and subsequent World Cup qualification. Unfortunately, Pat Boden, her daughter Vicky and I spent the following hours riding around on the Munich tube system having forgotten the name of the nearest station to our hotel, whose name we also couldn't remember. But no matter, this was the one we'd all waited for. However, once the World Cup unfolded in Japan the following year, it was Germany who found themselves in the final and not England.

♦　　♦　　♦

I didn't make it over to Japan but I would have been there had England reached the final in Tokyo. Gary Tipper had generously reserved and paid for a place on a corporate trip, which would have been waiting had England beaten Brazil and then made it past the semi-final. However, four years later my benevolent pal spent his money on a trip to a group match against Sweden in Cologne allowing Bibby and I to sample the delights of Deutschland once more.

The World Cup in 2006 had certainly changed from the first one I had attended in Spain an alarming twenty-four years earlier. While there were, at most, approximately 10,000–20,000 England supporters in 1982, various estimates claimed that approximately 80,000 supporters had made the trip across the Channel in 2006.

As if England didn't have enough support, the day before the game we stumbled upon four totally wasted Norwegians, resplendent in their national team's shirts, who just about managed to tell us through their collective alcoholic haze that they, ''ave come over to shupport England cos we hate Shwedes!' England drew 2–2 with Sweden in the Cologne's 'Klippity Kloppen Stadion' and, subsequently, we went on to see off the mighty Ecuador in the first knockout stage. Then it was Portugal.

Once again Gary came through with another trip and so Bibby, Charlie, Mr Tipper and I went back over to Germany on Saturday 1 July 2006, for the quarter-final against Portugal in the 'Carcharadon Carcharias Stadion', Gelsenkirchen (the home of 'Shark 04'). This was a day trip which left Wythenshawe's Bernard Manning International Airport at 9.30 a.m. and arrived back at 1.30 on the following morning. What happened in between ultimately turned into a nightmare. The flight took us back to Cologne and then transferred via coach to Gelsenkirchen. On arrival at the Marriott Hotel near the ground (located right next to the old World Cup 74 stadium) we picked up our match tickets. We were told by Gary's contact that we would also have tickets for both the semi-final and the final should England make it. This could be my only realistic opportunity to see England go all the way and with this in mind the match took on an even greater personal significance. Not only did we need victory to avenge the penalty defeat to Portugal in Euro 2004, but we also needed the win which would enable Bibby and I to go to Munich and then on to Berlin for the ultimate football experience. All in all, it was a reasonably important match. England were just two games away from the ultimate football experience but, once more, they failed us. It was typical that a couple of Manchester United players would mess it all up, with Rooney's antics and the disgraceful provocative behaviour of Ronaldo. This left us with ten men, an uphill struggle, the now seemingly obligatory penalty defeat and ignominious exit.

37

My Maine Road Career

"Get off the field," said Billy McNeill and how right he was,' is a piece of paraphrased commentary from the last match of the promotion season game back in 1985 when City played Charlton. Sixteen years later I found myself echoing those very sentiments during the pitch invasion which followed the 2000/01 season's final game (a 2–1 home defeat against Chelsea) and for good reason. Three days later I was to realise a lifetime's ambition and play on Maine Road's hallowed turf in a charity match that I had been invited to play by 'Our Saviour' Gary Tipper. Mr Tipper was given the nickname with due reverence during the 1990s when he put together a consortium to challenge for the ownership of City following the departures of Peter Swales and Francis Lee. My affluent pal was hoping to majestically propel the club away from the depths it found itself in at the time. He even made the *MUEN* front page headlines with the lead story, 'Cheshire Businessman Bids for City'! Despite his lofty status, our esteemed friend continued to drink in the Beehive when we would greeted with, 'Mornin' Saviour.'

I was to follow in our great family tradition of playing at Maine Road. My dad had informed me that he once played at Maine Road in the 1950s and, while it is an old joke, he did play bugle in the band at half time during an England international. And so, on the evening of 22 May 2001, it came to pass that I became the first ever Worthington to actually play football on Maine Road's hallowed turf (apart from our Frank that is). Before the match I didn't know in which position manager Tipper was going to play me, so I was worried about what I should have for my pre-match meal. I thought if he plays me up front I'd better have an Alan Shearer, so I made myself chicken and beans. Then I thought: what if he plays me in midfield?

Thinking of Gazza in his prime, I nipped over the road and ordered pudding, chips, peas and gravy from the chippy (with a kebab on the side, just for good measure). But then after I'd eaten all that, I started panicking, thinking, what if he wants to play me in defence? So I ordered a three-course Indian takeaway and washed it down with a couple of pints of lager, just like City's former Trojan centre-half Andy Morrison.

We sashayed into the home dressing room, which curiously still displayed the last remnants of Joe Royle's final, failed whiteboard tactics (he was sacked a few days later). It detailed an optimistic proposal on how the gallant Jeff Whitley would smother Chelsea's expensive and cosmopolitan midfield into submission single-handedly.

As we were deemed the home team, we put on our City home kit and took on board the instructions from manager Tipper which included the usual classics like, 'Go out there and give 110 per cent,' and thereby setting us an impossible task from the outset.

The game was fantastic. Not perhaps as a spectacle (although the scoreline ended up 4–2 in our favour), but certainly as an experience, I enjoyed every minute of it. Having played Sunday football for the best part of twenty years, the thing that struck me most was the actual size of the Maine Road pitch. I took three corners in the first half and really had to give the ball a good whack in order to get it into the danger zone. The most delightful aspect of the pitch was the actual playing surface and, despite the repaired blemishes, it was like playing on a gigantic bowling green.

Even though this was a charity match it was very competitive (City home kit versus City away kit) and the game was of a fairly high standard. My own personal highlight came early on as I somehow managed to volley over a 20-yard far-post cross with my usually dud left foot (as opposed to my usually dud right foot) which went into the Platt Lane net, via the head of one of our incoming strikers for the opening goal. By the end of that night of copious drinking, the cross in question had somehow become a 45-yard Tueartesque overhead kick which I had put over, having dribbled past four players and cheekily nutmegged the referee in the process.

Unfortunately, it was all over in a flash. My last abiding memories were of overlapping our midfield near the end of the game. I did this in a manner that would have put any of those great City full-backs of the past – Geoff Hammond, Lauren Charvet or Richard Edghill – to shame. Having said that, I was only overlapping the forty-seven-year-old – but still impressive – local radio commentator Jack Dearden; perhaps my late athleticism looked better than it might have appeared.

It was a night I'll never forget. This was also the night when five-year-old Sam Gilsenan was watching in wonderment as I dazzled all before me at Maine Road.

◆ ◆ ◆

By the time the final game at Maine Road arrived at the end of the 2002/03 season, I was taking Sam to the stadium with me; he was big enough from the age of three. His home debut was a 1–1 draw with the mighty Walsall on 26 February 2000 and, had he known any better at that age, he might have sacked it there and then.

There had been a long build-up to the final game down 'The Moss' and I'd braced myself for an emotional day. It wasn't just Maine Road we were leaving; we were also saying goodbye to twenty-odd years of drinking in the hallowed Beehive boozer on Claremont Road. It was also adios to thirty-odd years of queuing outside the ground for tickets and souvenirs, chippy food and Polos and, indeed, everything I could ever want that was associated with my beloved football club. It was an emotional occasion for more than one reason. After the match there were tears in my eyes as I handed Paul Gilsenan's boy back over a Kippax turnstile into the awaiting arms of his mother.

Maine Road had brought me some marvellous times: times of great pride and joy. They were the halcyon days, when the club and my dad were both at their prime in tandem, when young men of the like of Bell, Lee, Summerbee, Marsh, Tueart, Barnes, Francis, Lake, Rosler, Quinn, Kinkladze, Bernarbia and Goater gave me all the pleasure I ever needed, when Helen Turner rang her bell with great gusto and the team played majestically to the swathing mass choir of the Kippax Street stand in full voice, 'We are City, super City from Maine Road!' You'll always remain in my dreams: Maine Road 1923–2003.

38

From Here to Paternity

In 1992, married life began well enough for Jane and I, but it was not without its initial difficulties. Within the first few years, Jane's dad contracted Alzheimer's disease. Being an only child, my wife helped to shoulder the considerable burden, together with her mother. It was a draining time, which took its toll on all involved. Life can indeed be cruel and this was illustrated by a fabulous father who had lived life down the straight and narrow; he'd seen active service in the hell of the South Pacific during the Second World War while serving with the Navy. Steve suffered for seven years before he slowly passed away aged seventy-five and although our lives weren't put entirely on hold, Jane's parents rightly took precedence over any aspirations we might have had for starting a family.

Luckily, my stint at Chester came to a close after six years. Jane and I were four years into our marriage when I secured an interview for a promotion to a post at Halton Borough Council. The recruitment panel asked about my knowledge of all things 'computery' and I managed to convince them that I was some sort of new technology whizz-kid who could lead their committee section to a bright and bold new electronic era: a sort of latter-day Gary Numan, but without the wig. Cheshire County Council had been a pioneer in the introduction of e-Government and my limited knowledge was vast when compared to my would-be suitors at Halton. My success really boiled down to my positive answer to the question, 'Can you turn a computer on? Good, the job's yours.'

The actual interview was held on 12 June 1996. I know this because it was the day after the Lancashire/Yorkshire Roses B&H semi-final that had been delayed due to bad weather. There had been some play on the day before the dark skies took hold, and Lancs were in the driving seat to win the game. But by the time I returned, it was Yorkshire who were odds-on favourites to progress to the final. Play was due to resume at 11.00 a.m. and I had just enough time to complete the interview and shoot back to Old Trafford. On my way up to the sixth floor of the Widnes Municipal Building's interview room, I chatted to a tall, friendly-looking bloke who had the hint of a Birmingham accent. I explained to him that I was there for an interview but was keen to get back to Old Trafford to catch the end of the game. The bloke also turned out to be a cricket fan and he was interested in the other delayed semi-final between Warwickshire and Northants. A few minutes later when I was called into the interview, there was the Brummie bloke sat opposite me asking the questions! I was offered the job later that afternoon, but not before I'd returned in time to witness Peter Martin smack the winning runs off the final ball of a fantastic day.

I settled in quickly at Halton Borough Council, a local authority which covered both 'The People's Republic of Widnesia' and its neighbour 'The Mighty Empire of Runcornia'. The council offices were based in Widnes, on the opposite side of the Mersey Estuary from Runcorn, a town I'd visited in the early 1970s as reward for finishing in the top twenty in the school year for a short, but grubby, little tale I'd written, entitled 'Mud'.

While the journey to my new work station was significantly less than that to Chester, I spent only two years there before moving on to a further promotion at Salford City Council. However, my days at Halton Borough Council were among the happiest of my working career. I landed at Salford with a bump, and while there was the consolation of meeting some sound Blues, like Mike Relph and Paul Templeton, Salford City Council was not the place to be during the late 1990s as it had far too many United fans. As City languished in the third tier of English football, United won the treble but we still had the final laugh at the end of that particular season, thanks to Paul Dickov and his last-gasp equaliser that enabled a dramatic promotion.

♦   ♦   ♦

It's true to say that when it came to procreation, Jane and I took our time about it. Katy was born when Jane was at the comparatively old age for a first pregnancy of thirty-eight and I was past my sell-by date at forty-two – it meant eighty years of parental inexperience between us. But surely we were wise enough to take on the responsibility that only parenthood can deliver?

Once we found out Jane was pregnant it was of some relief to me. As I was virtually the only one left among our circle of friends who was yet to prove his manhood, I had the sneaking suspicion that I might be the one firing blanks. Gilly wasn't the only one who suspected this. In July 2003, we all piled over to the Isle of Man for a weekend of various excesses in celebration of Gary Tipper's fortieth. Throughout the trip, Carl 'Shag' Hendry had decided that, 'Worthy is a Jaffa', and banged on about it all weekend, so much so that it became a catchphrase. But I knew this wasn't the case as Jane was already several weeks into 'pudding club' membership. The week after the IoM trip, I embarked on the journey of a lifetime. Julie, my elder sister, was temporarily living in India with her husband and young family, and she'd invited Jane and me over. We'd already paid for the flights when we discovered Jane's impending delivery of an heir to the Worthy MCFC programme collection. After much soul-searching, we decided that Jane wouldn't go due to the threat of malaria. We also decided that it would be rude for me to stay at home, so I left my pregnant wife behind to fend for herself.

On Monday 14 July 2003, I flew to Mumbai. I'm not going to bang on about my Indian holiday, although it did provide a fittingly spiritual prelude to one of life's great experiences. Seven months later came probably the most profound experience of anyone's life: the birth of your first offspring. Jane had gone into Wythenshawe Hospital on Monday 1 March 2003 to be 'seduced' as I kept calling it. She was due a week or so earlier but, with no sign of action, I went to see City at an away game. Luckily it was just up the road at Bolton's Reebok Stadium.

Twenty-four hours before the actual arrival, Jane and I spent an unsuccessful day in the maternity ward, only to be told to go home as the doctor was sure that nature would take its course before long. Early the next day I was inconsiderately awoken by the strains of Jane's bathroom yelps. Her waters had broken, but this time I was ready. I'd spent all the previous day sitting by Jane's bed without so much of an offer of a cheesy 'Wotsit' from the nurses, despite Jane being fed with envious regularity. When I got home later that evening I was in a ravenous state. Remembering the Scout motto 'Be Prepared' (as opposed to 1st Wythenshawe's unofficial Scout motto of 'When in Cornwall, rob it blind') I packed my cricket cooler box with the usual goodies. These included Scotch eggs and door-stopper butties made from that most underrated, yet totally versatile and economical of meats that is corned beef. Back at the hospital, Jane and I spent from 7.30 in the morning until about 5 o'clock in the evening waiting for a grand entrance. As my uncomfortably bloated wife sucked in copious amounts of gas and air to lessen the pain, I casually munched on my sandwiches. The spectacle of Jane in labour wasn't *quite* as entertaining as the cricket, but at least I was dry and warm.

Anyone who questions the concept of 'love at first sight' has never had a child. When my little lady popped out to say 'hello' it was *the* most surreal moment and my first thought was just how beautiful she was. We couldn't have been happier with our little angel. She weighed in at a massive 9lb 7oz. We'd debated names long and hard before the birth, but without success. Therefore we were both eager to name her straight after the event and so 'we' quickly decided upon the obvious choice of Katy Bell Lee Summerbee Tueart Anelka Wright-Phillips Hareide Ingebrigtsen Worthington. Life would never be the same again; it would be unimaginably better.

The first City fixture with my shiny new daughter safely tucked up in her shiny new cot happened to be the inaugural visit of United to our shiny new ground at Eastlands. Perhaps it would be a good omen for the future if the Blues could produce a special win? Lee Athletic started that Sunday the right way with a 2–1 victory. City added to my celebrations with a 4–1 win in my daughter's first game and first derby match on the planet. It also meant that the City of Manchester Stadium was now baptised.

39

A Sad Finale

Prior to the distractions of childbirth I was able to devote every Sunday morning to the pursuit of success with Lee Athletic. Following Bibby's strict disciplinarian regime, I'd started to mould my own management style, putting an emphasis on freedom of expression. My initial frustrations at not being able to assemble a team with the ability I would have wished for were offset by the fact that the team that I inherited and helped to perpetuate certainly had a few laughs. If we couldn't win trophies I tried to ensure that it would be enjoyable in other ways, by 'trying our hardest' on the field, taking the mickey out of the opposition in success, and laughing at ourselves in adversity. Enjoying the game and each others' company, rather than having matching kit and a few brand-new footballs every month was important.

In terms of playing ability, we might not always have had the best, but we did have some fabulous individuals among the 300 or so that wore the kit in the twenty-seven years the club was established. The problem was that we never had the best XI together at the same time. Our most successful player was Howard Kemp, who scored the semi-final goal that took Oxford City to the 1994/95 FA Vase final at Wembley. It was our only claim to fame and a pretty tenuous one at that. Over the years Lee attracted many talented lads. Unfortunately, they never really lasted long enough to build a successful team. But through our sound organisation, we soon acquired a solid reputation and players gradually began to arrive who were of better quality than I was used to having at my disposal. Through his network of contacts in the postal service, Flynny was able to identify some good new footballers.

He was instrumental in the acquisition of the 'Smackhead Twins', Russell 'Dinger' Bell and John Kettlewell, who had arrived at Lee as a double act from the Broomwood Estate. This is an area in South Trafford that was full of 'rough diamonds' like these two. As well as team manager and kit-washer extraordinaire, one of my other many tasks on Sunday mornings was to collect these two indolent, yet lovable, loafers. Having won the weekly race of being chased in my car across the estate by a pack of wild mongrels, their residences were always easy to find as they were the only ones on the street with half an overgrown hedge missing at the front. They also had their over-exaggerated house numbers carelessly daubed in orange paint on the wall next to a front door that was, in turn, etched with frenzied claw marks while various discarded parts of several Ford Escorts lay strewn around the balding front 'lawn'. I knew that if I didn't pick them up, the chances of them arriving on time were nil. It was slightly ironic that Russell could never emerge from his pit on time because he was a postman in those days!

If Russ was bone-idle then it could be said that John was even worse. I remember him once telling me that he used to run for Sale Harriers. I could only assume that this must have been in the 5-metre jogging event because he had an economy of effort in everything he did, except rolling a joint; he was always first to 'spark-up' in the dressing room. Lethargy was always reflected in his irregular attendance at games when I couldn't be bothered going round.

John had his own unique and esoteric slant on things. Just as the team were starting to progress, he broke his leg during a 3–1 victory. It took us over an hour to persuade him to go to casualty for treatment. The following week I picked him up and he was wearing a full-length leg plaster cast. Only seven days later it had been mysteriously reduced to below the knee. I asked John why the hospital had cut down his cast and so soon?

'Oh, they didn't,' he replied, 'it was getting on me tits so, I sawed it off meself.' The following week John had hacked the rest of the pot off altogether and didn't go back to the hospital for a check-up.

Over the following years I had a few key players who suffered serious injuries but shared a similar disregard for their own well-being. Terry Doyle once broke three ribs, one of which punctured his right lung, after he was squashed by a goalkeeper who used Terry as his landing pad. Our ailing striker was quickly bundled onto the back of Greeny's milk float and rushed to hospital. After the game the lads had a whip-round and I nipped over to Wythenshawe Hospital to deliver his 'Get Well Plastered' tray of Stella Artois. When I arrived the injured player wasn't in his bed, but I heard noises from the balcony just outside. There was Terry with a large plastic tube sticking out of his chest and a fag sticking out of his mouth. You could actually see the smoke in the tube as he dragged away without a care in the world.

'Don't you think it would be best to lay off the fags while you have just the one lung?' I asked in genuine concern.

'Nah, it'll be sound. You need to chill out a bit more Worvy,' was his insouciant response.

One person who wasn't so casual about his severe injury was Jim 'The Jeweller' Grant. Tackling wasn't really Jim's forte. He broke his right 'tib and fib' in a midweek night match. As Jim writhed in agony on the floor, the ref took the offender to one side, tutted and sternly said, 'Watch it, lad. You could really hurt someone one day tackling like that!' As Jim couldn't be moved, he was becoming a bit of a nuisance, so I had a word with the opposition manager. It took all of ten seconds to agree to 'up pegs', take the nets down and move them to the adjacent pitch so we could get on with the game. Although nobody bothered to stay with Jim until the blasé paramedics arrived some 25 minutes later, we could clearly see that he was okay while lying on the floor over on the other pitch. Besides, one of their players was kind enough to put a coat over him – well, at least until he was promptly subbed and needed it back. Poor old Jamesy! When the ambulance arrived, it couldn't drive onto the fields. Instead, they wheeled him back on a stretcher over the bone-dry rutted grass, which he later described as, 'A rodeo ride more painful than the break itself.' The cry of, 'Let's do it for Jim,' certainly had an emotional effect – we promptly lost the game 5–0.

With such ambivalence rife among my players, and indeed the management, it was hardly surprising that we weren't the most successful of teams. To make matters worse, we also had players who sometimes played against us while playing for us; players such as Ian 'Salty' Salt, for example. This was a lad who turned sulking into an art form. When the ref asked the players to tape up items of jewellery before the game, I often wished this would also extend to Salty's mouth, as his grief towards everyone around him was incessant. Having said that, some of Salty's moaning was often witty. He complained to the referee about the wall not being back 10 yards. The ref said that it was, to which Salty replied, 'I hope you're not a carpet fitter.'

Another player, 'Mad' Martin Burns, was a complex character who was only psychopathic on the football field. The rest of the time he was mild-mannered and jovial. But give him a pair of football boots and, within seconds, he charged into tackles like a horny bull. It was suggested that Burnsy took his brain out and placed it in a bucket before each game. There was an occasion when Burnsy was taking a long throw into the opposition penalty area. Their right-back thought it a good idea to stand close to the line in order to hinder Burnsy's follow-through. Burnsy thundered towards the line and launched the ball into the box, which was headed straight in. As we celebrated I glanced over to the touchline, where the full-back was now rolling around the floor in agony. As Burnsy had released the ball, he'd also released his right leg and booted the defender right in the baubles.

My Town Hall buddies, Jerry Sweeney and Steve Annette, also turned out for Lee occasionally. The latter was a top striker who had announced in the dressing room prior to one game that his wife was pregnant. Minutes later he was celebrating a goal and ran over to the touchline with a clenched fist to announce, 'That was for my embryo!' We also had a 'crazy' full-back called Dave Hickman, whom we nicknamed 'The Matador.' This was because it was as if he was waving an invisible cape at wingers, while they gleefully went past without hindrance. Hickey wasn't just clueless on the pitch, he was a bit of a mentalist off it. On the way to one away game he managed to get lost despite being in the middle of the team car convoy.

Lee was often a team of characters, but eventually the majority drifted into other things. After 375 appearances, the diminutive Stewart Freeman departed to concentrate on his new job as head garden gnome at Wythenshawe Park. Terry Hyland and Ian Greenwood left the club for pastures new, which meant I'd lost several of my main friends. But others remained, such as the ever-enthusiastic Phil Knowles, Jim Grant, Andy Smith and Gillespie brothers, John and Pete.

Despite the vicissitudes of inevitable domesticity that threatened our long-term viability, their shackle-breaking loyalty allowed the main thread of Lee Athletic to carry on into the next decade. The long-suffering Pete Moore continued to take care of all things secretarial. All we had to do was to put out eleven players every week. Between us all we'd built a new team, a team that was going places, even if they were the same places we'd visited in the South Manchester area to the point of complete and total boredom during the previous eighteen years.

Come the new millennium, and things were decidedly on the up. In 2000 we posted the club's record ever win: a 14–3 demolition of the

Bull's Head. We also made it to the League's Supplementary Cup final. Our improvement had been manifested in the recruitment of new players, such as Colin Baker, Paul Massey and Paul 'Sprossy' Sproston. Sprossy had a sharp tongue to go with his sweet feet and sugar-coated, if elongated, forehead. He was a clever lad and a clever player and he once came on as a substitute and pulled off a sublimely slick and coruscating backheel near to our touchline. Never one to let such a piece of Brazilian skill pass without comment, Sprossy exclaimed, 'There's no substitute for class.'

'Yeah, and there's no class from the substitute,' replied the equally quick-witted John Gillespie. Sprossy was to play a pivotal role in the cup final against that season's divisional champions, the Buck. There was a big crowd at Broadheath Central that day, if only because most of us folk on the touchline were well overweight. Many former Lee Athletic players turned out to see if their old club could finally win a trophy.

I'd written my pre-match speech in advance and had even consulted my loyal assistant manager Phil about tactics. I'd also prepared some pre-cut orange segments in an I Can't Believe It's Not Butter tub. When I opened the container at half time, nobody could quite believe that it wasn't oranges. I'd pulled out the wrong tub from the fridge at the last minute and all it contained was margarine! As for the game, it turned out to be a thrilling, if ultimately disappointing, experience. Sprossy had come on as sub and scored a wonderful goal to bring it back to 4–3. But with a few minutes left to play, the same player missed an absolute sitter and success eluded us.

A couple of years later, it looked as if glory would finally be bestowed upon Lee Athletic. Prior to the 2002/03 season we'd managed to acquire the Smith brothers from Wythenshawe League team – and my dad's local – the Park. Not only were Clark, Carl and Clive first-rate, but they were built like the proverbial outdoor lavatory constructed in the traditional kiln-fired, oblong clay units and bonded together with hardened mortar. With the later acquisition of Scott Blower and a promising young striker named Craig Scott, all of a sudden we had a team. That year there were four clubs in contention for the title but we were never in pole position. Towards the end, we found ourselves right in the mix. By the time we won our final game at home, we'd already secured promotion to the First Division on goal difference. A few weeks earlier, we'd recorded an 8–0 victory in the wilds of Turn Moss. Sale United needed a point from their final game to take the title, but defeat against the Wheatsheaf would give us the championship with the same points as three other teams. Crucially, we had the best goal difference.

Lee Athletic took a huge army of travelling supporters to watch that last Sale United match of the season and to a man, all four of us invaded the pitch in celebration as the Wheatsheaf scored the winner. Being crowned as champions was perhaps the best fortieth birthday present I could have had, although Jane took me on a surprise trip to New York a few weeks later and that topped it by a mile.

The following season Lee Athletic almost made it into the Premier League, missing out on promotion by just three points and finishing fourth – our highest-ever league standing. It was a pity that we ultimately failed because it would have realised my ambition of having at least one season with Altrincham's impressive and prestigious élite.

Rather than push on to even greater heights the season after that, things started to unravel. Key players stopped turning up due to the usual losing struggles with hangovers. Things were so desperate that I'd been forced to resurrect my playing career due to a lack of options in the dressing room. Not only that, but none of the stalwarts were getting any younger and we had an average age of thirty-five (thanks to the inclusion of a couple of teenagers). Finding new players to replace the old became an almost impossible task and I became more and more frustrated as we started to slide backwards once more. Every other defeat I threatened to quit, until one Sunday my threat was not an idle one.

It all came to a head against Sale United in a League Cup tie. They were by now a division below us, but on the half-hour mark the underdogs were 4–0 ahead. Several key players including my captain, my midfield general – Sean 'Eisenhower' Durden – and my star striker had failed to materialise and we'd started the game with only ten players. At half time, rather than listen to my team talk, a young player wandered off smoking a fag while chatting to his mates with a disdainful grin. When I called him over, he ignored me and, when I persisted, he gave me some abuse, and I flipped my lid. The pair of us had to be separated on the spot. I decided enough was enough. After all the time and effort I'd put into the running of Lee Athletic, the least I demanded from the players was a modicum of respect. Rather than making matters worse, I walked off into the sunset never to be seen again. It was a desperately sad end to a long association with the club as player, player/manager and manager.

With the help of the ever-enthusiastic stalwart Andy Smith, Phil kept Lee going for another two seasons. Many things can be preserved in alcohol, but unfortunately Lee Athletic wasn't one of them and the club folded just after the 2007/08 season got underway.

Lee Athletic ran for the best part of twenty-seven years and had something approaching 300 players who wore the strip in its various multi-coloured (other than red) guises. Now the old team photos of Lee hang forlornly against the damp and the cobwebs that insist upon clinging to my garage walls. They are pictures that bear testament to times gone by and of the great days of my youth that give me so many fond memories.

40

All's well that ends well?

In the 2003/04 season, the Blues' migration to the new City of Manchester Stadium at Eastlands was smooth enough. The ground was full to its 47,000-plus capacity for the first season and most of the second, but by the time the third arrived the crowds had began to dip. One of the absentees was my dad. He hadn't wanted to move in the first place, continually insisting that, 'Maine Road's my ground.' Despite holding a season ticket for the first couple of years, he wasn't happy with the new stadium and the extra bus journey it took to get there (despite the free bus pass). He also missed a convenient and comparable boozer to match the Beehive, so he sacked going altogether. It was a sad loss, but for my dad and numerous other supporters of his generation, such a radical change at that stage of his life was too much to bear. Following our nomadic approach while travelling to away games in the 1980s and 1990s, Bibby and I found our spiritual home within the Cheadle Branch of the Supporters' Club. We enjoyed some fabulous trips with some wonderful people.

City managed to gain entry to the UEFA Cup during the first season at Eastlands. This arrived through the slightly embarrassing route of the mysterious Fair Play League. In the qualifying round we dispensed of the mighty TNS of Wales before sending Lokeren of Belgium packing in the first round proper. This was mainly due to a 1–0 away win in the small Belgian town and the overland trip to Lokeren on the Cheadle Branch coach had its usual amusing moments. Probably the best of these came when branch secretary Tommy Muir found out that there was a United supporter in our midst, promptly removing his shoe and chucking it off the ferry and into the sea!

Prior to the match a Belgian was cycling past one of the many packed-out bars in Lokeren's main square, but a drunken City fan staggered out and knocked the poor 'local' off his bike. Several concerned Blues rushed to the aid of the ruffled Belgian cyclist and helped him to his feet, only for one of the rescuing City fans to ask, 'Hang on a minute. Don't I know you?'

'Yeah, mate. I'm from Wythenshawe,' answered the victim, 'I've just nicked this bike for a laugh!'

The first leg of round two ended in a 1–1 draw at Eastlands against Poland's Pride, Groclin Wikipedia (as we called them), to leave the second leg hanging in the balance when we set off in an old bucket of a charter plane that the Wright Brothers might have recognised had they still been alive. After the two-hour flight from Manchester with Swiss Tony's 'Luxury' Tours – during which a number of oxygen masks somewhat alarmingly dropped down without a suitable explanation – we boarded a coach from the airport to our hotel. By the time we all piled on, it was standing room only. We were on the way into Poznan city centre when one of the lads from the Irish branch spotted a giraffe chewing on a tree behind a barbed wire fence.

'Feck me. Look at dat. Dare's a feckin' giraffe!' he exclaimed to his mates, with great excitement and incredulity. After a few seconds he soon continued, now in falsetto, 'Feck me, dare's a feckin' loyon,' and, moments after that, he added with further enthusiasm and increasing volume, 'Look behind it, dare's a feckin' elephant!' His excitement and bewilderment was soon broken when I rudely commented, 'Feck me, so that'll be the feckin' zoo then?' The lad had somehow confused the potholed road into Poznan with the plains of the Serengeti.

Unfortunately, this game proved to be the end of our brief European adventure – City's first *real* one since 1978 – as we only managed a 0–0 draw and lost on away goals.

♦   ♦   ♦

Kevin Keegan left the club in March 2005 and after a couple of years in charge, May 2007 saw the departure of the highly enthusiastic Stuart Pearce and his soporific brand of football. To be fair, and through lack of financial resources, he was severely restricted in what he could achieve. But when did fairness ever have a positive bearing on football? City fans should not forget the former electrician's role in today's optimism. Had City gone down in 2006/07 – which was always a possibility– and had John Wardle and David Makin failed to generously prop up the club with their own personal funding, there would not have been a subsequent buyout and we would probably be languishing once more. Pearce paid the price with his job as a result of the introduction of the former Thai Prime Minister, Dr Thaksin Shinawatra.

If I have to live in an age where money is king of footy, then it's best for my club to have lots of it. Despite his financial therapy, Thaksin's first season was totally in keeping with the cock-up traditions of the club, as Sven-Göran Eriksson was installed under a wave of optimism. That term we even recorded our first win at Old Trafford since Denis Law's nonchalant backheel which consigned United to the Second Division in April 1974. It took twenty-seven attempts to finally come away with a victory; I attended all twenty-seven. For a gloriously protracted honeymoon period it looked as though City might conquer all, but after Christmas 2007 it all went wrong, as usual. Only City could get knocked out of the FA Cup thanks to a balloon, which changed the flight of the ball that set up Sheffield United's first goal in an eventual 2–1 defeat. Having spent the first half of the season in the top four, we slumped to such a degree that we were hammered 8–1 in the final game of the season at Middlesbrough. Another nice day out on Teesside.

Nevertheless, and in true City tradition, Sven was soon sacked and a former Red, Mark Hughes, entered the club under yet another wave of optimism. Several weeks later I was sitting in my office minding my own business when Phil Knowles rang to tell me that rumours abounded that Thaksin had been bought out by a consortium of fabulously wealthy Arabian businessmen. The prospective buyers were reportedly worth a mind-boggling £560 billion, and had stated that they were willing to finance City into the position of the biggest club on the planet. A bit of a 'Brucey Bonus' was taking shape.

Before the day was out, City had put in cheeky little bids for United target Dimitar Berbatov and a couple of other top names. A few hours later we actually signed the mercurial Brazilian striker Robinho from Real Madrid, despite him being a seemingly nailed-on transfer target for Roman Abramovich. By the time I went to bed at five past midnight, the deal had been done and the words, 'Robinho is now a City player,' had been uttered. Our new owners had bought Brazil's then striking protégé from Real Madrid, right from under the noses of Chelsea. The British transfer record had been smashed, proving beyond doubt that these were no 'fake sheikhs'. It was difficult getting off to sleep that night after such an extravagant statement of intent.

With a triumphant FA Youth Cup winning team, a hungry new manager with a shipload of money to spend, things were looking rosy for the 2008/09 season. But it wasn't just football I had to look forward to. A few weeks after the sensational takeover, Jane and I were celebrating the birth of our beautiful new daughter, Molly. Her arrival might have cut short my foreign jaunts. However, my darling wife is well aware that such adventures keep me happy and I more than appreciate her more-than-generous licence to roam. Although City still failed to win a trophy with such fabulous financial backing, we were at least treated to a UEFA Cup run which took the Blues on to the quarter-final. I took advantage with five more overseas adventures along the way. Perhaps my most 'humorous' incident came after the Schalke 04 game while staying in a luxurious hotel room in Cologne with Phil Knowles. After our exuberant victory celebrations I went for an uncharacteristic late night/early morning sleepwalk. Apparently I'd got up for a pee and taken several wrong turnings. I awoke to find myself marooned and incarcerated on the freezing cold staff staircase wearing just a pair of boxer shorts and a puzzled expression. Failing to attract any attention by shouting at the top of my voice and banging desperately on the locked doors of all six echoing stair landings; I was finally able to regain my liberty after 30 shivering minutes by setting off the fire alarm at 4.00 in the morning. Call me 'Mr Popular'.

Having acquired several notable new recruits, particularly the addition of Carlos Tevez from United (who sadly for them, couldn't afford to sign him up) in 2009/10, City were a hard team to beat. But too many draws meant a premature ending to Mark Hughes' brief stint in charge. The stylish Italian Roberto Mancini (affectionately Christened 'Bobby Manc') took over the helm. When he arrived, the Blues were still in two cups and the hunt for that elusive trophy remained a possibility. In the Carling Cup, City made it all the way to the semi-final (the club's first for twenty-nine years) only to lose a two legged tie 4–3 in injury time at 'Sold' Trafford. It was a bitter pill to swallow. 'Hope' has been a four letter word when it comes to MCFC. When hope becomes realistic, disappointment becomes so much harder to bear.

After the match, our new boss commented that we'd just have to win the FA Cup instead. Needless to say we didn't. As things stand, I'm forty-eight years of age and, for one reason or another, I still haven't seen my club lift a major trophy. Take my word for it I'd have loved City to have won things, especially during my young, free and single years. But the way it's panned out is the way it's panned out, and that's showbiz. Like England and Lee Athletic in tandem, my football career has been more about camaraderie than success. As my dad always puts it, 'Failure breeds character.' Perhaps I'd have preferred a little less character.

However, even after a lifetime of disappointments I still believe. Come the time City are finally triumphant, begrudge us not. For Manchester City's many loyal supporters, success will have been earned the hard way. For the record, please discard everything I previously said about losin' my religion. All my hopes and dreams have finally arrived on the backs of our Arabian knights. There *is* a God and He loves me – of that you'd better believe. The future's bright, the future's City. It might just take a little bit longer than I imagined.

♦   ♦   ♦

And so, finally, to the big question: has this been a 'Worthy' journey? I'd like to think so otherwise my life would have been a bit of a waste of time. If you have enjoyed reading this book as much as I have enjoyed writing it, then maybe it was half good. Writing my autobiography has been a self-gratifying and cathartic exercise and, at the very least, Katy and Molly will have a dubious account of what their dad was all about in his younger days to treasure . . . mostly, having a laugh.

FIN

Acknowledgements

Mark Bowden; Terry, Tracey, Ben & Megan Hyland; Phil, Jennifer, Josh and Emma Knowles; Noel Bayley; Joanne Gilsenan (née O'Neill); Gavin O'Neill; John & Joanne Eaton; Neil, Judith, Matthew, Stephanie & Biff Burrows; John Maddock; Peter Barnes; Darren Hendley; Ian Greenwood; Gary, Frank, Ben and Callum Tipper; Jim, Sarah, Adam & Beth Grant; Johnny Copper; Andrew 'Charlie' Charles and Joe & Olivia Charles; Flynny, Sue & Chloe; Stewart, Julie, Michael, Vicky & Ashley Freeman; Mark, Julie, Joesph & Rebecca Taylor; Sean, Catherine & Anna Durden; Janet Evrington; Football Tony & Christopher Morehead; Sean and Pete Morehead; Mark Todd; Pat, Mike, Thomas & Vicky Boden; Shirley & Frank Hendley; Dave Clee; Mike Relph; Rita Relph; Graham Moore; Pete Moore; Sheila Moore; Ron Frohlich; David Frohlich; Lilly, Joel & Hugh Frohlich; Pete Gillespie; Dave Blinkhorn; Stephen Dodds; Alan Sparrow; Phil Borrows; Ian Thorpe; Russ Bell; John Kettlewell; Lee Jenkins; Kevin Cummins; Janet Royle; Ian & Ted Prince; Jim & Helen Yates; Steve Annette; Jerry Sweeney; Khalid Ahmed; Roger Fielding; Mike Iveson; Craig Ainsworth; Phil Elgee; Jaine Duffy; Gulderen Harwood; Bernard McAlinden; Deb & Dave Harris; June Kenny; Geoff Garrett; Mrs Garrett; Lynn & Paul Star; Kevin Clarke; Geoff Smith; Graham & Sue Lister; Kevin McLaren; Gary Lawlor; Steve Graham; Dave Graham; Harry Boyle; Lee Crewe; Mark Proudlove; Kevin Cook; Gary Blissett; Joe Lawson; Big Ian Eastaugh; Steve, Ann & Lara Maher; Dave Littlewood; 'Tesco' Ian Shelmerdine; Paul Templeton; Keith Clare; Alan Heason; Pete Daniels; Mike McHugh; Neil Watts; Lyn Slamon; Nicky Park; John Troy; Steve Whyatt; Jimmy Johnson; Gill Ferguson; Andrea Grant; Sonja Booth; Suzanne Ellis; Vinny O'Neill; Debbie Darbyshire; Nicola Sands; Alan Wright; Dave Beveridge; Barry Gibson; Stuart Drysdale; Steve Baker; Nicholas Phythian; Paul Sposton; Andy & Jason Smith;

Clive, Carl & Clark Smith; Billy Kenny; Dom Cosseron; Colin Baker; Chris, Deborah, David & Natalie Hulme; Tony Collins; Wayne Smith; Alan Ford; Steve Zanft; Ann Ashton; Martin, Jane & Isaac Creavy; Cliff Doyle; Bob Dillistone; Derek Fisher; Karl 'Shag' Hendry; Glynn Sloan; Steve McDonagh; Paul Carey; Jimmy Pannett; Marky Morgan; Vinny Nash; Charlie McCormick; Jock Brocklehurst; Neil Kenny; Ian Salt; Codger; Les Hare; Glynn Sloane; Pete Stringer; Wilf Goodwin; Andrew Haymes; Vinny Unsworth; Barry Hope; Vicky Sugars; Mr Davies; Martin Burns; Graham Bantham; Ian Doyle; John & Alex Scott; Alex Murray; Simon Daysh; Mark Sowerby; Paul Ramsey; Nice Guy Greg; Andy Smallwood; Danny Belston; Riser; Mike Billinge; Paul Billinge; Mark 'Rosey' Burns; Stevie Coward; Steve Shelton; Tony Hawkes & Damo; Hodge; Dave Parr; Steve Wilcox; Andy Fannon; Ian Whitfield; Mark Sellwood; Martin Eaton; Alan Potter; Gary Griffiths; Howard Jones; Jeff Palfreyman; Roy Nutter; Neil Blinston; Simmo; Ole Morten Egedal; Elizabeth Egedal; Jan Sramek; Espen Fodstad; Tor Sønsteby; Ketil Aune; Richard Stott; Steinar Sel; Christian De Lange; Egil Svarstad; Ole Fuglestad; Ken Ball; Mark Howell; Nicola Ierston; Tony Jefferson; Nigel Larkin; Warren Heppolette; Stuart Cowley; Pecker & Pecker's dad (Pecker Snr); Steve Kay; Mickey Vernon; Mike Greenwood; Paul Davies; Hammy & Dimitch; Richard Isaacs & Andy Smith II (the sequel); Pete the window cleaner; Steve Fox; Jon Vali; Damian Eaton; Chris Braithwaite; Andy Buckley; Fred Eyre; Vincent Turner; Steve Wadsworth; Alan Wadsworth; Joe Lawson; Billy Roddy; Dave Shepherd; Steve Wilcox; David Tomlinson; Pete Johnson; Andy Seddon; Mike Summerbee; Tony Book; Frank Carrodus; Garry Cook; Terry Stanton; Fred and Frieda Stanton; Madge Steele; Muriel Pearson; 'Blue Peter' & Matt Gillinge; Sminge & Rob Clements; Rob Dale; Baz Riley; John Dutton; Alan & Mike Derbyshire; Steve Slater; Swiss Family City Fans; Dave Wallace; Gary James; Mark Halsey; Tony Welsh; Paul Phoenix; Alfie Noakes; Bobby Nobby; Ross McFarter; Arch Stanton; everyone and anyone who has ever entertained me while playing for City (and the vast majority who haven't); all supporters of MCFC (the only football team to come from Manchester); everyone who has ever been associated with the mighty Lee Athletic Football Club; anyone who ever went to Chorlton High School during the 1970s that didn't victimise me and anyone I might have forgotten (soz). Thanks also to Michelle Tilling, Richard Leatherdale and everyone at The History Press. Finally, mum and dad, Joanne and Julie, Katy, Molly, Sam Gilsenan and my ever-patient and loving wife Jane, without whom I would be a single man and a sad one at that.

Thank you for the music . . .

The Stranglers, Puressence, The Chameleons, David Bowie, Mew, The Psychedelic Furs, Japan, Magazine, The Smiths, Joy Division, The Sex Pistols, Public Image, New Order, Ride, Embrace, Oasis, The Stone Roses, Morrissey, The Catherine Wheel, The Charlatans, JJ72, Doves, Iggy Pop, Elbow, The Happy Mondays, The Boxer Rebellion, Choir of the Young Believers, BRMC, Longview, VAST, The Soundtrack of Our Lives, Kraftwerk, Ultravox, B Movie, Roxy Music/Bryan Ferry, James, OMD, John Foxx, Gary Numan/Tubeway Army, Glasvegas, White Lies, The Buzzcocks, Skids, Marilyn Manson, Love Spit Love, The Longcut, Snow Patrol, HRH Grace Jones, Thirteen Senses, Ash, Bill Nelson, X-Ray Spex, The Killers, The Damned, Visage, Echo and the Bunnymen, Talking Heads, The Mock Turtles, The Fall, Echobelly, Mull Historical Society, The La's, Cast, The Teardrop Explodes/Julian Cope, Mansun, Martha and the Muffins, The Wonder Stuff, Siouxsie and the Banshees, Haven, Interpol, The Sea Horses, The Rolling Stones, Badly Drawn Boy, Nash the Slash, Supergrass, The Verve, Reef, The Pretenders, Pixies, The Rezillos, China Crisis, Kate Bush, Jah Wobble, Immaculate Fools, The Human League, Heaven 17, Penetration, Eels, Bauhaus, Belasco, Fad Gadget, Gomez, The Proclaimers, The Cult, Weezer, Blancmange, Garbage, The Clash, The Ramones, T. Rex, Talking Heads, The Cranberries, Crispy Ambulance, Mercury Rev, Simple Minds, Dead Kennedys, The Sun and the Moon, The Reegs, Blondie, Bow Wow Wow, Stiff Little Fingers, Devo, XTC, The Undertones, Talk Talk, The Ruts, The Jam and The Beatles. Some were better than others, others were better than some, but every goddam one of 'em gave it a good go and that's the main thing.

We Could Be Heroes?

His Highness Sheikh Mansour bin Zayed Al Nahyan, Colin Bell, Dennis Tueart, Francis Lee, Mike Summerbee, Tony Book, Georgiou Kinkladze, Shaun Goater, Paul Dickov, Paul Lake, Stan Bowles, Rodney Marsh, Paul Walsh, Peter Beagrie, Niall Quinn, Craig Bellamy, Carlos Tevez, Tommy Muir, David Bernstien, Brian Horton, Malcolm Allison, Paul Power, John Gillespie (*the* best player ever to play for Lee Athletic), Jean-Jacques Burnel, Mark Burgess, Richard Butler, Quagmire, Andy Sipowicz, Peter Kay, Edison Arantes do Nascimento (Peel), Willie Bald, Muhammed Ali, Sugar Ray Leonard, Ricky Hatton, Daley Thompson, Ray Makin, John Wardle, James H. Reeve, Dave Ward, Freddie Flintoff, Ian Botham, David Lloyd, Neil Fairbrother, Ian Austin, Jonathan Meades, the New York Giants, Irvine Welsh, James Lee, James Woods, Clint Eastwood, John